WHEN THE WOLVES BITE

WHEN THE WOLVES BITE

TWO BILLIONAIRES, ONE COMPANY,
AND AN EPIC WALL STREET BATTLE

SCOTT WAPNER

PUBLICAFFAIRS
New York

PublicAffairs
Hachette Book Group
1290 Avenue of the Americas, New York, NY 10104
www.publicaffairsbooks.com
@Public_Affairs

Printed in the United States of America

First Edition: May 2018

Published by PublicAffairs, an imprint of Perseus Books, LLC, a subsidiary of Hachette Book Group, Inc. The PublicAffairs name and logo is a trademark of the Hachette Book Group.

The publisher is not responsible for websites (or their content) that are not owned by the publisher.

A catalog record for this book is available from the Library of Congress.

ISBNs: 978-1-61039-827-5 (hardcover), 978-1-61039-828-2 (ebook)

LSC-C

10 9 8 7 6 5 4 3 2 1

CONTENTS

AUTHOR'S NOTE

This book would not have happened without the gracious coopera-
tion of the three major parties involved in this story—Carl Icahn,
Bill Ackman, and, of course, Herbalife's now former CEO, Michael
Johnson. All agreed to speak on the record about their roles. Some of
the events depicted have not been reported until now, a testament to
the commitment each of the players, and others, made to the integrity
of the story. In some places, you'll notice direct quotes that were taken
from the many hours of interviews I conducted with each partici-
pant. In other instances, quotes or specific events and dates are uti-
lized from the overwhelming amount of information available from
public sources; these are thus footnoted. Other facts are taken from
direct conversations with the key parties or those close to the story.
I'm grateful for their support of this project.

INTRODUCTION:
THE MASTERS OF THE UNIVERSE

Not since the Rockefellers and Vanderbilts has one group of investors exerted more influence on Wall Street than does the current class of financiers known as shareholder activists.

This class of super-investors, which includes Carl C. Icahn, William A. Ackman, Daniel S. Loeb, Nelson Peltz, and others, is defined by an interest not just in owning a piece of a company, but also in using their influence and money to change the way it operates. And no company, large or small, is beyond their reach. Apple, PepsiCo, Yahoo, DuPont, JC Penney, and Macy's are among the businesses that have been targeted in recent years.

While the 1970s and 1980s marked the rise, dominance, and ultimate fall of the corporate raiders, arbitrageurs, and junk bond kings of the day, during the current Era of the Activist, barely a week goes by without one of the aforementioned financiers revealing a stake in a company's stock and an ambitious plan to propel it higher.

Activism isn't just proliferating—it's exploding.

In 2012 there were seventy-one activist campaigns with a total of $12 billion invested, according to the new regulatory filings with the Securities and Exchange Commission. By 2015 the numbers had surged to eighty-three filings totaling nearly $31 billion and counting. As the number of dollars has grown, so has the size of the targets, with the average market caps of their companies increasing from more than $2.3 billion in 2012 to nearly $6 billion in 2015.

1

As a finance reporter, this exclusive, iconoclastic world is an obsession for me. It has been ever since January 25, 2013, when Icahn and Ackman engaged in a wild, intensely personal war of words on live television and brought Wall Street trading to a sudden standstill.

Consider the moment: Here were two billionaires hurling insults while the world watched and trading stopped. CEOs from Davos to Dallas dropped what they were doing to watch it. It was a moment in time—organic, bizarre, and completely unplanned. I should know—I was hosting the live TV show when it happened.

The rise of shareholder activism and the power of these new Masters of the Universe are equally as stunning. Ten years ago, activist hedge funds had less than $12 billion under management. Today, it's more than $120 billion, with more than ten funds now managing more than $10 billion each.

Why? Some cite the ongoing bull market—the raging rally of stocks since post-crisis 2008—as the catalyst. Companies were flush with cash and could borrow it at record low interest rates, and shareholders were hungry for a bigger piece of that pie. Enter the shareholder activist to get it for them, typically using a familiar playbook—usually a spin-off, share-buyback, or cost-cutting initiative—always in the name of unlocking more value for all shareholders.

There is also a case to be made that activism as a technique has become popular because in many cases it has worked. Big investors with big ideas and big names driving share prices higher while forcing CEOs to maximize returns for their shareholders—or else.

The activist aggregator, 13D Monitor, found that between 2006 and 2011 the average one-day "bump" for a stock once an activist had revealed their position was 2.65 percent, with the average return over fifteen months reaching 15.24 percent, dramatically outperforming the payout of the S&P 500 over the same time frame.

But do those gains come at a cost?

Leo E. Strine, the influential Chief Justice for the Delaware Supreme Court, wrote about activist hedge funds in February 2017's *Yale Law Journal* in his 133-page paper titled "Who Bleeds When the

Wolves Bite? A Flesh-and-Blood Perspective on Hedge Fund Activism and Our Strange Corporate Governance System." "There is less reason to think (activists) are making the economy much more efficient, and more reason to be concerned that they are perhaps pushing steady societal wealth on a riskier course that has no substantial long-term upside," he suggested.

Distinguishing between so-called human investors—those of us who save for college or retirement—and the "wolf packs" of activist hedge funds who attempt to instill change in a corporation, Strine argued,

> What is commonly accepted about activist hedge funds is that they do not originally invest in companies they like and only become active when they become dissatisfied with the corporation's management or business plan. Rather, activists identify companies and take an equity position in them only when they have identified a way to change the corporation's operations in a manner that the hedge fund believes will cause its stock price to rise. The rise that most hedge funds seek must occur within a relatively short time period, because many activist hedge funds have historically retained their position for only one to two years at most.[1]

Judge Strine is not alone in his criticism of the perceived short-term nature of activists. Jeffrey A. Sonnenfeld, Senior Associate Dean of Leadership Studies at the Yale School of Management, argues that "too often activists pressure companies to cut costs, add debt, sell divisions and increase share repurchases, rather than invest in jobs, R&D and growth," and that any value created by activists is "often short-lived and sometimes comes at the expense of long-term success, if not survival."[2]

Others lament the activist class's herd mentality—too much money chasing too few good ideas. Laurence D. Fink, the noted and outspoken CEO of the world's largest asset manager, Blackrock, decries the quick-fix approach as damaging to the corporate structure at large. In February 2016, in a letter sent to hundreds of chief executives, he urged them to focus on "long-term value creation" rather than on buybacks and other initiatives.

The famed corporate lawyer Martin Lipton, known as the creator of the "poison pill" defense tool, designed to protect a company from a hostile takeover, would declare that hedge-fund activists are ruining America, rather than helping it. But even Mr. Lipton would certainly attest that there's no denying the rock-star status these activist investors have achieved, mostly for their methods, but sometimes as much for their madness—their noise and provided platforms.

Never was that more apparent than in the years-long public battle over Herbalife, which began on a cold December day in 2012 and rages on to this day. This is the inside story of how it all went down— the fights, the factions, the money, and the mayhem of an epic Wall Street war.

1

THE PROFILE

Herbalife Chief Executive Officer Michael O. Johnson had been waiting for weeks, hoping its arrival would help unmask the man who had threatened to destroy him. It was spring 2014, and the most closely followed multilevel marketing company on Earth was under siege.

For the better part of eighteen months, Wall Street's resident rock star, the hedge-fund manager William A. Ackman of Pershing Square Capital Management, had waged war against the company, burning through tens of millions of dollars of his firm's own money, with no end in sight.

Ackman was tactical and tenacious, driven and determined, at times even obsessive in his torment, yet to the executive who'd spent the bulk of his time bobbing and weaving to avoid the onslaught, Ackman was, at the same time, bewildering.

What drove him to attack so viciously, Johnson often wondered. What really made Ackman tick?

One Sunday afternoon three weeks into May, some of that suspense was finally about to end, with the delivery of a document so sensitive its mere existence would be kept a secret until this writing. Even some of Herbalife's most senior leaders were initially kept from viewing it.

The thirty-page workup read like something out of a spy novel, but it wasn't a work of fiction. It was an in-depth psychological profile of Ackman himself, the kind the FBI might do when chasing a hardened criminal. The secret dossier titled "Preliminary Report on Bill Ackman" described an adversary who was "fiercely competitive" and "extremely smart," fueled by ambition and a quest to win at all costs.

Herbalife's vice president of global security, Jana Monroe, had commissioned the effort with one goal in mind—to get inside Ackman's head, to uncover the who and why, his methods and motivation.

"My assessment early on was that he was going to be in this for the long haul," Monroe said of the report's critical findings. She was "looking at his attacks on the company and figuring out where they might go so that we could be preemptive rather than reactive."

Monroe had spent thirty years in law enforcement, including more than twenty inside the Federal Bureau of Investigation. Five of those years were in the elite serial crime unit called the National Center for the Analysis of Violent Crime, in Quantico, Virginia. A real-life Clarice Starling, Monroe was on the teams investigating serial killers Ted Bundy and Jeffrey Dahmer, was an early reader of the Unabomber's notorious manifesto, and knew penetrating Ackman's mind would help the company understand the threat it was facing.

"It was clear (from the report) that this was someone who wears his competitiveness on his sleeve—it's not just business, it's personal, it's me. I'm the one who knows how to make the right investments," said Monroe.

The report was prepared by Dr. Park Dietz, one of the nation's leading forensic psychiatrists, a man who has spent decades profiling evil—from serial killers and stranglers to stalkers and school shooters.

Dietz had never met Ackman before, but the Herbalife affair reminded him of the Tylenol tampering case from the 1980s and the incidents that followed—in particular one involving a man who shorted shares of a drug manufacturer then phoned in a hoax to drive the stock price lower.

"Part of what interested me was the resemblance to a case that had fascinated me decades earlier," Dietz said. "I always thought that was an interesting kind of crime."

But Dietz knew getting deep into Ackman's psyche would be difficult.

Unlike most of his prior cases, he couldn't interview his subject and would instead have to scour the internet for old stories and television clips in order to study the major events of Ackman's life.

"Most of it was journalistic," Dietz said. "It was whatever was available—trying to look at his biography, the major newsworthy events and how he'd reacted to prior wins and losses. The task is to try and learn their life story with the available data and look for patterns in the behavior of that person in the life span."

Over dozens of highly descriptive pages, the document, which took nearly six weeks to prepare and cost Herbalife around $100,000 to commission, dissected Ackman and the characteristics that have made him the most famous financier on Wall Street—his history and tendencies, priorities and psychology.

It described a man "aggressive and competitive in all things," with a "grandiose sense of self" who "craves association with other 'special' people and institutions."

"Greed would be an accurate descriptor," it read, "but only because the number of digits followed by a dollar sign is a metric by which he measures his place in the world and expects others to measure him." The document described Ackman as a person who "requires constant admiration, adulation and publicity," who "uses publicists and other contacts to shape and control press reports; chases celebrity and sees himself as a celebrity whose image is to be shaped and tailored by those loyal to him."

"My basic view was that he saw Herbalife as a target that offered him the potential to reap rewards for his investors while appearing to be a crusader for the downtrodden," said Dietz.

"To me, he didn't seem to have much personal awareness," said Monroe of her own research. "His performances weren't very convincing."

Line by line, the document tore Ackman open, depicting a merciless megalomaniac who "uses philanthropy to deflect critics" and is "inclined to arrogant, haughty, disdainful, condescending, patronizing behavior and attitudes that he seeks to mask." Ackman, it said, "blames others for his defeats and mistakes" and "looks for loopholes in the law and ethics that he can exploit."

It threw shade on Ackman's uncanny resiliency, saying he "believes he is in the right and stubbornly, inflexibly, sticks to his position." He is "very controlling," it read, "and believes he can do most things better than anyone else in the room."

Another paragraph attacked Ackman's ability to deal with defeat, saying he is "very sensitive to criticism and failure, which causes shame, humiliation, and rage, producing long-remembered 'injuries,' but he always seems to have a bigger quest lined up to take his mind off the pain and distract others from the shame."

The report concluded with the following passage:

Ackman's public persona is an illusion manufactured to project onto a large screen his fantasies of unlimited success. As long as the public accepts the illusion, he can function, but he experiences any and all criticism or resistance as a threat to expose the insecure boy behind the curtain. He has no capacity to manage the feeling of shame that this creates, and he reacts to the feeling with rage.

By some measure, the document confirmed what Herbalife had believed from the beginning, but Johnson and his team thought building a more complete composite of the enemy would help determine the best way to fight back—what flanks to cover and how to manage the campaign.

"We were trying to determine what his motivation was," said Herbalife's chief financial officer, John DeSimone. "How we could get through this and what the endgame might be. We didn't know who Bill Ackman was—the man—the tactics and the strategy he might employ."

But beyond laying out a portrait of the enemy, the document also defined a road map for Herbalife to follow should the situation with Ackman suddenly—and dramatically—change.

Under the headline "Strategic Priorities," it advised Herbalife executives to "keep open a door to genuine alliance" with ground rules "closely negotiated."

"If a path to engagement opens," it advised, "appeal to Ackman's charitable persona by shifting his focus away from Herbalife's marketing and finances to the products. . . . Consider inviting Ackman to Herbalife to learn more about the business, the products, the people." The report even suggested that "Ackman would be drawn to a meeting that gave him a photo op and bragging rights for associating with someone he considers a bigger celebrity with the right image, perhaps President Obama, Michelle Obama, Oprah Winfrey, Jerry Bruckheimer, Mark Zuckerberg, Bill Gates, Melinda Gates, Warren Buffet, or the current or most recent Presidents and Past Presidents of Harvard, Yale, or Princeton." The document also recommended Herbalife "see Ackman's highly public campaign for what it is: an opportunity to tell the world about (the company)."

"Create a big, positive narrative around (CEO) Michael Johnson," it recommended. "THIS is the good guy. . . . Convey his energy, enthusiasm, and vision for Herbalife."

It advised Herbalife to "right-size the threat" and to "keep the focus away from Ackman personally and on the substance of his criticism. Any publicity centered on Ackman, even negative publicity, can play into his public persona as an 'activist shareholder.'"

The battle with Ackman had consumed the company since December 2012, when Ackman had first laid out his stunning case and his billion-dollar short. Now—*finally*—for the very first time, Johnson and Herbalife's other executives felt they could begin to understand why the war had happened in the first place.

It was a war that began with little more than a phone call.

2

THE PITCH

William Ackman was sitting in his office at 888 Seventh Avenue, on Manhattan's West Side, when the phone rang. It was early summer 2011, and a woman named Christine S. Richard was on the line, a hint of urgency in her voice.

"Bill, I think I found the next MBIA," she said through the receiver, knowing the acronym would instantly pique Ackman's interest.

MBIA was the bond insurance behemoth that had arguably put Ackman on the map. He'd battled with the company from 2002 to 2009, ultimately winning a $1.4 billion windfall, but not before a sprawling struggle in which he became the subject of investigations by both New York's attorney general, Eliot Spitzer, and the Securities and Exchange Commission.[1]

It was a long and drawn-out affair that had begun when Ackman, a relative newcomer on the hedge-fund scene at his fledgling firm, Gotham Partners, went short on MBIA stock, betting its shares would plummet if the then white-hot housing market weakened. In addition, he'd bought something called credit default swaps—insurance policies, in effect, that would pay off even further if the company went bankrupt, as Ackman expected. Ackman had accompanied his investment with a fifty-page missive titled "Is MBIA Triple A?" that took aim at the company's pristine credit rating—in essence, its lifeblood.[2] Ackman systematically took the company apart, accusing MBIA of misrepresenting the value of its assets and listing several accounting shenanigans and other transgressions he claimed could lead to a liquidity event—the death knell for a business where confidence in the company's credit means everything. MBIA chief executive officer Gary C. Dunton admitted as much about the firm's prized triple A rating, once telling the *New York Times* reporter Joe Nocera that it was the most critical thing MBIA had. "Our triple A rating is a fundamental driver of our business model," he had said.[3]

Simply put, MBIA would be toast without it, and Ackman knew it, which is why he also did something almost unheard of at the time for a short-seller—he released his scathing report over the internet in a public "fuck you" of sorts to the company. Ackman *wanted* people to read it—for the market and investors to doubt the firm's solvency—and he didn't stop there. Ackman went to the SEC and New York State insurance regulators, hoping they'd come to the same conclusions he did, slap the company around, and cause the stock price to plummet.

The effort, though intense, was mostly for naught, as month after month, then year after year, Ackman pressed his case, and MBIA managed to fight him off.

Finally, the tide began to turn in Ackman's favor when the SEC and Mr. Spitzer began investigating MBIA's accounting practices in 2004.[4] One year later, the company would be forced to restate its earnings for an eight-year period, though the stock held up reasonably well during this process, which tested Ackman's resolve.

The investment finally paid off in 2007, when the onset of the financial crisis crushed stocks like MBIA under the weight of the subprime housing bust. Lehman Brothers and Bear Stearns would eventually go belly-up, and many wondered if companies like MBIA were next.

Sure enough, MBIA shares *did* suffer. By December 2007, shares had fallen more than 56.3 percent, including more than 25 percent in a single day, as confidence in the sector quickly began to evaporate.[5] It may have been a lucky break, but Ackman had finally received his bounty. He made more than $1.4 billion on MBIA and earned a reputation as one of Wall Street's hot shots.

Richard hoped Ackman was ready for another go-around.

It wasn't an easy sell. The more than half-decade war with MBIA had left its battle scars, or "brain damage," as Ackman described it. He'd told those close to him, even some of his own investors who were clamoring for the next big hit, that he'd almost certainly never do such a public short campaign again. It was just too exhausting.

"I didn't want to do another public short," said Ackman. "It's a huge strain on the organization, and you get a lot of this negative press, and everyone hates you. That's really the answer."

No one understood the ordeal more than Richard herself. She had documented the whole MBIA saga while an investigative reporter at Bloomberg News, exposing some of the company's major issues. She later wrote a book about Ackman's crusade, *Confidence Game: How a Hedge Fund Manager Called Wall Street's Bluff*. It told of a relentless investor willing to go to great lengths to win, even if it meant waiting years to do so.

The MBIA story, and all of its gyrations, had taken its toll on Richard too. After taking a leave of absence to write the book about Ackman's quest, she left Bloomberg altogether to take a job with the Indago Group, a small and somewhat secretive boutique research shop that counted some of New York's top hedge-fund managers as clients, including Ackman.

Richard and the firm's founder, Diane Schulman, a former TV producer and licensed private investigator, were paid top dollar for their exclusive investment ideas and had been given the catchy, if kitschy, nickname "The Indago Girls" by their mostly male clientele. Schulman had helped the investor Steven Eisman, famous for his role in Michael Lewis's *The Big Short*, do some digging for his short bet against for-profit education stocks.[6] Eisman had made a killing on the investment, giving Schulman and Indago some well-deserved street cred in the ego-heavy hedge-fund world.

Schulman had given Richard a list of companies to comb through—some Chinese internet firms and the like—but they were too opaque and obscure and hard to do good research on. However, there was another name on Schulman's list that Richard vaguely recognized from some reporting a former colleague had done years earlier—the name she'd tell Ackman that day on the phone in the summer of 2011. It was Herbalife.

Herbalife was a publicly traded nutrition company that sold health shakes, teas, and vitamin supplements. When Richard gave him the name, Ackman paused for a moment, as if he'd never heard of the company before. Even if he had heard the name, he probably didn't know its ticker symbol or exactly what it did. That would change, and soon.

Richard briefly ran through some of the research she'd already done on the company, telling Ackman how she thought it could be a pyramid scheme.

Now Ackman seemed intrigued.

Richard had spent hundreds of hours poring over pyramid-scheme cases, finding many troubling similarities to what she'd dug up on Herbalife. She didn't have to look too hard either. Multilevel marketing (MLM) companies have been heavily scrutinized since the early 1970s, mostly for their controversial pay structures in which people are compensated for how much product they actually sell along with how many new folks they recruit into the business. Other short-sellers have given the industry a quick scan plenty of times throughout the years, believing the twisty businesses enrich only those who get in early, while the rest of the suckers who sign up late get screwed. Some have even been called pyramid schemes by the government, were later sued, and then were permanently shut down.

In one of the first such cases, a company called Koscot Interplanetary, which sold beauty services and cosmetics, was targeted by the Federal Trade Commission (FTC) and accused of being a fraud.[7] Those who signed up were encouraged to spend $2,000 for essentially nothing more than a fancy title and the right to earn commissions. They were then prompted to spend another $5,400 to buy the actual cosmetics. Members who joined would earn bonuses on new recruits who came aboard, as long as they also made similar investments.[8]

But on November 18, 1975, Koscot was ordered by the FTC "to cease using its open-ended, multilevel marketing plan; engaging in illegal price fixing and price discrimination and imposing selling and purchasing restrictions on its distributors; and to cease making exaggerated earnings claims and other misrepresentations in an effort to recruit distributors."

Other cases soon followed, providing Richard with a treasure trove of material. Even in recent years, there have been companies with some of the same eyebrow-raising characteristics. In June 2007, the Federal Trade Commission sued the MLM company BurnLounge, which operated online digital music stores. Following an investigation, the FTC concluded BurnLounge was a pyramid scheme since the majority of its members were compensated more for recruiting new members into the business than for actually selling services.[9]

In July 2007, a California court barred the company from operating and froze the assets of one of its promoters, pending a trial. More than fifty thousand people were said to have been affected in the scam, with more than 90 percent of them losing money.

The FTC shuttered several more MLMs, including the Global Information Network, Trek Alliance, and a company called Five Star that marketed leases of "dream vehicles" for free, as long as they paid an annual fee and recruited others into the opportunity. After a trial, the US District Court for the Southern District of New York determined Five Star was a pyramid scheme since people didn't make anything near the money they were promised.

As for what had been found on Herbalife, "Send me something," Ackman told Richard, who made an appointment to visit him face-to-face the next time she was in the city.

The day of the meeting, Manhattan was sweltering, the humidity barely budging even after a midday downpour, when Richard, still soaking wet from the storm, took the elevator up to the forty-second floor, and the offices of Pershing Square, Ackman's firm.

Richard exited the elevator bank, walked through the glass doors into the pristine, white-washed offices, and was escorted to Ackman's conference room overlooking Central Park, the spectacular view mostly obscured by the angry weather outside.

It was there that Richard waited for her prized audience.

Finally, after several lonesome minutes, Ackman flew into the room in a whirlwind, trailed by an assistant, who handed him a tote bag overflowing with papers, along with a golf umbrella. Clearly distracted, Ackman quickly apologized and said he was unable to stay because of a pressing family matter, leaving Richard disappointed and drenched.

But before rushing for the exit, Ackman asked one of his top analysts, Shane Dinneen, and a Pershing Square attorney named Roy Katzovicz to sit in for him and hear Richard out. Seated around the conference table, Richard reached into her bag and pulled out the report, its edges wrinkled and weathered from travel, all the while trying to quiet her jangling nerves. Richard may have been an accomplished journalist who'd made a living writing about hard-to-understand subjects on Wall Street, but she felt out of her league in front of guys who were Ivy League analyzers of arcane numbers and corporate balance sheets.

Richard took a deep breath and began, focusing on Herbalife's questionable compensation plan for its legion of distributors. She likened their constant push to recruit new clients to running on a treadmill, as members made purchase after purchase of the company's products in a quest to move up the food chain to where the real money was made. "It's so manipulative and disrespectful," said Richard as she described the structure, zeroing in on claims made by some of Herbalife's top sellers, who boasted in marketing videos of the fancy cars, boats, and mansions they'd attained through selling the company's shakes.

While Richard spoke, Dinneen appeared to do some calculations in his head, considering many of the key questions anyone on Wall Street would ask before making an investment: How big was Herbalife? Who were its customers? Who were the largest shareholders? And so on.

The men in the room seemed interested but not overly enthusiastic. Still, they peppered Richard with questions for the next ninety or so minutes, before the meeting eventually wrapped. Dinneen seemed the most taken by what he'd heard, but wanted to do his own research before fully buying what Richard was selling. It wasn't that he didn't believe Richard's work—it was just the way he operated.

Dinneen, who had fiery orange hair and a slim, athletic build, had started at Pershing straight from Harvard, where he graduated at the top of his class. He was intensely competitive, to the point where he'd go for a run in Central Park and almost toy with the other joggers— setting a pace to goad them, then blow by them in a flash, leaving them standing still.

In the office, Dinneen showed the same kind of determination. Colleagues said he came across as aloof and dispassionate, and he would often walk around stone-faced and openly try to "one-up" other analysts in Pershing's weekly investment meetings. But there was no denying Dinneen's brilliance and intellectual endurance.

Ackman was drawn to it. He'd taken to Dinneen in part because he'd done the bulk of the work on one of Pershing's biggest-ever winners, an investment that would go down as one of the greatest in hedge-fund history. In 2008, Pershing Square had bought shares in General Growth Properties (GGP), a mall operator that was teetering on bankruptcy. Ackman had eyed the stock for months, but Dinneen repeatedly urged that they hold off on buying until shares dropped even more. It proved to be prescient advice. When the real-estate bubble popped in 2008, General Growth's stock dropped below $1 a share. The company would end up filing for what was then the largest real-estate bankruptcy in US history. Ackman pounced, investing at the bottom, helping to bring the company out of Chapter 11. The trade was a home run, turning the original $60 million into a stunning $3.7 billion.[10]

Dinneen's work on GGP had earned the analyst star status at Pershing Square, at least with his boss. If Herbalife was really the fraud Richard had described, Ackman wanted Dinneen to be the one to determine it.

Dinneen dove in, doing a bottom-up analysis of Herbalife and reporting what he'd found to Pershing's investment committee, which met weekly on Tuesdays. During those sessions, a half-dozen Pershing analysts would sit around the conference table and pitch their ideas while the others, including Ackman, scrutinized them.

Paul Hilal, a Pershing Square partner who'd met Ackman at Harvard, seemed especially ambivalent about the idea. He also made it no secret, to anyone who would listen, that shorting Herbalife was a risky endeavor since the laws prohibiting and defining pyramid schemes were especially murky and hard to fully understand.

Scott Ferguson, another senior partner with an Ivy League pedigree, had more "personal" concerns. Ferguson openly worried that Herbalife distributors who were making several millions of dollars a year selling the company's products wouldn't take kindly to some Wall Street asshole trying to shut the whole operation down. He feared they could become violent, once telling Ackman he was scared that one of them would even try to shoot him.

Ackman wasn't one to come across as timid, but he was skeptical of the trade and how or even *if* it could pay off. When Richard returned a few weeks later for her long-awaited face-to-face, she found Ackman far from ready to commit to adding Herbalife to the Pershing portfolio. "What is this?" he asked about one section of the report. "What does that mean?" he'd interrupt as he flipped through Richard's work.

It was just the way Ackman's analytical mind—and mouth—worked. He could pick apart a pitch quickly, deciding within seconds if it had merit or not. He'd pull facts with astounding regularity from the depths of something he'd read or researched several years earlier. As most in the office had quickly learned, debating Ackman could prove futile for the unprepared. Ackman's intellect made him enough of an adversary.

Then, there was his presence.

At 6'3", with piercing blue eyes, a barrel chest, and the fully-grayed mane of a man twenty years his senior, Ackman was imposing, as much for his physical appearance as for his quick, unsparing wit. Richard knew that as well as anyone, having interviewed Ackman while working on *Confidence Game*. Now, she found Ackman anything but sold on her short idea.

Ackman noted that Herbalife had been in business for thirty years, appearing wholly unconvinced government regulators would put a dagger into the company now. "Why would anyone care?" Ackman wondered. And even if Richard's thesis was right, Ackman questioned whether there would be a catalyst to prove it publicly, which is what was needed to bring down their stock price and make the investment a financial success.

There was also the lingering MBIA hangover—the toll that the whole affair had taken on him personally and the fact that he had no real desire to repeat such a saga.

The meeting ended with Richard pledging to keep Ackman informed of any new developments she'd found, which she periodically did until the end of the year.

Richard kept digging, taking a particular interest in Herbalife's mushrooming nutrition clubs, a part of the business its CEO, Michael Johnson, had declared in 2009 was "the greatest source of our growth over the last three to four years."[11] By 2011, Herbalife had more than sixty-seven thousand nutrition clubs around the world. Herbalife billed the clubs as social hangouts where people could gather, try a nutritional shake or tea, and learn about the company and the business opportunity it presented.

The clubs had started in Zacatecas, Mexico, in 2006, and quickly caught on in nearby communities. When Johnson and the company's president, Des Walsh, visited one during a routine business trip to the country, they were so taken by what they saw they came home determined to replicate their success in the United States, which they did. In fact, the clubs had grown so prolific in recent years they accounted for 35 to 40 percent of Herbalife's global sales.

Richard had a different view and thought the clubs were shady, if not downright sinister. Just like she'd done as an investigative reporter, Richard had gone out in the field and done surveillance on nutrition clubs in Pennsylvania, Rhode Island, and New York City. She was disturbed by much of what she'd found. The establishments were almost always rickety-looking storefronts, mostly in heavily Latino neighborhoods. There were no signs or official Herbalife markings, and doors were always kept closed, with the windows fully covered by curtains. "Welcome" signs were prohibited, along with anything else that could give the appearance of a typical retail operation, including those now ubiquitous credit card logo stickers on the front door, which were also banned.

Herbalife billed the establishments in its own internal documents as places "for meeting and sharing the Herbalife products in a social atmosphere as well as explaining the business opportunity." But to Richard, the clubs appeared to be a scam—a place where visitors stopped in for a shake or tea and were then suckered into buying thousands of dollars' worth of Herbalife products with hopes of striking it rich.

Richard told Ackman's team of what she'd found, but the investor still remained reticent to get involved. That is, until January 5, 2012, when Herbalife was declared "an illegal pyramid scheme" in a Brussels court.[12] The case was brought by a Belgian nonprofit called Test-Aankoop, and though Herbalife fought the accusations vigorously, a judge rejected the company's claim that its salespeople could be considered "retail customers" and not simply distributors of its products. Furthermore, the judge argued, based on the evidence presented, Herbalife's only actual customers were Herbalife's salespeople themselves. The company appealed, and for most people that day, the news was but a blip, getting almost zero media coverage.

Ackman and Dinneen, though, were among the few who took notice. Richard mentioned she'd booked a trip to visit another Herbalife nutrition club in Omaha, Nebraska, in the following week, and Ackman told Dinneen to go see for himself what was really going on.

On the morning of January 11, 2012, Richard and Dinneen walked into a nutrition club in Omaha and found several people drinking Herbalife teas and shakes. They'd met the club's operator, a man named Jose, who claimed to spend $3,000 a month on products to serve and sell in the club. But after watching Jose's customers come and go and calculating how much his supposed "regulars" were spending, it appeared to Richard as though the man was making about $3,450 a month in revenues, barely enough to get by after paying rent and other expenses. Jose complained about how difficult it was to recruit without signs and the other markings of a traditional business establishment.

Richard concluded that the entity looked unviable.

Dinneen came home from Omaha more convinced than ever of Herbalife's misdeeds, and continued to pitch the idea and his own new findings in the Tuesday meetings.

By mid-February, Richard and Schulman's full investigative report on Herbalife was ready to drop. They sent it to Ackman and other big-name hedge funders on the payroll, hoping at least one would bite. The document, dated February 22, 2012, was damning. It was a hundred pages long and began with the statement, "Herbalife would be an impressive American success story, if it weren't based on a lie." It continued, "Far from being a shining example of corporate beneficence, Herbalife is a story of stunning deception. It is a pyramid scheme whose revenue comes not from retail sales of its products, as it contends, but from capital lost by failed investors in its business opportunity."[13]

Richard and Schulman charged that 98 percent of investors in Herbalife's business, some 11 million people since 2004, had failed, losing a combined $11 billion. They documented what they'd found at the club in Omaha, and at others in Pennsylvania and Rhode Island, saying they were nothing more than a "stage set" for a "get rich quick and achieve the American dream" scheme.

They took aim at Herbalife's so-called Chairman's Club members—the top-level distributors who'd earned millions over the years and boasted about it openly. Richard and Schulman wrote of a video presentation they'd found in which a slippery-sounding distributor named Doran Andry told a group of wide-eyed new sellers that they could earn $55 million in "passive, residual income" after ten years through the same nutrition-club operations Richard and Schulman thought were bogus. "This opportunity called nutrition clubs is an opportunity for you guys to make tens of millions of dollars or hundreds of millions of dollars over the course of a lifetime," he told the group.

The women had also gotten their hands on Herbalife training materials that described "magic numbers" needed to reach the higher levels of the pyramid. They argued that the system of internal milestones was rigged from the beginning. "While the vast majority of people who become Herbalife distributors fail," they wrote, "a tiny fraction of those at the top of the pyramid are enormously successful. Their stories are held out as examples of what is possible for any Herbalife distributor."

They sneered at the longevity of many top distributors, claiming, "as in all pyramid schemes, the opportunity is greatest for those who get in early," making the point that it was the suckers who joined later who were often left holding the bag, or, in this case, thousands of dollars' worth of Herbalife products. The nutritional supplements, they showed, were often dumped on eBay and other internet sites when they couldn't be sold as expected.

The report documented other similar companies either fined or shuttered by regulators over the years and concluded by calling Herbalife "a predatory money trap." "The fraud is both obvious and complex," they wrote. "We have uncovered strong evidence that Herbalife operates as a pyramid scheme."

The women were hopeful that Team Ackman would read the document and be so compelled by it that they'd be willing to start shorting Herbalife shares on the spot. There was only one issue—Ackman's lawyers initially wouldn't let him read it, as they were worried about some obscure legal language that protected Herbalife's distributors. Pershing's attorney initially redacted nearly every line in the report, giving Ackman a black-marked copy to see. Ackman wasn't happy, but the move was a sign of just how sensitive Pershing's management was to potential lawsuits that might pop up.

Even so, Dinneen, who'd seen the Omaha club for himself and then continued to do his own research, sometimes sleeping under his desk between long days at the office, was more convinced than ever that Herbalife was the perfect Pershing target.

Ackman, however, who was ultimately the only voice that really mattered, still wondered about a catalyst, knowing that no matter how good a story was, there had to be a mechanism to make it work. The MBIA struggle had underscored it, and winning with Herbalife, he thought, would be no different.

Pershing's investment committee continued to meet, and though some, including Dinneen, argued vociferously in favor of betting against Herbalife, Ackman refused, perhaps swayed by the misgivings of others and by his own desire to not be the front man in another public feud, no matter how compelling the story.

Not that Ackman didn't want to be the center of attention again. Quite the opposite. He lived for it.

3

THE ACTIVIST

Bill Ackman smashed a return into the net, served up an expletive, and returned hastily to the baseline for the next point. It was just a friendly tennis match on Ackman's spectacular Bridgehampton property over the summer of 2016, but the investor was as dialed-in as ever. There were grunts and grimaces, the atmosphere nearly as tense as Wimbledon. Ackman liked pushing himself against players with pedigrees—former pros or aspiring ones who could run him around his Har-tru clay court. He may have been in all-whites instead of a business suit, but Ackman was no less determined to win. Ackman was always on.

"Bill plays tennis the same way he invests," said a friend and some-times on-court opponent of Ackman's. "He's looking for home runs and outright winners. He needs to win every point, game, and match he plays."

Those who know him best say that he has always been this way—fiercely competitive no matter the sport or challenge at hand.

"He likes to win and is always optimistic that he *will* win," said Mike Grossman, a childhood friend and one-time doubles partner who met Ackman at a local tennis club when he was thirteen years old. "We did win most of the time, and when we didn't he always thought it was an aberration," Grossman said.

Ackman was raised about thirty miles from Manhattan, in leafy Chappaqua, New York, known for being home to Bill and Hillary

Clinton and the kind of Westchester town dotted with old-monied mansions and a place where children of privilege were expected to do well in life.

Ackman was no exception.

The youngest child of Lawrence and Ronnie Ackman, young "Billy," as he was known back then, grew up in a well-to-do and loving family with all the accoutrements one might expect from such a statused upbringing. There were sleepaway camps in the summer, where Ackman enjoyed camping, canoeing, and kayaking along with baseball and other sports.

Taller than most boys his age, Ackman ran cross-country and captained the tennis team at the nearby prestigious Horace Greeley High School, where he excelled. Even then, Ackman showed the traits that have made him the most talked about investor on Wall Street.

"He was always larger than life. Very opinionated, self-confident, brash, blunt, honest, and polarizing," said Grossman. "Some people loved him, some people didn't, but he made his presence felt and always had an unshakeable faith in himself."

While sports may have been Ackman's early passion, business was never far behind. Ever the aspiring entrepreneur, as a young teen Ackman had his own car-waxing operation, along with a few other side ventures, to make some extra cash.

"He was a big-time capitalist and always interested in how money could be made," said Grossman.

He also could look across the dinner table each night for inspiration.

Ackman's father had become CEO of the family's real-estate brokerage firm, named Ackman-Ziff, which traced its roots to the early 1920s. Ackman's grandfather had started the business with a brother, somehow surviving the Great Depression and World War II while building the firm up to focus on the lucrative business of property finance.

While Ackman took a modest liking to real estate, it was hardly a given that he'd follow in his father's footsteps. A straight-A student, Ackman graduated fourth in his class of 280 at Horace Greeley, as he was quick to tell anyone who asked.

Grossman said Ackman seemed destined for success and wasn't afraid to bet on it or talk about it. "I gave him a T-shirt for his sixteenth birthday, and the expression I had put on the shirt read, *a closed mouth gathers no foot,*" he said. "He got a kick out of it. He's genuine. He's real. There's no BS with Bill. He's a genuinely honest, high-integrity person. He'll tell you exactly what he thinks—there's no playing games or politics. What gets underestimated is his high level of integrity."

Ackman demonstrated his self-belief by wagering his father $2,000 that he'd score a perfect 800 on the verbal portion of the SAT. Ackman had been acing practice tests in the weeks leading up to the exam and figured he'd nail the real thing too. But the night before the test, Ackman's dad, perhaps figuring the pressure of the test was enough weight on his son's shoulders, along with having no real desire to lose a cool two grand, abruptly canceled the bet. Ackman got a 780, missing *one* question. He missed three on the math part, scoring a 750, and still seems pissed about it.[1]

Since Ackman's older sister, Jeanne, had begun studying at Harvard College a year earlier, it seemed only natural that Bill would follow suit. Sure enough, in the fall of 1984, Ackman enrolled in Cambridge, and it didn't take long for the outspoken freshman to make an impression on the more seasoned student body. Friends say Ackman was outgoing and opinionated—unafraid to start a debate or express his passions and points of view.

"Bill was polished at a super young age," said Whitney Tilson, a star investor and public commentator who first met Ackman in 1986 on Harvard's campus. "Just off-the-wall smart, ferociously competitive, off-the-charts confidence, which some might call arrogance, always an incredible talker."

Those attributes would come in handy during a college job Ackman took selling ads, alongside Tilson, for the "Let's Go" series of travel guides that were popular with backpackers.

"Whoever could sell the ads the quickest was going to make the most money," Tilson said. "We were in a little room, no windows. I could listen to Bill's calls and he could listen to mine. We were supposed to make $5,000 each—that's what they made the previous year—but we ended up making twelve to thirteen thousand dollars each. We sold a half million dollars' worth of ads in the course of a summer. That's real money for college kids."

Ackman excelled in the classroom too, and on the adjacent Charles, where he rowed crew. He said he became one of the best "strokes" on the Harvard team—the member of the squad who guides the boat and sets its pace. And though he'd never make it to the top boat, where all the glory was, Ackman claimed he was happy just to be recognized at all.

But while driven to succeed at Harvard, Ackman had no clear direction of what he wanted to be in life, other than to make a lot of money. After graduating, he went to work in the family business. His job was to find financing for developers to build new projects or to help developers who wanted to borrow money. Ackman was convinced by his father that the experience he'd get at the firm was better than that at most other jobs, and being the son of the CEO couldn't hurt either.

Ackman did the job for two years, but found the work uninspiring. He figured it would be more fun to be on the other side of the phone—the "players" actually looking to do the deals, rather than the guy trying to service ones. And though real estate may have been an interest, it wasn't a passion.

Still, Wall Street was barely on Ackman's radar. He'd occasionally pick up the *Wall Street Journal* for kicks, but he hadn't aspired to be the next Warren Buffett—at least not yet.

After those two years at his father's firm, Ackman returned to Cambridge to attend Harvard Business School, where he found his true calling. It was Wall Street where Ackman decided that he would make his mark.

Having some close-to-home connections helped. One night, Ackman's dad made an introduction during a cocktail party to a man named Leonard Marks, a successful investor who urged the young wannabe to read Benjamin Graham's definitive value-investing bible, *The Intelligent Investor*, which Ackman readily did, along with several other books on the subject. It was the same Ben Graham who'd inspired Mr. Buffett many years earlier, so Ackman was more than eager to dive in.

It wasn't long before he'd put the words of wisdom he'd read on paper into practice.

At Harvard, Ackman used $40,000 he had saved from the job at Ackman-Ziff and, in October of 1990—at the bottom of the recent stock-market cycle—opened a Fidelity account in his own name and began investing for the first time. His first stock purchase was Wells Fargo for $47 a share, as he believed the bank was better than its competitors because of its more conservative loan book. It didn't hurt that the aforementioned Buffett, whom Ackman was all but idolizing at this point, had recently bought shares too and at a higher price. Ackman would also buy stocks in real-estate firms and retailers, using the knowledge he'd soaked up over the years from his father. One of those trades was in the department store chain Alexander's. Ackman bought shares for around $8 apiece when the company filed for bankruptcy. Months later, he nearly tripled his money, selling them for $21.[2]

Always on the hunt for insight, Ackman read every word of Buffett's annual letters to learn as much as he could about the art of investing. In a twist of fate, the Oracle and his young believer would actually have a chance meeting at Fordham University in New York City, where both were attending an event. Ackman's seat that day in the auditorium just happened to be next to Susan Buffett, Warren's then wife, who took an interest in the young investor and saved a place for him next to the couple at lunch. At the meal, seated right next to the man himself, Ackman peppered Buffett with questions about the markets, he later recalled. But it wasn't a story about the markets that stood out. As Ackman tells it, after returning to his seat with a plate of food, including a brownie for dessert, Mr. Buffett salted the *entire* dish, including the dessert.

Some of the actual investing conversation must have stuck as well because back at HBS, Ackman approached a classmate named David Berkowitz about starting their own investment fund.

"David said a lot of smart things," Ackman told the *Washington Post*. "And I thought this is a sharp guy. We became friendly."[3]

Berkowitz studied engineering at MIT, and Ackman thought he was brilliant. Berkowitz, who'd come from a family of more modest means than that of the Westchester-reared Ackman, was interested, but nearly backed out at the eleventh hour.

Berkowitz eventually agreed to join forces on the fund with the stipulation that the two neophytes would need to raise at least $3 million to get going. Ackman had already raised money from the father of a classmate and two professors at Harvard, including $250,000 from Martin H. Peretz, who taught social studies and was then the editor-in-chief of *New Republic* magazine.[4] Peretz, who now serves on Pershing Square's advisory board, wasn't shy in urging Ackman to start his own fund rather than work at a larger institution. It was then that a friend of Ackman's then girlfriend's mother introduced the boys to George Rausch, an heir of the Ryder truck family. Rausch agreed to give the boys $900,000, bringing their total assets to $2.9 million—still slightly below Berkowitz's threshold. Finally, Ackman was introduced to a member of the infamous Durst family who agreed to give the boys $250,000. It was enough to push Berkowitz over the goal line.

Ackman's father had kicked in money too, and with a total of seven initial investors and $3.2 million in assets under management, Gotham Partners Management opened in New York City, with the fledgling firm renting space in the famed Helmsley Building, at 230 Park Avenue, where other startups had also set up shop.[5] Sharing a single office, the two men had desks, a Bloomberg terminal, and no windows. In other words, they had arrived.

One of Gotham's first investments was in Circa Pharmaceuticals, which had seen its shares plummet. Ackman saw it as a real-estate play, believing the property assets were worth more than what the stock was currently trading for.[6]

"Wall Street was just dumping the stock," Berkowitz said at the time. "But it still had significant assets."[7] The investment was a hit with Gotham. They sold after several months with a 63 percent gain.[8]

With Berkowitz the operator and Ackman the investor, the two newbies on New York City's hedge-fund scene were off and running, albeit somewhat more slowly than they'd hoped. The fund fell 3 percent in its first month—not exactly the start they were hoping for. Things would quickly turn, though, and Gotham would end its first year up more than 20 percent.[9]

Word began to spread about the dynamic young investors, eventually reaching a man named Daniel H. Stern. Stern was a partner at the storied Ziff Brothers Investments and had seeded several up and comers, such as Barry Sternlicht, who started Starwood Capital, and Daniel Och of Och Ziff Capital Management. With Stern's blessing, the Ziffs gave Ackman and Berkowitz $10 million to play with. They also agreed to pay Gotham's expenses until the young firm got up to scale.

It didn't take long for Ackman and tiny Gotham to flex their muscles.

In 1994, when Ackman was just twenty-seven, he launched an audacious effort to control one of New York City's most iconic landmarks. Earlier that year, Gotham had quietly grabbed a nearly 6 percent position in the real estate investment trust (REIT) that owned Rockefeller Center and had fallen into bankruptcy protection.[10] Ackman partnered in the investment with the Leucadia National Corporation, which owned a 7 percent stake and backed Ackman's ambitious turnaround plan.[11] A bidding war soon ensued, with the twenty-something Ackman up against such real-estate heavyweights as Sam Zell and Tishman-Speyer—not to mention David Rockefeller himself. And though Ackman would eventually lose his bid, the tussle alone, and the young activist's rabble-rousing along the way, had pushed the value of Rock Center's REIT sharply higher. It paid off handsomely for Gotham.[12]

It was also Bill Ackman's first foray into activist investing.

The Rockefeller play helped Gotham finish 1995 with a 39 percent return, while earning the young investor a nice payday along with some lucrative reputational capital with Leucadia's president, Joseph S. Steinberg.[13]

In 1997, after a few more up-and-down investments, Ackman and Berkowitz invested in Gotham Golf (the name of which was purely coincidence), which controlled about two dozen golf courses around the country.[14] Ackman was betting that its real-estate assets would keep appreciating in value. When they didn't, Ackman and Berkowitz doubled down, continuing to buy golf courses, which only increased the company's growing debt load.

Though Gotham Partners had returned a strong 19.65 percent net of fees in 2001,[15] by 2002, the size of the golf position had quickly become an anvil around the fund's neck. Losses were piling up, and investors had begun asking for their money back.[16] These payouts, known as redemptions, were a hedge fund's worst nightmare. This was especially true for Gotham, which had a highly concentrated portfolio made up of only a few names and positions, some of which were illiquid and not easy to unwind.

Ackman and Berkowitz tried to merge the failing golf company with First Union Real Estate Equity & Mortgage Investments, an REIT holding that Ackman had bought in 1998, but the plan was derailed when an investor sued to block the transaction.[17] The situation grew more precarious by the day, with Ackman holding out hope for a lifeline. He thought he'd found one in the famed investor J. Ezra Merkin, who agreed to put $60 million of fresh capital into Gotham Partners.[18] Merkin had invested $10 million in one of the firm's credit funds in the past and had even shaken hands with Ackman on the new money.

The only question was the timing. Ackman and Berkowitz needed the money quickly to avoid showing losses. In the meantime, they turned to their other positions to help ease the strain the redemptions were causing.

One such "long" they were banking on was an investment in a controversial company called Pre-Paid Legal Services. Pre-Paid was a multilevel marketing company that sold services to individuals and small businesses and had more than 1.3 million members nationwide. Not everyone was a believer though. The company was heavily shorted on Wall Street, with skeptics charging that Pre-Paid's services were actually worthless and that the company was fraught with accounting issues.

Ackman and Berkowitz disagreed, however, and had become the company's staunchest supporters, holding one million shares of stock.[19] In fact, the two men thought so highly of the company that Pre-Paid had become Gotham's biggest position, with 13 to 15 percent of the fund's capital dedicated solely to the investment.

On November 19, 2002, with a wave of redemptions rolling in, Gotham put out a report titled "A Recommendation for Pre-Paid Legal Services, Inc." on its website.[20] On the document's front page, Ackman and Berkowitz said, "We believe that much of the press coverage of Pre-Paid, has been unfair, unbalanced, and in many cases simply wrong. It is our intent in this report to both lay out in detail the bullish case for Pre-Paid and to refute many of the bearish arguments."[21]

Ackman said Gotham held more than one million shares of Pre-Paid Legal's stock and that "based upon our research and analysis, and after giving due weight to the shorts' arguments, we believe that Pre-Paid is a highly attractive business that is extremely undervalued."

In one section under the heading "How do the Shorts Sleep at Night?" Ackman called Pre-Paid "one of the most heavily shorted of all companies listed on a US exchange," saying, "We are at a loss to understand what the short sellers are thinking. They must believe that the business is going to implode . . . and soon."

Ackman's advocacy was working. Pre-Paid Legal's shares began rising. Ackman began to hope that his Hail Mary play was working. But just a few weeks later, on December 6, New York's Supreme Court formally blocked the golf company merger, meaning Gotham Management wouldn't get the tens of millions it was counting on to help with its finances.

The ruling left Gotham Golf on the brink of bankruptcy. Even worse, Ackman had to tell Merkin they could no longer take his money.[22]

Three days after the devastating court decision, Ackman tried to salvage another of the fund's large positions when he released his blistering report on MBIA, questioning its Triple-A bond rating and beginning the seven-year legal and financial saga. But for now, Ackman couldn't afford to play the long game—he needed a win just to stay in business. Though the stock initially fell when Ackman went public, it quickly rebounded, leaving Ackman and Berkowitz in something of a stranglehold.

It soon became clear that the only viable option was to wind down the firm.

Over the next two weeks, Gotham sold more than 20 percent of its position in Pre-Paid Legal. Company insiders started bailing too, raising questions in the media as to whether Gotham had grown so desperate it had pumped and then dumped the stock.[23] Ackman refused to comment publicly on the suggestion, which was raised in a Sunday *New York Times* piece, on the advice of a public relations consultant.[24]

In January 2003, after ten years in business, Gotham Partners Management, whose assets had grown from $3 million to $300 million, and which had scored annual gains of 20 percent since inception, began the process of winding down. It was a difficult, even embarrassing, decision, but at the time Ackman said that "to wind down seemed the fairest thing to do."

Embarrassment would be the least of Ackman's worries a few weeks later, when New York Attorney General Eliot Spitzer began an investigation into Ackman and Berkowitz, probing the MBIA short and the alleged sketchy trading in Pre-Paid Legal. Ackman felt the probe was a witch hunt that was only initiated because of MBIA's contacts high up in Albany, the state capital.

The Spitzer investigation dragged on for months, leaving Ackman not only out of a job but also under the government's glare and on the defensive. Spitzer was a pit bull. He'd already earned the title "The Sheriff of Wall Street" for taking on the big banks and dealing out more than $1.4 billion in fines over analyst research reports. Many wondered whether Ackman would be Spitzer's next piece of roadkill. On May 28, 2003, Ackman made the trip to Lower Manhattan, to 120 Broadway, where Spitzer's office was located, for a nearly eight-hour deposition.[25]

Joined there by his attorneys from the New York law firm Covington & Burling, Ackman was peppered about his report on MBIA, running through the intricacies of his detailed allegations against the company and what they all meant. Lawyers from the A.G.'s office then turned to Pre-Paid Legal, asking, among other things, where the investment idea had come from in the first place. "David Berkowitz came up with it," Ackman said. "I don't know where he got it."[26]

Ackman was asked about the timing of the Pre-Paid stock sales and news reports that the firm was selling even as it was "touting" the position on its own website. Ackman took issue with the characterization and defended the sales, saying a disclaimer on Gotham's website made it clear that it could alter its position on the stock at any time. He also explained why he couldn't go public to explain the sales when they occurred, arguing that given Gotham's precarious financial position, the news could have caused a run on what was left of the fund. Ackman claimed that Gotham was unexpectedly forced to sell in order to meet the flood of redemptions and that they simply had little choice.[27]

"David and I talked about it," Ackman said. "We decided to sell, and we sold."[28]

Though the investigation would ultimately find no wrongdoing, the whole ordeal left Ackman reeling, professionally and personally. He sold whatever of Gotham's assets he could—as quickly as he could—to help pay back his investors. One such investment was called Hallwood Realty, a Dallas-based REIT whose shares were trading near $60. Ackman believed they were worth $140, but since the firm was facing a wave of redemptions, he wasn't in a position to stall for a comeback. So, the thirty-something investor picked up the phone and cold-called a man nearly thirty years his senior—a man considered one of the most powerful investors on Wall Street.

His name was Carl C. Icahn.

Icahn had built a reputation over his decades in the business as one of the shrewdest dealmakers on the Street. He chewed people up and spit them out for a living, and was always looking for his next score.

Ackman asked Icahn if he could help, a tinge of desperation in his voice.

Perhaps sensing Ackman's weakened position, Icahn said he was interested, and the two quickly struck a deal for Hallwood.

The agreement, dated March 1, 2003, stipulated that Icahn would pay Ackman $80 a share[29]—a generous premium from the current stock price, but still below what Ackman thought the investment was really worth.

Knowing the elder investor's penchant for making money, Ackman had Icahn's lawyer, Keith Schaitkin, write in a provision the men called "schmuck insurance" to protect Ackman from looking like an idiot if Icahn quickly flipped the stock for a much higher price. The deal said that if Icahn sold the shares "or otherwise transfers, or agrees to sell or otherwise transfer, any of the Sale Units," within three years, Icahn and Ackman would split any profits above a 10 percent return, with the money due within two business days. In addition, Ackman added a clause that said if the deal became contentious, the loser would cover the other's legal fees.

Schaitkin had pulled a near all-nighter drawing up the agreement.

Ackman considered the two men partners, hopeful that the older investor would turn Hallwood into more money for both of them.

On July 29, 2003, the deal was done. Icahn put out a press release at 1 p.m. Eastern time proposing to buy Hallwood himself in a hostile bid of $132.50 per share, or $222 million. The price was a stunning 87 percent premium over where Hallwood shares had closed trading in March when he and Ackman had drawn up their agreement.[30]

Hallwood rejected the offer and in 2004 agreed to merge with another firm for $137 a share, which Icahn, as a shareholder, voted against. Nevertheless, Icahn scored a windfall, pocketing the difference of the $80 a share he'd paid Ackman for the stock and the final merger price in the $130 range.[31]

Ackman thought he was entitled to a piece of that money, but after the two-day timeframe required in his original contract with Icahn, no wire transfer had been made.

Ackman called Icahn to check on his share of the profits, detailing the conversation in the *New York Times* in 2011.

"First off, I didn't sell," Ackman said Icahn told him.

"Well, do you still own the shares?" Ackman said he asked.

"No," Mr. Icahn said. "But I didn't sell."

The conversation quickly devolved, with both men threatening to sue each other.

In 2004, Ackman did just that, contending breach of contract.

In a statement, Icahn said, "Hallwood was acquired in a merger transaction that we voted against. We did not believe that the agreement covered such a situation, based on cases in a number of states, and it was very clear from my negotiations with Bill that he was not to be paid under these circumstances."[32]

But in 2005, a New York court disagreed with Icahn, as did an appeals court the following year.

The two men did try to come to a resolution, meeting at Icahn's favorite Italian restaurant, Il Tinello, an old-school joint on West 56th Street where waiters still wear tuxedos and a dish called Pasta alla Icahn sits on the menu. Over Caesar salad and Dover sole, Icahn offered to give $10 million to a charity of Ackman's choice to settle the tiff for good. But Ackman refused, arguing that the money belonged not to him but to his investors.[33]

The battle remained in the courts for another half-dozen years until finally, in October 2011, Icahn was ordered to pay Ackman $9 million—the original money he was owed, plus interest.

Icahn was none too happy. He tore into Schaitkin. Admittedly, in his haste to draw up the deal quickly that evening eight years earlier, Schaitkin had clumsily left the contractual definition of a "sale" open to a court's interpretation. The careless mistake gave Ackman a legal opening and left Icahn fuming. "He started to lecture me," Mr. Icahn told the *New York Times*. "And I said, I've been in this business for 50 years, and I've done OK without your advice."[34]

After reluctantly paying Ackman his money, Icahn, who could hold a grudge with the best of them, quietly advised Schaitkin to keep his eyes open for an opportunity to get Ackman back.

Aside from the legal squabble with Icahn, 2004 was a milestone year for Ackman. He had rebounded from the Gotham blowup, and with $50 million in new seed money from his old buddy at Leucadia

National, Joseph Steinberg—the man he'd partnered with on the old Rockefeller deal—Ackman launched Pershing Square Capital Management and named the firm for the area in Manhattan near Grand Central Station where its first office was.

Fancying himself an activist, Ackman followed a standard modus operandi: take a large stake in a publicly traded company, then loudly push for change through the media and elsewhere in hopes the company would cede to his demands.

In early July 2005, Pershing Square took a 9.9 percent stake in the fast-food chain Wendy's International and sent a letter to the company's management urging them to spin off the Tim Horton's doughnut chain. Ackman argued that a new publicly traded listing of Tim Horton's would help Wendy's stock go up in value by giving the company more control over its performance.

On July 29, only weeks after Ackman's first letter, Wendy's agreed to a spin-off, with its chairman and CEO, Jack Schuessler, saying in a conference call, "We really believe the two brands are moving apart. I think Tim's is growing faster and Wendy's is maturing." Ackman, who was also on the call, said, "I think management did an excellent job. . . . We're excited to be shareholders."[35]

Wendy's shares spiked 14 percent on news of the spin-off of Tim Horton's to a new fifty-two-week high of $51.70.[36] The stock had been barely above $30 when Ackman initially invested.

That same year, Ackman took a $500 million stake in Wendy's competitor McDonald's, urging it to follow a similar strategy and spin off some of its company-owned franchises. The plan was roundly rejected by McDonald's management that November.

Undeterred, in January 2006 Ackman upped the ante and unveiled his plans for the company during a live presentation at a conference in Midtown Manhattan called "A Value Menu for McDonald's." Ackman served up his plan, along with McDonald's hamburgers, to the audience, making many of the same arguments he'd made the previous fall.

Once again, McDonald's said no, but it did agree to buy back $1 billion worth of stock and license fifteen hundred of its restaurants to franchisees. In 2007, Ackman cashed out of the Golden Arches, selling his entire stake in the chain while pocketing a return of almost 100 percent.[37]

The victories in Wendy's and McDonald's, along with other high-profile plays in the department store chain Sears and bookseller Barnes and Noble, had made Ackman a celebrity on Wall Street. As more people began following his every move, Pershing Square's assets grew, and grew rapidly. By 2007, they had ballooned to almost $5 billion. The legend of Bill Ackman was growing with both the public and his peers. It would lead to one of the biggest bets of Ackman's career.

On July 16, 2007, Pershing Square unveiled a position in the retailer Target, claiming in the filing that the stock was undervalued.[38] Ackman had accumulated a 9.6 percent position in the company, proclaiming that shares, which he'd bought in the high $60s, were worth more than $100.[39]

On the surface, the investment appeared to follow others Ackman had made up to that point, focusing on an undervalued name with a strong real-estate presence. But the structure of the investment was different, most notably for who was involved. For starters, Ackman had hit up many of his friends in the hedge-fund industry for the capital, including Daniel S. Loeb of Third Point, Greenlight's David Einhorn, and York Capital's Jamie Dinan. The plan was to start a separate fund called Special Purpose Investment Vehicle, or SPIV, that Ackman said would only invest in a single yet unannounced company.

Though Ackman told the group of investors he wouldn't reveal the investment in advance, he raised $2 billion from fifteen different money managers in a matter of weeks, a testament to his growing prowess in the industry.

"He was able to raise money, in a blind pool, from the smartest guys in the business," said one of those who gave Ackman a chunk of cash. "Two billion in fourteen days, and he told us the stock is broken, that it's an iconic company and easy to fix."

But the investment was a disaster from nearly the beginning.

Though Ackman would get Target to sell a portion of its credit card business, the timing of the investment was far from perfect. It was made right before the Great Recession, which threatened to bring down the global financial system. Stocks plunged, including Target's, which crushed the value of Ackman's investment. Target also refused Ackman's demands to spin off its real-estate assets, saying the plan was "risky and speculative."[40]

Ackman launched a proxy fight, hoping to grab five seats, including one for himself, on the company's board of directors. "The deficit of experience on Target's board had contributed to the company's underperformance," wrote Ackman in a letter to shareholders.[41]

On May 29, 2009, at the Target Annual Meeting in Waukesha, Wisconsin, Ackman addressed shareholders, twice appearing to choke up while quoting John F. Kennedy and Martin Luther King Jr.[42]

"We launched this contest to make sure Target is never known in the future as a once-great company," he told the room before the results were revealed. When the official numbers came out, 70 percent of shareholders had voted to keep the incumbent board members, handing Ackman a sweeping and resounding defeat.

The corporate governance expert Claudia Allen told the *Minneapolis Star Tribune* that the vote was a milestone for the company, if not for activism itself. "It's a referendum on the strategic direction of the company," she said, "and management and the board obviously made a more compelling case."

After the vote, the headline in the hometown paper blared, "Shareholders: Target 4, Ackman 0."

Target may have won its first-ever proxy fight, but it was a costly affair—reportedly $11 million in expenses, not to mention hundreds of hours of agita. But the battle, and subsequent stock slide, would prove even more costly for Ackman and his band of billionaires.

The Target trade would end up losing nearly 90 percent of its value, pissing off many of the original investors. To make matters worse, many felt Ackman wasn't contrite enough afterward. Ackman acknowledged as much in a letter to the group that offered an opportunity to withdraw what was left of the money and waive performance fees for future investments if they chose to make them.

"In my effort to get last week's letter out promptly," he wrote, "I neglected to apologize. I am deeply disappointed by (the) dreadful performance and I apologize profusely for the fund's results to date. . . . Bottom line, PSIV has been one of the greatest disappointments of my career to date."[43]

To some, the words rang hollow, and they'd never forgive Ackman for the devastating loss of capital.

By late 2010, Ackman was smarting.

He'd not only hurt people who were his friends, but the Target investment also called into question his own abilities to manage risk. Some investors later told me they thought the plan was doomed from the start.

Whether it was to prove his mettle in the retail industry or to simply right the Target wrong, on October 8, 2010, Ackman revealed he'd taken an almost $1 billion stake in JC Penney, the 111-year-old company that had been floundering for the better part of two decades. Ackman had convinced Penney's board to oust longtime CEO Mike Ullman and replace him with Ron Johnson, a hotshot from Apple who was credited with helping design the tech company's snazzy retail stores.

Johnson quickly blew up Penney's "old" identity. He redesigned stores to have a "town square" feel, even pushing the idea of free ice cream and haircuts while you shopped, which seemed almost comical to some observers. Johnson introduced a "store within a store" concept, where the big box itself would have dozens of brand-name boutiques inside it to draw in shoppers with a wide array of interests. And, in the biggest upheaval of all, Johnson ended JC Penney's sales and signature coupons in favor of a more democratic "fair and square" pricing plan.

The plan bombed.

Sixteen months after Johnson took the helm, JC Penney shares had lost 50 percent of their value. More than nineteen thousand employees had lost their jobs. Sales dropped a stunning 25 percent.[44] Johnson was later fired, leaving JC Penney in shambles.

Ackman found himself ducking for cover. Among CEOs, Ullman was well liked and well respected. By taking him down, Ackman had angered a whole community of highly influential people.

Starbucks' founder and CEO, Howard Schultz, went on CNBC and unloaded on the investor. "Here's the situation," a clearly agitated Schultz said. "This is the truth. This is not fiction. Bill Ackman was the primary engineer and architect of recruiting Ron Johnson to the company. He and Ron Johnson co-authored a strategy that has fractured the company and ruined the lives of thousands of JC Penney employees. . . . Bill Ackman has the blood on his hands for being the architect and the recruiter of Ron Johnson and then the co-author of the strategy."[45]

Ackman would call JC Penney "probably the worst investment I've made."[46]

By mid-2012, with the Penney's debacle escalating and the Target wound still fresh, Pershing Square Capital was underperforming the S&P 500 Index and the Dow Jones Industrial Average.[47]

Bill Ackman was feeling the heat.

4

SELLING A DREAM

The ambulance eased its way through the security gate of 33064 Pacific Coast Highway in Malibu just before 11 a.m. Paramedics had received a frantic call about a man lying "lifeless and unresponsive" in the queen-sized bed in the master suite with no obvious signs of trauma on the body.[1]

Once inside the sprawling $27-million estate by the sea, medics pulled the six-foot, 190-pound man dressed in a black T-shirt and bikini briefs to the carpet, tried CPR to no avail, and pronounced the man dead on the scene at approximately 11.15 a.m.[2]

There, deceased in his mansion and already in rigor mortis, was forty-four-year-old Mark Reynolds Hughes, the flamboyant founder and chief executive officer of Herbalife International, Inc.

It was May 21, 2000.

Hughes' wife, Darcy, told the two LA police detectives who arrived at the house that her husband was drinking wine the night before and had fallen asleep following a birthday party for his eighty-seven-year-old grandmother. Darcy had tried to rouse him from the couch near midnight, then again at 1 a.m., but couldn't, and so she went to sleep. When she awoke the following morning, she'd found Hughes facedown in bed, thought "he did not look right," and immediately called 9-1-1. Security guards had first tried to revive him but couldn't.[3]

Nearly one month later, following a formal autopsy, the LA County coroner ruled Hughes had died of an accidental overdose following a four-day binge of alcohol and a toxic level of the prescription anti-depressant Doxepin. His blood-alcohol level was 0.21 percent, more than twice the legal limit.[4]

According to the coroner's report, Hughes had a history of binge drinking, had suffered from pneumonia the prior February, used two inhalers for asthma, and was on a handful of prescription medications. Darcy Hughes told investigators her husband was normally very health conscious and didn't use narcotics but that he smoked six to eight cigars a day.

It was an untimely death for a man who, in many ways, had become larger than life.

Hughes left an estate worth nearly $400 million.[5] He controlled more than half of Herbalife's publicly traded stock and owned homes in California and Hawaii. He was a revered figure within Herbalife, as much for what he'd made of the company as for what he had made of himself, even if Hughes' real persona was hazier than most knew.

Hughes told people he'd grown up in a mostly Latino part of La Mirada, in Southeast Los Angeles County, but in reality, it was a predominantly white middle-class neighborhood. It was the kind of place where most families had what they needed and kids didn't long for much.[6]

Hughes was brought up with two other boys by Jo Ann and Stuart Hartman, but even that was complicated. Stuart Hartman was one of two men who claimed to be Mark's biological father.[7] The Hartmans lived in La Mirada until the early 1960s, when the family packed up and moved ninety minutes up the 101, northeast to Camarillo, where Mark's father had started a new business supplying the US government with airline parts.[8] The new venture prospered, and with their improving financial situation, the family traveled, had a Cadillac in the portico, and had plenty of toys for the boys.[9]

But the good times were short-lived.

The Hartmans often fought over how to discipline the children, until ultimately they divorced when Mark was thirteen. During a deposition, Stuart told of a woman hooked on painkillers who occasionally used the family grocery money to support her costly and growing habit. Following his parents' split, Mark would go with his mother to live with her family, taking her maiden name with him.[10]

But while the surroundings may have been new, trouble never seemed too far away. As a teenager with his home life deteriorating, Hughes was busted multiple times for drugs and then shipped off to the CEDU institute in the San Bernardino Mountains to get clean. There, he befriended a staff member, whom he would accompany on the center's fund-raising trips to the ritzier parts of Los Angeles, like Bel-Air and Beverly Hills. On one such trip, the young Hughes coaxed $500 out of California's governor at the time. His name was Ronald Reagan.[11]

Then, on April 27, 1975, when Hughes was just nineteen and still at CEDU, his mother died from an overdose. Hughes told people she was thirty pounds overweight and had tried every quick fix in the book before reverting to diet pills, which had killed her. It would have been a heartbreaking story—had it been true.[12] The official toxicology report showed Jo Ann Hartman had a deadly level of the painkillers Darvon and Percodan in her system. She was just thirty-six years old.[13]

"That's why I dedicated my life to finding a better way to help people manage their weight," Hughes later said of his mother's passing, pushing the phony story until well after her death.[14]

In the mid-1970s, Hughes began selling weight-loss products for the Slendernow brand, which was owned by the Seyforth Laboratories.[15] Its founder, Mark Seyforth, was a pioneer in the fast-growing direct-selling industry, where products are sold by individuals acting as independent contractors.[16] People who signed up would either use the products themselves or sell them to family, friends, and co-workers, sometimes trying to recruit new salespeople into the operation. Their pay structure was controversial. Seyforth had invented a system where the independent contractors, called distributors, were compensated for what they sold as well as for how many new recruits they brought in. This multilevel marketing (MLM) structure was booming at the time.[17] Mary Kay Cosmetics, Amway, and Tupperware were well-established brands with histories dating back to the 1950s, but in the 2000s the practice was experiencing a rebirth, and these familiar companies were doing well, along with hundreds of lesser-known brands. At the same time, the structure was often criticized. Skeptics said MLMs were nothing more than pyramid schemes.

In 1975, the US government decided to take a closer look at the industry. On March 25 of that year, the Federal Trade Commission (FTC) sued Amway.[18] The FTC said the company's distributors had made deceptive statements about the business opportunity and that distributors were really only selling to others inside the Amway network and not to real customers.

The case dragged on for four years, but in 1979, Amway won when a judge ruled that the company's distributors were selling to legitimate customers. Amway could continue to operate, but, as part of the deal with regulators, was forced to put in a series of safeguards to better protect consumers. The court required that 70 percent of all products sold had to be to customers outside the Amway network. Sales reps had to document at least ten real retail sales per month, and, to protect new recruits from being scammed, Amway had to buy back any unsold inventory their sellers might have purchased for a full refund.

The so-called Amway Decision cleared the way for other MLMs to prosper, and Hughes seemed a perfect match for the controversial, yet mushrooming enterprises. Hughes became one of the top one hundred earners for another weight-loss company, Slendernow, in the years before it went bankrupt. He'd do a stint with yet another MLM selling exercise equipment before he appeared ready to start his own operation.[19]

Hughes had traveled to China, where he'd observed the Eastern philosophy of medicine and thought combining it with the West's burgeoning supplement industry could be a good business opportunity.

In February 1980, Mark Hughes founded Herbalife International, Inc. out of the back of his car, making the products in an old wig factory in Beverly Hills.[20]

He was just twenty-four years old.

Herbalife's early products were a meal-replacement shake called Formula 1, an herbal tablet called Formula 2, and a multivitamin, which the company claimed would help people lose weight.[21] The products were expensive, with the full line costing about $3,000. To counter the hefty cost, Hughes gave customers who agreed to become distributors a 25 percent discount, figuring they'd be able to purchase more if they got a deal. And, taking a page from the old Seyforth plan, Hughes paid distributors commissions based on how many new recruits they brought in. The more people who signed up and bought Herbalife products, the more money people could make, and the faster they'd climb the Herbalife food chain. The most successful distributors could earn commissions on what they sold and on their "downline," which referred to sales made from the recruits below them. Top sales people could move up to the President's Team and, ultimately, to the promised land—the Chairman's Club, where nearly every member was a multimillionaire.[22]

In Herbalife's first five years, revenues went from $386,000 to an astonishing $423 million, with Hughes serving as the company's leader and CEO, which in this case might as well have stood for Chief Evangelical Officer.[23] Hughes looked the part too. He was well tanned, with dark, feathered hair; he wore expensive suits, spoke with the cadence of a preacher, and pitched Herbalife at flashy spectacles inside local sports arenas.

"Trust me . . . I can tell you with absolute sincerity," he said at one event. "Anything is possible if you just keep using and talking and do it over and over and over and over again. The wildest dreams you've ever thought of can come true in Herbalife."[24]

Hughes was almost messianic in the way he preached Herbalife's virtues to his growing numbers of believers. Herbalife events were shown on cable television, with Hughes clad in a tux, wearing his trademark lapel pin that read "Lose Weight Now, Ask Me How?"[25]

"You can go as far as you want to go . . . because that's the way it is in Herbalife!" he'd exclaim.

Customers ate it up, and by 1985 Herbalife had more than seven hundred thousand distributors around the world, many of whom were sold on the promise of amazing wealth.[26]

"I used to drive a truck, and I made $80,000 last month," said a female distributor at one Herbalife extravaganza. "You want to join this sucker or not?"

"We haven't been in the business a year, yet our ninth royalty check was $40,883, and we're excited!" said a couple that same night.

Hughes chartered DC-10s, flying planeloads of distributors off to faraway places, including Sydney, Australia, for an extravaganza at the famed opera house. At one such fete, Donnie and Marie Osmond entertained. Ray Charles and Natalie Cole performed at another.[27]

It seemed as though nothing could stop Hughes, or Herbalife.

"Let me tell you what we're going to do with a company called Herbalife," he'd say. "We're going to take the company, customer by customer, and distributor by distributor, and we're going to take Herbalife around the entire world."

By the mid-1980s, Hughes was a player in the Los Angeles entertainment scene. He owned two Rolls-Royces and had bought an estate in Bel-Air for a reported $7 million from the entertainer Kenny Rogers.[28] Raucous parties were the norm.

In 1984, Hughes married Angela Mack, a former beauty queen from Sweden. Wayne Newton played at the reception. Mack was the second of Hughes's four wives.[29]

But in March of 1985, Herbalife was in trouble.

The California attorney general sued the company, charging it with making false claims about its products. The suit also claimed Herbalife was an illegal pyramid scheme.

In May of 1985, Hughes was called to testify before Congress, where he was grilled for two days by a Senate panel about Herbalife's research and testing. Lawmakers had been urging regulators to take a stronger stance on the diet and supplements industry, and Herbalife—along with its swashbuckling CEO—seemed as good a target as any.

While Hughes sat on the hot seat inside the hearing room, outside, a legion of Herbalife distributors marched in support of their leader. Hughes was defiant, telling questioners of the diet experts who'd already testified, "If they were such experts on weight loss, why were they so fat? I've lost sixteen pounds in the last few years!"[30]

The exchanges were testy.

Senator Warren B. Rudman, a Republican from New Hampshire, peppered Hughes on how he could possibly be an expert on the business when his own formal education history had stopped in the ninth grade.

Hughes replied, "I defy anybody to be able to produce the results that this company has."

"Do you believe it's safe to use your products without consulting a doctor?" Senator William V. Roth asked.

"Sure," replied Hughes. "Everybody needs good, sound basic nutrition. We all know that."[31]

Hughes tried to reassure his customers that despite the growing criticism, the business would survive.

"There are going to be a whole lot more articles that are going to come out about this company," Hughes told his loyalists. "And they're not all going to be positive. Some are going to be very negative. They're going to take some shots at us. They're going to say some things are wrong with our products. They're going to say some things are wrong with the ingredients."

On October 16, 1986, Herbalife settled with the state of California. The company agreed to pay an $850,000 fine and to stop some of its controversial marketing practices. The company didn't admit any wrongdoing, and after the settlement Hughes claimed victory.[32]

"I'm pleased to announce that after a year and a half, with many many discussions with the Food and Drug Administration, the California Attorney General and the State Department of Health, that all three of these agencies have independently determined that Herbalife have been, and still are, safe for the American public—and that all of our claims, products and marketing materials are now in complete compliance with the letter of state and federal law," he said.

Just one week later, on October 25, 1986, Hughes took Herbalife public on the Nasdaq exchange, making himself enormously rich.

Hughes continued to expand Herbalife, focusing on overseas markets. In 1990, Herbalife opened in France and Germany, then, in 1992, in Italy, Japan, and Hong Kong. By 1996, Herbalife was in Greece and South Korea and spreading quickly. Hughes was earning $17 million a year, making good on his promise "to take Herbalife around the entire world."[33]

In February 2000, during the company's five-day twentieth-anniversary celebration at the Los Angeles Forum, a video high-lighted the company's history—its rise from the back of Hughes's car to global powerhouse. Hughes handed out million-dollar checks to top sellers, while tears rolled down his cheeks. Hughes seemed over-whelmed by how far Herbalife had come.

Just three months later, he was dead.

At the time of Hughes's death, Herbalife had one million dis-tributors in forty-eight countries and $1.79 billion in annual sales.[34] Investors, though, seemed unimpressed, as Herbalife shares under-performed. A Los Angeles Times story documenting his death said that in the months prior Hughes had tried and failed to buy out the com-pany himself, unable to raise the necessary financing. Herbalife shares had slipped to nearly $10 a share.[35]

With its patriarch gone, it wasn't long before Herbalife began to suffer.

After sales grew 18 percent from 1996 to 1999, they rose just 7 percent in the first quarter of 2000. Shares dropped 40 percent after hitting a fifty-two-week high that January.[36] Herbalife's bottom line was suffering, and things weren't much better at the top. Herbalife went through four CEOs in three years. Distributors were essentially doing whatever they wanted, even if it meant pushing the legal limits. One especially questionable practice involved a business opportunity called "Newest Way to Wealth," which was run by a handful of pow-erful distributors who pushed an opportunity to "work from home."

Ads were pitched on the radio and cable television by popular person-alities. People who answered the spots were asked for their contact in-formation, which was then sold to distributors. The distributor would then call the prospective recruits, who would have to buy thousands of dollars' worth of products if they decided to join. These dubious busi-ness practices would eventually force Herbalife to close the Newest Way operation, but not before facing a class-action lawsuit.[37]

Plus, there were doubts as to whether Herbalife could survive without Hughes at the helm.

Then, in 2002, JH Whitney & Company and Golden Gate Capital, two West Coast–based private equity firms, took Herbalife private for less than $350 million and began a search for a new CEO—someone to lead the twenty-three-year-old company back to prominence.

On April 3, 2003, the firms announced who they'd found. He was a confident, smooth-talking fitness buff named Michael O. Johnson, and he was then president of Walt Disney International. "A proven winner" is how the official press release described Johnson's hire.

"I basically sat with the private equity guys in my Disney office and we talked from 6 p.m. to 11:30 p.m. and talked about what the potential could be," Johnson said.

Though he had no MLM experience to speak of, Johnson seemed the perfect fit for Herbalife. He'd done triathlons and was an accom-plished cyclist who looked like he could give Lance Armstrong a run for his money. "I felt a kindred spirit with the product." Johnson said after being hired.[38] Johnson was also just the kind of leader Herbalife figured it needed. He was a type-A talent, a spark plug of enthusiasm who was active and aggressive.

"I think I've always been that way," Johnson said. "That's the way I operate best."

They were traits, Johnson said, that came from his father, who ran a successful manufacturing business in the family's hometown of Jackson, Michigan. The elder Johnson made crankshafts for diesel trucks, and his company had become the largest maker of the prod-ucts in the world. He was a Depression-era man who was as tough as nails.

"He was a very aggressive, successful guy," Johnson said. "I probably get a little of that from him."

As a young man, Johnson seemed destined for his own slice of success. He had good grades in high school, played sports, and had plans to go to the University of Michigan. But in Johnson's junior year of high school, tragedy struck. His brother—one of five siblings—was killed in a skiing accident in Taos, New Mexico. Johnson's life went into a spiral.

"We grew up in two's," Johnson said, meaning they were often paired with the sibling closest in age to themselves. "And my brother and I were really close."

Johnson's grades suddenly fell apart, leaving his dream of the fabled university in shambles. Johnson ended up at the local junior college, and in 1973 he moved to Dillon, Colorado, to work at a saloon with a friend. He would end up running the place.

"I carried around a business card that read, 'Bus Boy with Keys,'" Johnson said. "I learned more about business there than anywhere."

With his life back on track, Johnson enrolled at Western State College of Colorado, majoring in political science with minors in business, history, and English.

"I took a lot of classes," Johnson remembered.

There were stints in sales, and one company offered a transfer to Los Angeles. Johnson jumped at the opportunity and moved to California in March of 1980. He soon grew bored with the new job though, and enrolled at UCLA, taking classes in marketing, script writing, and film.

"I didn't know anybody in LA," Johnson said. "I slept at a friend's place."

Johnson took a series of jobs to make ends meet, selling light shows to the big-name musical acts of the day and working in magazines before finding his way to the more glitzy and glamorous world of entertainment. After several interviews and offers, Johnson chose Disney, where he settled in to the company's home video department.

Johnson would spend seventeen years in Burbank, and was considered a marketing whiz. He'd engineered the expansion of Disney's video business, growing it from thirty-four markets when he took over to more than eighty by the time he left. Johnson had succeeded future Disney CEO Robert Iger in the unit, and he helped turn Disney into the number one distributor of home entertainment in the world.

At Disney, Johnson was known as the "shake guy" because of his love for smoothies with a blast of protein powder, and he burst with energy.[39] He sounded like a motivational speaker when he talked, and he still loved the University of Michigan, frequently flying back to Ann Arbor on Saturdays for the football team's home games.

Still, the messy MLM business was a far cry from the wholesome home of Mickey Mouse. Johnson knew it and initially declined the job when approached by the search firm Heidrick and Struggles. "A woman approached me and I said, Herbalife? Are you kidding me?" Johnson said. "I looked at it much in the same way others did at the time." Johnson didn't know much about Herbalife or its business, but had heard enough about its checkered past to pause. "The image was a little, let's be honest, challenged," he told an interviewer.[40]

Johnson had thought about leaving Disney before but had always passed, even turning down big jobs at AOL and Hertz. "I even got a reputation in the recruiting business as the guy who'd never leave Disney," Johnson said.

But the Disney gig had started to develop its own issues. "I had a huge title that didn't have the proper authority to go along with it," Johnson said. "I was getting increasingly frustrated."

Before accepting the Herbalife job, Johnson did his own research, hoping to dispel any of the concerns he had about the company's past. "I snuck into an Herbalife meeting in the Bonaventure Hotel in Los Angeles and saw the people in there, and I saw a highly motivated sales force," Johnson said. Johnson's recon went a step further, even signing up as an Herbalife distributor to see for himself what the products were all about.

"I had my trainer do the same thing," Johnson said. "We would share notes. I got a case study on the lawsuits the company had faced. I looked at the company and just didn't understand all of the machinations of how the company worked."

The private equity shops that owned Herbalife offered Johnson a piece of the business, and he ultimately caved, sensing he could do for Herbalife what he'd done at Disney—expand the brand's international presence. He also realized he'd never be Disney's top dog, since Iger had been bumped up to president and seemed the heir apparent to its current CEO, Michael Eisner.

Johnson figured he could be a positive influence on Herbalife's rank and file.

"My personal enthusiasm for fitness and wellness gives me a special attraction to Herbalife's mission," Johnson said in a press release announcing his hiring. "Herbalife is a well-established organization with terrific products and a powerful world-class sales network comprised of more than one million distributors."[41]

Herbalife's powerful distributors welcomed their new, well-established leader after years of unrest.

"I'm extremely pleased to welcome Michael Johnson to the Herbalife family," said longtime distributor Leslie Stanford, who was also on the company's board of directors. "His entrepreneurial spirit and personal passion for wellness is an ideal match with the legacy of this company and will allow him to work well with distributors."[42]

But Hughes's death—and the chaos that followed—revealed just how powerful Herbalife's top distributors had become. After he died, fourteen top distributors led Herbalife sales meetings—a testament to their influence.[43]

Johnson had no idea what he was getting himself into, which became clear fairly quickly. Shortly after taking the job, Johnson tried to introduce a new product without first consulting distributors. It failed. Distributors didn't trust him, and they wondered whether he was the right guy for the job.

Johnson wasn't sure either, and figured he'd made a mistake taking the job.

"It was very, very rough," Johnson told *Fortune* of the transition from Disney. "There were a lot of issues I didn't understand. A language was spoken that I didn't get."[44]

After only a few months, Johnson was ready to quit.

"There were practices that were taking place that were legal, but I'm not sure they fit what we wanted to be as a company," Johnson said. "I had some ideas in my head that maybe I wasn't right for this job."[45]

Ready to walk, Johnson called a mentor, who pushed him to stay. Johnson went home, wrote a business plan that night, and decided to stick it out.

One of Johnson's immediate goals was to downplay the shady sales pitches some distributors had been making during the Hughes years. Herbalife had already banned the sketchy "Newest Way to Wealth" lead-generation practice, and in early December 2004, Johnson settled the class-action suit against the company for $6 million, figuring it was time to move on from the past.

Nearly a week later—and a year and a half after Johnson was hired—Herbalife, which now had $1.4 billion in annual sales, went public again, this time on the New York Stock Exchange, offering 14.5 million shares for $14 apiece. The company raised $200 million.[46] Johnson hoped the IPO would help the company move beyond the scrutiny of years past. He also had even bigger aspirations—to turn Herbalife into a truly global powerhouse.

He outfitted soccer icon David Beckham and his Los Angeles Galaxy team in Adidas jerseys with "Herbalife" emblazoned on the front, knowing the sport was part of the fabric of Europe and Latin America and was growing in popularity in Asia.

"Adidas produced more than 600,000 Galaxy jerseys in its initial run, and everyone on every one of those is a mobile Herbalife billboard," said Johnson during an earnings call.[47] A few years later, Johnson upped the ante by cutting a deal with another of the game's legends—Lionel Messi, whose professional club, FC Barcelona, is one of the most successful and popular in the game.

Johnson was also intent on pushing Herbalife as a life brand—a place to make money in the business opportunity and *save* it too for when times got tough. On December 16, 2008, during the middle of the Great Recession, and with Herbalife's stock price tanking along with the rest of the market, Johnson and his executive team went to the New York Stock Exchange for an Investor Day event. Inside an NYSE conference room, Johnson threw to a video, where a narrator pitched Herbalife as a safe port in the now gathering financial storm.

"Why Herbalife?" the voice asked.

> Well, now is the perfect time. I mean, you've seen the news. Let's face it. It's a scary time. The economy's in trouble. Gas prices are at an all-time high. Everybody needs money. Markets are crashing. People are losing their homes. Their jobs. People can't buy groceries. People are looking for something they can depend on. A better life. Herbalife has the perfect, inexpensive, healthy meals. We have the best nutrition products in the world. Changing people's lives. A better life, that's why. Why Herbalife? Herbal-nomics. It's recession proof.[48]

Though Johnson had tried to downplay the role of recruiting—or, at least, the shady methods of recruiting used by some distributors to attract new members—he made it clear to the group what the practice meant to the company's growing bottom line.

"We're focusing on recruiting and the growth of our distributor base," he told the meeting. "This is absolutely foundational to us. It is making sure that we get our message to distributors, that this company stands 100 percent behind them, that we are confident that you can create an income working at Herbalife, that you can build a business, that you can build an opportunity for part-time or full-time income and for generations to come."[49]

Johnson's strategy seemed to be working. From 2008 to 2011, total shareholder return in Herbalife stock rose 870 percent as sales soared.[50] Not even the Belgian pyramid-scheme lawsuit, brought against Herbalife in November 2011, could derail its growth. That year, Herbalife had $3.45 billion in sales.

Then there was Johnson's *own* incredible success. In 2011, he was the highest paid CEO in America, taking home a whopping $89 million, including stock options, a testament to Herbalife's meteoric growth under his guidance.[51]

By mid-2012, Herbalife had operations in ninety countries and an envious track record on Wall Street. It had turned in eleven straight record quarters, with shares quadrupling over the prior two years. The steady performance led CNBC's Jim Cramer to once proclaim during an interview with Johnson, "This is arguably the greatest stock we have ever talked about!"

Johnson seemed on top of the world. Herbalife was humming, and investors had taken notice.

5

THE PHONE CALL

Michael Johnson climbed atop his $3,000 Bianchi mountain bike and set out for the office from his Malibu home. It was May 1, 2012, and in just a few hours, Johnson and his team would run through the previous quarter for sell-side research analysts on Wall Street.

Cycling the thirty or so miles down the Pacific Coast Highway to Venice Boulevard, then onto Olympic, where Herbalife's headquarters were located, was a chance for the CEO to clear his head—to break from the routine and get ready for that morning's somewhat mundane earnings call with analysts.

Johnson was a grinder. Besides being a regular on the triathlon circuit, he regularly competed in one of the most grueling events in the country—a bike race called the Leadville 100 MTB, a hundred-mile trek through the Rocky Mountains, including frequent climbs, some as high up as 12,600 feet.[1] Those who finished the race in less than twelve hours—after managing to wind through the uneven and dust-covered backcountry—got a buckle for their efforts, and a lifetime's worth of pride. Johnson had scored the brass bounty every time he'd competed and viewed anything less as unacceptable.

Quarterly conference calls weren't nearly as grueling or rewarding and had become a formality. Johnson expected nothing different this time around as he pulled into L.A. Live, the complex downtown where Herbalife's headquarters was located and headed upstairs to his desk with his bike in tow. Once upstairs, Johnson cleaned up, then ran through the prepared remarks he'd read for analysts in a matter of hours.

At just before 8 a.m. local time, Herbalife's executives gathered in a conference room to get things going. Seated side-by-side at the long rectangular table was Johnson, President Des Walsh, Chief Financial Officer John DeSimone, and Chief Operating Officer Richard Goudis, along with legal advisor Brett Chapman and a few others. It was expected to be an upbeat affair, as the night before Herbalife had reported strong numbers for the prior three months.

Johnson began with a few minutes of prepared remarks—a typical run-through of the quarter that was and what the Street could expect from future quarters to come:

> Our financial and business trends continue to be strong. Yesterday, we announced a 24 percent increase in earnings per share, driven by a 24 percent volume point growth. Each of our six regions experienced strong volume point growth in the quarter. Five of the six regions had double-digit volume increases. Four of our regions—Asia, North America, China, South and Central America—exceeded 20 percent growth. Mexico had a 16 percent increase in volume points and Europe, Middle East, and African markets were up 6 percent. Before I elaborate on the quarter, let me say thank you to our distributors, employees, and vendors around the world. The consistency of our growth and financial results is due to your dedication and hard work.[2]

Johnson had just passed his ninth anniversary leading Herbalife—a pretty good feat considering he'd almost quit within a few months of taking the job. In reflecting on nearly a decade at the helm of the company, Johnson noted how much Herbalife had changed through the years and how more people than ever seemed to be using its products every day.

"We call that daily consumption," he said. "It is one of the key drivers of our growth. Today, we estimate that more than a third of our volume is being transacted through daily consumption."[3] It was

Johnson's way of saying the company's business model wasn't simply the distributor-to-distributor enterprise that had drawn so much criticism in years past. Herbalife not only had real customers, he intimated, but the numbers were growing—and growing fast.

Johnson then handed the duties off to Walsh, who echoed Johnson's assessment of the business and lauded the company's rapidly rising nutrition clubs, which were helping to fuel the meteoric growth.

"We estimate that in the first quarter of 2012, there were approximately 33,500 commercial or non-residential clubs," Walsh said. "As we mentioned in our last quarter, and at our recent Analyst Day, we believe that approximately 34 percent to 41 percent of our overall volume is currently driven by daily consumption business methods."[4]

Walsh was especially upbeat about the strength overseas. Volumes in Brazil grew 22 percent in the quarter, he said, and by 26 percent in Russia. Planned Herbalife extravaganzas in South Korea and Singapore were expected to draw twenty thousand and twenty-five thousand participants, respectively, a sign of how popular the company was becoming around the world.

Following the remarks from Walsh and CFO John DeSimone, Chapman, who was leading the call, cleared in one of the analysts from the awaiting queue. Mike Swartz from SunTrust Robinson Humphrey asked a few basic questions, with Walsh running through his typically rosy view of the world. When Walsh clicked off the line, Chapman welcomed in the next caller—a man whose name alone made some in the room straighten in their seats.

"Your next question is from the line of David Einhorn with Greenlight Capital," said Chapman.

"Oh, shit," DeSimone admitted thinking when he heard the name come out of Chapman's mouth. Though Johnson himself had never heard of Einhorn before that moment, most of the investing public certainly had. Einhorn was a famed hedge-fund manager who many on Wall Street considered to be a genius. He'd called out Lehman Brothers during the financial crisis and dumped all over Allied Financial before that, and had made a fortune doing it. He was a billionaire who seemed to like toying with people he thought were suspect. He'd also recently made the papers for shorting Green Mountain Coffee, but Johnson and Walsh, in their distant Los Angeles offices and surrounded by the associated cultural mores, had been too removed from the Wall Street scene to really notice.

"I got a couple of questions for you," said Einhorn. "First is, how much of the sales that you'd make in terms of final sales are sold outside the network and how much are consumed within the distributor base?"[5]

It seemed a simple and straightforward query—how many sales were being made to "real" customers outside of Herbalife's web of distributors versus those made from one distributor to another.

But Walsh, who spoke with an accent reflecting his Irish heritage, appeared flustered by a question that should have been a layup.

"So, David, we have a 70 percent custom rule, which is—which effectively says that 70 percent of all product is sold to consumers or actually consumed by distributors for their own personal use," said Walsh, virtually stammering through the answer.

"What is the percentage (of product) that is actually sold to consumers that are not distributors?" Einhorn pressed.

"So, we don't have an exact percentage, David, because we don't have visibility to that level of detail," said Walsh.

"Is there an approximation?" Einhorn continued.

"So, well, again, going back to our 70 percent rule, we believe that it's 70 percent or potentially in excess of that," Walsh answered.

"Des Walsh was a great spinmeister and very smooth," said Herb Greenberg, who covered Herbalife as a reporter for CNBC and hosted a network documentary about the company. "I can understand why they put him as their front man. He has that Irish charm, could be very disarming. He had the right answer to every single question."

Except, this time, he didn't. The 70 percent number was wrong, at least by the way Herbalife accounted for which of its members were distributing the company's shakes as a business and which ones weren't. It seemed Walsh had clumsily cited the Amway threshold from the 1970s instead of a number reflective of Herbalife's current business.[6] Walsh knew he'd screwed up, but in the heat of the moment, he didn't immediately correct himself.

That wasn't the only problem. Back on Wall Street, Herbalife shares were in free fall. From the moment Einhorn had appeared on the call, Herbalife stock, which opened the day at $70, began falling—first 10 percent, then 20 percent, then even more.[7] By lunchtime on the East Coast, not even an hour from when the call had started, CNBC's Greenberg dialed in live to talk about the slide with Sue Herera, one of the network's longtime anchors.[8]

"We were in the Denver airport and got the message to call in to the network immediately," remembers Greenberg, who was also blindsided by Einhorn's questions. "I was more intrigued that they took his questions, because typically companies would screen those out. I thought, boy, if Einhorn is there, that is interesting."

Greenberg recapped some of the questions Einhorn had asked, while showing a real-time stock chart documenting the stock's sharp decline. The reporter had long been skeptical of multilevel marketing companies in general and laid out for viewers why the questions were so damning for the stock, which was now plunging.

"You have a situation where is this a pyramid sort of operation, or is it a genuine business selling products to you and me—that is the crux of the issue here," Greenberg told Herera.[9]

There were nine Einhorn questions in all that morning, which must have felt like one hundred to the overmatched Herbalife executives, before the quizzing mercifully ended.

"OK, thanks so much guys," Einhorn said, cordially, if unfulfilled.

At the end of the trading day, Herbalife stock closed at $52—a stunning 40 percent drop—one of the worst declines in its history as a publicly traded company.

Blood was in the water, and the hungry sharks on Wall Street sensed it.

At 2:20 p.m., a headline on the *New York Times* website blared, "Einhorn Questions Prompt Selloff at Herbalife," with the *Times* reporter Michael J. De La Merced writing, "When David Einhorn speaks, investors around the markets listen.[10] So when he asks critical questions on a company's earnings calls, shareholders apparently panic."

Panic is exactly what happened next inside Herbalife headquarters, where executives were now wondering what to do. Johnson urged everyone in the room to remain calm, reminding the team that they didn't even know if Einhorn was short on the stock and that other analysts were still in the queue, waiting for their turn to ask questions of the team.

Walsh, who was always the rosiest of Herbalife's top executives, now claims he wasn't as concerned as the others. Walsh felt Herbalife had nothing to hide and that the team of c-suiters knew the business far better than some interloper three thousand miles away.

That Herbalife would even give the famed hedge-fund manager a platform in the first place is a decision that would haunt the executive team afterward, especially since earnings calls are typically reserved for company investors and the analysts who followed the company for their clients. Taking Einhorn's call without even knowing his position in the stock, including whether he even had one, was a calculated risk, and management knew it. They also felt they had no choice.

In just two days, CFO DeSimone was scheduled to meet with investors in New York and Boston, and he was worried that keeping Einhorn off the call—and Einhorn's attempts to join a secret being kept from other investors—could trigger a violation of SEC disclosure rules. Since Johnson had never even heard of Einhorn, he deferred to DeSimone to make the call on the fly. DeSimone figured that if Einhorn actually *was* shorting the stock, they might as well know about it right there and then.

But Einhorn wasn't your average skeptic. He had earned the reputation of being one of Wall Street's undeniable superstars from all of his earlier exploits.

Einhorn, who grew up outside Milwaukee and went to Cornell University, had founded Greenlight in 1996 with a former colleague, Jeff Keswin, and $900,000 in assets under management. Einhorn and Keswin set up shop inside the Manhattan offices of Spear, Leeds and Kellogg, using the free desk space to save money while sharing the lone photocopier with the five other firms on the floor.[11] It didn't take very long for the duo's investment chops to pay big dividends. In its first year, Greenlight didn't suffer a single losing month, returning 37.1 percent in the final three months alone.[12] The following year was even better, with returns for the now $75 million fund reaching 57.9 percent, partly from a successful short position in the restaurant chain Boston Market. Einhorn returned 31.6 percent in 2001 to firmly solidify his place as one of the hedge-fund industry's up-and-comers.[13]

Former associates say Einhorn liked the ground-game aspect of investing, the weeks of analyzing companies down to the nitty gritty. It was that sort of bottom-up attention to detail—the mining of corporate balance sheets and financial statements for hours—that would pay off in 2002 when Einhorn shorted the finance company Allied Capital at $26.25 per share, claiming it defrauded the Small Business Administration through questionable lending practices.[14] Einhorn went public with the investment on May 15 of that year at the Ira W. Sohn Investment Research Conference in Manhattan, an annual charity get-together where the biggest names in the business appeared onstage to reveal their best investment ideas. The forum frequently moved stocks, which is exactly what happened after the fresh-faced investor grabbed the microphone three-quarters of the way through the event and unleashed his takedown. Einhorn branded Allied a fraud, likening it to WorldCom, the now defunct telecom firm whose CEO, Bernard J. Ebbers, went to prison for accounting fraud and other crimes.

It was the first time Einhorn had stood before a group of that size to deliver such a meaningful speech. Wearing a blue suit and multicolored necktie with a buttoned-down collar, the visibly nervous investor took the stage and, with his name tag slightly askew, led the captivated audience through Allied Capital's business and the reasons he was short during the fifteen or so minutes allotted for the presentation.

Einhorn's delivery was so effective that the next day, Allied shares were primed to plunge more than 20 percent at the open of trading on the New York Stock Exchange. However, the shares didn't even open out of concern among investors that selling would lead to a panic and that shares would fall even further.[15]

But beyond a sudden and swift stock move, Einhorn's presentation had set off a firestorm. The company attacked Einhorn personally, accusing him of manipulating the market. CEO William L. Walton accused Einhorn of trying "to scare people, make a quick buck and move on."[16] Allied hired private investigators, who illegally obtained phone records of Einhorn and his firm through a process called pre-texting, where someone impersonates another individual to obtain confidential information.

It was a full-on war. Allied said Einhorn was engaging in a "campaign to spread misleading or false statements." Walton even convinced the Securities and Exchange Commission to investigate the brash hedge funder, but Einhorn was undeterred.[17] Over a span of five years, Einhorn fought back. He released hundreds of documents detailing the alleged fraud, painstaking work that paid off in June 2007, when the SEC found that the company itself had broken securities laws related to the value of illiquid securities. By 2009, Allied shares had sunk to $1.56 a share.[18]

Allied would eventually end up bankrupt, and the legend of Einhorn was born. He would later recount the tale in his book, *Fooling Some of the People All of the Time.*

But if Allied gave Einhorn a certain mystique on Wall Street, his crusade against Lehman Brothers, just months before the firm collapsed, made him seem like a seer. On May 21, 2008, once again under the lights of the Sohn stage, Einhorn publicly revealed his Lehman short in a fifteen-minute presentation titled "Accounting Ingenuity." Einhorn tore apart the bank's balance sheet, questioning the true value of its assets and whether it was hiding risks from investors and the markets. He ridiculed CFO Erin Callan's recent descriptions of the company's financial performance, drawing parallels to his scathing Allied thesis. He then summed it all up by saying the bank needed to raise capital and raise it now. Shares fell more than 6 percent after Einhorn spoke.

Afterward, a Lehman spokeswoman said, "We will not continue to refute Mr. Einhorn's allegations and accusations. He also makes allegations that have no basis in fact with the same hope of achieving personal gain."

Four months later, Lehman Brothers collapsed in the largest bankruptcy filing in US history, with $639 billion in assets and $619 billion in debt.

Now one of the most feared financiers around, Einhorn set his sights on the coffee company Green Mountain, laying out his case at the Value Investing Congress, an industry conference, in a 110-slide PowerPoint presentation titled "GAAP-uccino," a reference to the company's accounting methods. Green Mountain's K-Cup coffee pods had become ubiquitous in offices and homes nationwide following the company's acquisition of Keurig and its popular single-serve machines. Einhorn pointed out that from 1991 to 2000, Green Mountain's revenues had grown 25 percent a year, but that growth had slowed to nearly half that in the ensuing years. The company operated under the familiar Gillette razor model, selling the Keurig brewer near cost and the disposable pods at highly profitable margins. By 2011, Green Mountain had sold more than thirteen million single-serve coffee brewers and a stunning nine billion K-Cups, with the in-home market now the company's most important growth engine.

There was only one issue. Einhorn thought it was wholly unsustainable. He concluded his presentation by mentioning an SEC inquiry into the company's revenue-recognition practices and suggesting that the issue was more problematic than the company was letting on. Einhorn concluded his presentation with a latte-art picture of a bear made in the drink's foam.

Shares dove 10 percent that morning, yet another victim of the "Einhorn Effect."

Einhorn was still headlong into the Green Mountain short when the name Herbalife came across his desk in late 2011, in the same report the Indago Girls had sent to Ackman. Einhorn had also read Christine Richard's initial work and, like Ackman, was also unconvinced the stock was a good short candidate. Richard had actually come to Einhorn first, but he politely passed on investing in the name. Shorts were never taken on lightly because of the damage they could inflict, and Einhorn wasn't one to jump in without being fully convinced.

Over the next several months, Richard kept checking in, until finally Einhorn capitulated and assigned a Greenlight stock analyst to have a look. The analyst visited Herbalife nutrition clubs and went to recruiting meetings around the United States, noticing some of the same practices Richard herself had raised red flags about in the research report. The analyst reported what she had seen to Einhorn, who was now intrigued enough to go see the operations for himself.

One morning, Einhorn and Richard boarded the #7 subway train from Grand Central Station to Corona, Queens, with plans to visit four or five nutrition clubs. On one visit, along a busy street loaded with bodegas and other storefronts, Einhorn and Richard entered a club that was only identifiable by a neon green light out front. Once inside, the two encountered a young man, probably in his early twenties, who, according to Einhorn, looked "fit and buoyant." The young man told the two that he had opened the club just a few months prior with dreams of reaching the upper levels of Herbalife's sales force—its Chairman's Club, where the real money would start rolling in. Einhorn and Richard sat and drank an Herbalife tea, along with aloe water and a nutrition shake.

Only, something seemed off. The man told Einhorn and Richard he'd worked nearly one hundred hours per week, beginning at breakfast, spending part of the day passing out flyers to people in the neighborhood hoping to attract new customers. They noticed that the man tracked everything in pencil in a three-ring spiral notebook and placed a small gold star—the stick-on kind an elementary school teacher might give—next to repeat customers or the ones who seemed the most promising. There was no cash register to be seen, as they were strictly forbidden because the nutrition clubs were to be viewed as social clubs, not retail stores.

Most troubling, Einhorn thought, was that the man appeared to be consuming most, if not all, of the products himself as his main food source, and slept each night on the dusty floor of the club. And the only people who ever showed up to buy products were other distributors.

Einhorn thought there was no way the man could even pay his monthly rent.

Einhorn and Richard drank Herbalife shakes and teas all morning long—enough so that after they had finished, the hedge-fund manager hit a nearby convenience store for a bag of chips or Cheetos to settle his stomach. Einhorn and Richard would meet several people that trip, all with the same goal—to strike it rich selling Herbalife products.

It was shortly after that visit, in the later winter of 2012, that Einhorn—who took on Allied and railed against Lehman—decided to short Herbalife stock, initiating a medium-sized position in the name.

But Einhorn's recon didn't stop there.

On March 23, 2012, the Greenlight analyst and Richard traveled to a Los Angeles hotel where Herbalife was holding its annual meeting, which is where company executives brief analysts and major shareholders on the state of the business and take their questions.

Following the morning festivities, which began with a 6:30 a.m. boot camp workout and a speech by Johnson, Richard and the analyst made their way to lunch, where DeSimone was making the rounds in a meet-and-greet. DeSimone sauntered to the table where Richard and the analyst were sitting and stopped to say hello. Richard asked him several questions related to the old Amway decision of the 1970s and the level of actual retail sales the company was making—the same sort of questions Einhorn himself would ask on the earnings call in May two months later. DeSimone immediately grew suspicious and asked who the women were. Richard said she was doing research for the woman sitting next to her. DeSimone quickly left the room and alerted CEO Johnson.

The next day, Herbalife held its President's Team Summit, an extravaganza where Johnson would hand out $52 million in bonus checks to more than 350 of Herbalife's top distributors.

"The air will go out of the room on a few of those announcements," Johnson told the investors, alluding to the sizeable payouts they awaited.

"Good morning, Herbalife!" Johnson exclaimed the next morning as he officially opened the festivities. The crowd roared, while some in the audience threw their arms in the air as if Johnson were the Messiah.[19]

Johnson laughed as he soaked up the adoration. "We've got something special at Herbalife," Johnson said "Can you feel it? Can you feel it?!"

Speaking for more than an hour, Johnson told of the company's journey, reminiscing about his time at Disney and how it could be repeated at Herbalife.

"I am more excited about this company today than I have ever been," he said. "I am more excited about the promise of Herbalife than I have ever been, at any time in this company."

Music roared. The crowd stood and clapped in unison.

"We give people the opportunity to improve their lives. . . . We give people an opportunity to change their lives," he said.

Each time Johnson spoke, the assembled rose to their feet.

As Johnson basked in the glow of adoration, he acknowledged Herbalife's doubters—those through the years who had criticized the company, and he urged his ranks to be at their best.

"We're going to get bigger, and more people are going to be skeptical about who we are and what we do. We have to be the best at what we do. We have to have the highest integrity at what we do. We don't need to make anything up."

Richard and the Greenlight analyst sat among the faithful, soaking it all in. Both returned to New York moved by what they had witnessed. Richard felt that Johnson had oddly sensed they were in the room when he'd called out the doubters, as if he were referencing them directly.

Not even two months later, Einhorn dialed in to the earnings call and began his now infamous inquisition. It was just a precursor of things to come. In just two weeks, Einhorn, along with John Paulson,

Jeffrey Gundlach, and several other star investors, was scheduled to present at another Sohn Conference in New York. If Einhorn had merely fired warning shots at Herbalife on the earnings call two weeks earlier, most expected that he'd use the big event to go nuclear and admit he was actually shorting Herbalife shares.

At 3:31 p.m. on May 16, 2012, Einhorn took the stage at Avery Fisher Hall inside Lincoln Center on New York City's West Side. Anticipation in the performance hall was thick. The overflowing room darkened, except for a spotlight on the lectern.[20]

Back in Los Angeles, the Herbalife executives were huddled in the conference room, listening to the presentation live thanks to a plant they'd put in the room. The operative had live-dialed Herbalife's LA headquarters from the auditorium, leaving the phone open to hear everything.

Up popped Einhorn's first slide.

"M-L-M," it read—an obvious reference, those in the auditorium thought, to multilevel marketing, the kind of business Herbalife was. The assembled journalists and a cadre of finance bloggers clutched their phones, ready to tweet the news when it became official.

Herbalife braced for the worst.

And then . . .

Martin Marietta Materials.

It was all a ruse.

M-L-M was the ticker symbol for the construction materials company and not an acronym for multilevel marketing. Einhorn was just screwing with the company, and laughed, as did all in attendance.

Herbalife shares spiked 15 percent almost immediately out of pure relief.

Michael Johnson, who should have been elated, had no idea what had just happened.

The previous weekend, he'd gone over the handlebars of his mountain bike while riding with friends in Cheseboro Canyon in Agoura Hills, broke several bones, and was airlifted to a hospital, where he lay drugged up with painkillers at the very moment Einhorn spoke.

While Johnson breathed a sigh of relief when he learned of the stunt, he was just happy to be breathing at all.

In reality, the fakeout was classic Einhorn. This was, after all, a guy who routinely played high-stakes poker in Las Vegas, once winning $4.3 million in the king of all tournaments, the World Series of Poker Main Event.

But what made Einhorn's appearance all the more remarkable that day was that he was out of Herbalife altogether by the time he entered the hall that morning, a fact no one in the room knew. Not the media, not the audience, and certainly not its most interested and intrigued member—Bill Ackman.

6

THE BIG SHORT

After returning an impressive 29.7 percent, net of fees, in 2010,[1] largely due to the GGP home run and gains in other stocks within his portfolio, 2011 had gotten off to a rocky start for Pershing Square and its principal.[2] The Target misfire dragged on the main fund's performance and had dented Ackman's reputation, but it was far from his only headache.

In November 2006, Ackman had invested in the bookseller Borders Group,[3] hopeful that the company could navigate the industry's fast-changing landscape and perhaps pull off a merger with its main rival, Barnes and Noble. The investment followed the classic activist playbook—buy into a perceived undervalued asset, exert some muscle, and watch shares rise substantially over time. Ackman knew flipping Borders wouldn't be easy, but if there was one thing he'd proven time and time again, it was that he had the endurance to wait. But whereas Ackman saw opportunity in Borders, others saw a broken story. Borders had missed the e-book revolution, and while competitors were either downsizing to meet the digital transformation or introducing new products, Borders continued to expand while amassing a heaping pile of debt. Ackman had held the stock for years, even boosting Pershing's position over time, convinced he'd made a good investment. But by May 2012, things looked so dire that Ackman was looking for a way out. He offered to play matchmaker and even help fund a transaction between Borders and Barnes and Noble, but a deal never materialized.[4] When it soon became clear that bankruptcy might be the only viable option, Ackman threw in the towel altogether and began dumping the stock. He sold one million shares at a reported $200 million loss, with the rest of the position soon to follow.[5]

By the fall of 2011, Pershing Square, which had $10 billion under management, was down 15.6 percent, net of fees, a disappointment by any measure and even more so for a money manager used to double-digit returns.[6]

Ackman didn't plan to remain in the red for very long.

In October, Pershing revealed a new 12.2 percent stake, or 20.6 million shares, in the railway Canadian Pacific.[7] CP shares promptly surged 10 percent on the news, and for the most part didn't stop. Between October and the end of December 2011, shares rose 18 percent, effectively making, if not *saving*, Ackman's year.

Feeling revived by the Canadian Pacific boon, Ackman entered 2012 eyeing a more prosperous outcome. The real question was whether JC Penney could help him get there. Ackman had amassed a 16.5 percent stake in the retailer back in 2010 and had waged a boardroom upheaval, installing his handpicked savior, Ron Johnson, as the new CEO.[8] Ackman's hopes were so high that the company could reverse years of sales declines that he boosted his stake to 26.7 percent, telling his investors in a letter, "We don't buy 26% stakes and join boards of directors unless we believe an investment has enormous potential."[9]

· Others apparently didn't share the optimism. By the spring of 2012, Wall Street was already losing faith in Ackman's turnaround plan, which only grew worse that May when JC Penney reported dismal first-quarter sales numbers. Comparable stores sales, the industry's key measure of revenue growth, declined 18.9 percent from a year earlier, with total sales declining more than 20 percent.[10] When Penney's stock opened for trading the following day, shares promptly dropped 19.7 percent.

To make matters worse, Johnson appeared delusional, claiming in a statement accompanying the earnings results, "Customers love the new JCP they discover in our stores."[11] Ackman appeared undeterred, telling a reporter that despite the obvious challenges facing the company and the early disappointments, Johnson was "the best guy to run the company"—and that JC Penney "isn't fundamentally broken."[12] Ackman had also put a $77 price target on the stock even though it was currently trading for less than $30.

Canadian Pacific, however, looked much more promising.

Ackman had become the company's biggest shareholder. He won a proxy fight for seats on the board and would soon ditch its CEO for his handpicked alternative.

By mid-2012, the large stakes in JC Penney and Canadian Pacific made up more than 40 percent of Ackman's highly concentrated portfolio.

Herbalife wasn't exactly out of mind, but with Ackman preoccupied by Penney's and Canadian Pacific, Shane Dinneen, the Pershing Square analyst who'd done more work on Herbalife than anyone, continued digging, unearthing new leads on the company's business that only made him more skeptical. Dinneen lobbied Ackman to add Herbalife to the portfolio as a short position, but Ackman showed no sign of budging—at least not until the morning of May 1, 2012, when Einhorn dialed into the earnings call.

Dinneen had dialed in too, heard Einhorn's pointed questions, and was devastated. With his shoulders slumped, Dinneen walked into Ackman's office down the hall and told his boss that Einhorn was on the Herbalife call and that they'd blown it.

"Shane comes in and is depressed and the stock is down and I was like, oh, this is good!" remembers Ackman. "David Einhorn is a great short seller. He's clearly going to be public. He'll be the catalyst."

Ackman convened the Pershing Square investment team to discuss whether to get involved. Present were Ackman himself, along with associates Scott Ferguson, Paul Hilal, Roy Katzovicz, Ali Namvar, Ryan Israel, Jordan Rubin, and Brian Welsh. Ackman told them of Einhorn's appearance on the conference call and that it was the perfect opportunity to short the stock.

"When you're sure someone else is taking the lead, number one you don't have to be public and you can abandon it at any time," said

Ackman. "It's not as big a commitment as when you buy 10 percent of the company and have to file. You can blow it out tomorrow."

While Ackman made his case to the assembled group, a debate ensued among some in the room as they wondered about a path to victory. Einhorn had already hammered the stock by 40 percent, some noted. Was there really much downside left? Others questioned whether regulators would have incentive to step in and shut the company down. It was a valid point for sure. Though some MLMs had been put out of business in the past, most of the larger, more recogniz-able names had survived, if not thrived.

As the debate raged, Ackman offered up a much more matter-of-fact question. If Einhorn had already done the heavy lifting and was shorting the stock, he offered, "How do we lose?"

He also figured the calendar was on his side. In a couple of weeks, Einhorn was set to present at the Sohn Conference, and just about everyone expected Herbalife to be his target. The implication was obvious: if Einhorn's questions alone had tanked the stock, one could only imagine what a public takedown could do.

With Herbalife shares getting killed on Einhorn's appearance on the conference call, Pershing Square began shorting Herbalife, initiating a small position at an average of $48 per share. *Shorting* means you're bet-ting against a stock, and while it can be highly profitable, it carries risk. That's because when you short a stock, you effectively borrow shares from another investor and sell them. If the shares lose value, you can them buy them back at a low price and pocket the difference. While gains can be enormous if the stock falls in price, losses can be endless if it goes up. There is no ceiling to how high a stock price can rise.

On May 16, the day of the Sohn event, Ackman traveled the eight blocks or so from his office up Columbus Avenue and into Lincoln Center to give a sixty-slide presentation on JC Penney. Ackman stayed on message throughout and made no mention of Herbalife during his fifteen minutes onstage. He then took his seat as Einhorn took his turn in front of the crowd.

When Einhorn walked onstage, nearly everyone in the room ex-pected the snarky short-seller to hit Herbalife with a sledgehammer.

But when Einhorn tricked everyone and called out Martin Marietta instead, Ackman was among those shocked. He headed straight back to the office, met with his team, and considered getting out of Herbalife right then and there rather than become the public face of the fight.

"There was a lot of skepticism in the room about going public," Ackman said. "We talked about it, and I said, look, Shane has done great work. Let's put together a presentation, because there's a certain discipline associated with that—let's just do it for internal purposes only and see what it looks like, then we can make a decision."

Ackman wasn't naive to the risks of going it alone, but countered that Pershing could easily fill the void left by Einhorn's exit.

"I said, I don't know what David is going to do, but there could be an upcoming catalyst," Ackman said he told the others. "We can be the catalyst."

Dinneen began working day and night on the presentation, even sleeping under his desk to turn over any stone he could find on Herbalife.

"And Shane kept finding things, and I kept learning things," said Ackman. "Then, we put more resources into it, and we hired a law firm."

Katzovicz, who was Pershing's in-house regulatory expert, called Sullivan and Cromwell, hoping to retain the firm to do the forensics on Herbalife's business even though it rarely worked on public shorts. Sullivan and Cromwell would have to investigate all of the possible scenarios Pershing could face if it took on the fight, the history of pyramid-scheme law, the likelihood that the government would intervene, and even the possibility that Herbalife could sue Ackman and Pershing Square.

"I said, I think this thing is really interesting. I've never seen anything like it," Ackman said he told the firm. "Why don't you go and do two weeks' worth of work on it and come back. If you think it's interesting, we'll keep talking. They started digging into it, and not only were they able to confirm our allegations, they found more damning evidence."

Even though pyramid-scheme law was more gray than black and white, the more dirt S&C found, the more convinced Ackman and the others in the office became that Herbalife was the fraud he and Dinneen had long suspected.

Ackman then decided to up the ante.

With the stock still hovering in the high $40s, Ackman proposed going nuclear—raising the value of the short position to one billion dollars—a massive 20 percent of the float, or the total number of shares available for trading. It was go big or go home—just the way Ackman liked it. And since Ackman was as much a showman as an activist, he proposed doing a splashy presentation in New York—a public execution for the whole world to see.

Some thought the plan was insane, that unveiling such a large position could easily invite thrill seekers to take the other side. But Ackman had an answer for that too. By shorting Herbalife and winning, he argued, Pershing Square would not only make money for its investors but could do good at the same time by stopping a predatory business that preyed on minorities and the less fortunate. Ackman said those who had the balls to take the other side would essentially be taking blood money, and who would want to carry that burden? The idea led to a debate over whether Pershing Square's real objective was to make money for its investors or to fulfill some altruistic or moral mission. Ackman won that argument as well, saying Pershing Square could do both.

He told Dinneen he wanted a presentation ready by June, just a few weeks away. Now it was Ackman's turn to plot the big reveal. He phoned a friend from the industry who just happened to have the perfect venue.

"Bill called me ahead of the 2012 Ira Sohn Conference and said I have something really great but I'm not sure it's going to be ready in time," said Douglas Hirsch, one of the charitable event's cofounders and a longtime friend of Ackman's. "Then later, in October, early November, he called back and said, hey, remember our conversation? Well, I have something I'd like to present, so we came up with the idea of a Sohn special event."

With Hirsch onboard, Ackman booked the AXA Center on Seventh Avenue. It was Ackman's go-to venue and large enough to hold the hundreds of people he hoped would show up. Timing was the only question. When October came and went, Ackman pushed the presentation to the week of Thanksgiving. But when Dinneen still wasn't ready come November, Ackman set a drop-dead date of December 20, just before many on Wall Street would take off for the holidays.

With the date fast approaching and the presentation looming, Dinneen worked around the clock to prepare the hundreds of slides they'd need for the deck. If they were going to bring Herbalife down, everything had to be perfect, including making sure enough people actually showed up to see it.

Ackman had a plan for that too.

On December 19, the day before the Sohn special event, Ackman called CNBC's hedge-fund reporter, Kate Kelly, to break the news about the big short. Kelly had a slew of big contacts in the industry and from Ackman's point of view was the perfect person to drop the bomb.

Just before 2 p.m., Kelly busted into CNBC's regularly scheduled programming with the "breaking news."

"I've just learned that Pershing Square hedge-fund manager Bill Ackman has a major new short position in Herbalife,"[13] Kelly said, while producers in the control room threw up a stock chart to watch the reaction on Wall Street. "Ackman considers Herbalife to be one of the single best investment short thesis he's ever seen from what we're hearing," said Kelly. "He has been short Herbalife for about seven or eight months and will unveil more details why at the Sohn Conference tomorrow morning."[14]

Boom.

The Kelly scoop immediately sent Herbalife plunging, falling 15 percent within seconds. Three thousand miles away, inside Herbalife's Los Angeles headquarters, CEO Michael Johnson saw the slide and went apoplectic.

"Who the fuck does this guy think he is," Johnson screamed to no one in particular, while a spokesperson with the company quickly drafted a statement blasting Ackman. Johnson continued his tirade. He was out for blood and didn't care who knew it. He also felt powerless to stop the stock's slide considering he was in Los Angeles and Ackman was in New York, where the story was just starting to spiral. Johnson wiped his schedule and called the Los Angeles offices of Moelis & Company, an investment bank that Johnson had done business with in the past. The firm's copresident, Navid Mahmoodzadegan, took the call. He knew Johnson well and urged the now frantic CEO to remain calm while the two figured out exactly what they were up against.

Johnson would have none of it, arguing that he wasn't about to let some asshole back in New York ruin his company in a matter of minutes. So Johnson did the unthinkable. He picked up the phone and called into CNBC's *Street Signs* program and unloaded on Ackman in a tirade reflecting his outrage.

"First of all, this is not about Herbalife's business model; this is about Bill Ackman's business model," Johnson railed into the phone, as Kelly and the program's host, Brian Sullivan, listened and watched the stock react in real-time. "This is wrong," Johnson said. "This is totally wrong what is taking place. This is blatant market manipulation. We're not a pyramid scheme— that's a bogus accusation. We have millions of customers around the world. We don't pay for recruiting. We've been in business thirty-two years. We just announced a hundred-million-dollar facility in North Carolina employing over five hundred people with the governor of North Carolina this morning. This is a legitimate company. Mr. Ackman's proposition that the United States would be better off when Herbalife is gone . . . The United States would be better off when Bill Ackman is gone."[15]

Just like that, one of the biggest battles Wall Street had ever seen was on. Ackman watched Johnson's explosion live and was taken aback at how angry he appeared, even feeling threatened by the outburst. Johnson was pissed, so much so, as the rage was spilling from his body, that he'd jumbled Herbalife's sales figures in an exchange with the CNBC on-air talent. Kelly had asked Johnson questions similar to those that Einhorn had asked about Herbalife's long-controversial sales figures.

Here's the transcript:[16]

> KELLY: "Mr. Johnson, questions have been raised by other major investors, including David Einhorn. Are the sales that go on about your products confined to your own distribution network? Is that the case, or is it broader than that?"
>
> JOHNSON: "We have millions of customers. Our customers are sometimes called distributors; that's the only confusion that we have, and they are distributors because they get a discount on our products."
>
> KELLY: "Can you give us a percentage figure though Mr. Johnson as to what percentage of your sales are outside that distribution network?"
>
> JOHNSON: "90%."
>
> KELLY: "So the vast majority?"
>
> JOHNSON: "Absolutely."

The number was not accurate. Johnson had fucked up, and he knew it—not that there was anything he could about it now.

Ackman pounced, claiming Johnson had lied.

"He really sounded like a thug," Ackman remembers. "It was clear to me that it was not the reaction of a normal CEO. He flat-out lied."

It all set the stage for the main event the following morning at the AXA Center.

On the morning of December 20, Ackman made the short trip from Pershing's offices to 787 Seventh Avenue, where the AXA was located, to give his presentation. Dinneen and a cadre of Pershing executives followed, taking a seat in the front row for moral support.

As the clock struck 9 a.m. Eastern time, the event began.

"Good morning, my name is Evan Sohn, and I'd like to welcome you to the first Sohn Foundation Conference Special Event."[17]

Standing backstage, Ackman believed the presentation he was about to give was the best piece of research Pershing had ever done.

There were no rehearsals—no dry runs in front of a mirror or practice speeches in front of his Pershing Square colleagues. Ackman had never felt more ready. He knew what was at stake and wasn't about to blow it.

After the brief introduction, Ackman, dressed impeccably in a dark suit and royal blue tie, quickly walked onstage clutching a clicker to advance the slides, and began.

"OK, so we've got a lot to cover today, and we're going to move pretty quickly,"[18] Ackman said as he pushed the button on his projector remote to reveal the first slide.

"Who Wants to Be a Millionaire?" it read.

"Herbalife . . . if you can dream it, you can do it," Ackman began, mocking a slogan from Herbalife's own marketing materials.

Ackman began by highlighting the company's remarkable growth, marveling how, in a little more than thirty years, Herbalife had gone from nothing to a $5 billion market cap company, becoming "one of the fastest growing companies in the history of the world."

"Has anyone in the room purchased an Herbalife product?" Ackman asked of the few hundred in attendance.

One or two hands went up.

"This is not a particularly well known company," he continued.

He called out the company's top-selling product, the Formula 1 meal replacement, comparing the shake's impressive sales figures to more mainstream household products like Clorox, Crest, and Palmolive.

How was Formula 1 "the only $2 billion brand nobody's ever heard of?" Ackman snickered.

"How is it possible that Herbalife sells six times more nutrition powder then Ensure, Slim Fast, and GNC's Lean Shake?" Ackman wondered. He even used Johnson's own words from the previous day against him, chiding the chief executive over the 90 percent figure he'd told Kate Kelly of CNBC regarding the company's sales.

Then Ackman played a video. It was a highly produced testimonial made by Herbalife itself featuring the top-selling Herbalife distributor Doran Andry that Richard had mentioned in her original research report. Andry had left a desk job at the age of twenty-two, saying he was taken by the business opportunity Herbalife presented. He'd climbed the Herbalife sales ladder, reaching the top-level Chairman's Club, and he had all the spoils to show for the ascent.

"This is a product that is changing people's lives," said Andry, showing off the Ferrari, Bentley, and expensive chopper-style motorcycle he'd gotten from working "two to three hours a week" as an Herbalife distributor.[19]

"In my very first calendar year, our income hit $350,000," Andry claimed. "And our second year, I turned thirty and Miko (Andry's wife) turned twenty-five, and our income hit $1,100,000. We had become millionaires."

Andry gave a guided tour of the opulent mansion he'd bought.

"You know, it's really amazing. I step out of the Ferrari, Bentley, whatever, and people go, what does that guy do for a living? And I go, I'm an Herbalife independent distributor. And people are absolutely amazed what I do. It's an incredible quality of life. All of you, if you just dream, can have all that we have, and much more."

Ackman mocked Andry's success, calling Herbalife "the best-managed pyramid scheme in the history of the world."

Then, it was Dinneen's turn at the lectern.

He attacked Herbalife's marketing and compensation structure, which he and Ackman said was a purposely convoluted web of misinformation based almost entirely on recruiting. The pay plan, they charged, essentially worked like this: when an Herbalife distributor recruited new members, or distributors, into the business, they received a commission when that person bought products from the company and continued to get paid when those original recruits found others to join. And as their so-called "downline" bought Herbalife products, a distributor would move up the Herbalife food chain to higher and higher levels, with the biggest sellers ultimately reaching the Chairman's Club level, where Andry and others were striking it rich.

There was only one problem, asserted Ackman and Dinneen. Almost all of Herbalife's new recruits actually failed at the business opportunity, they claimed, losing thousands of dollars in the process, with many dropping out altogether within the first year. They also charged that the only sales the company was actually making were from distributor to distributor, one of the key hallmarks of a pyramid scheme.

"Do we even know if any retail customers exist?" Dinneen asked, almost rhetorically.

Over three and a half blistering hours, Ackman, Dinneen, and Pershing Square attorney David Klafter shuttled through 343 slides. Herbalife shares, which had fallen 12 percent the day before on the Kelly scoop, plunged nearly 10 percent more while Ackman and company made their case. In the space of twenty-four hours, billions of dollars in Herbalife market cap had evaporated. Ackman made it clear he didn't expect the stock to stop there.

Minutes after leaving the stage, Ackman calmly sat for an interview with CNBC's Andrew Ross Sorkin and said of the stock, "If it's found to be a pyramid scheme, it's a zero."

A zero. Think about that. Ackman wasn't just betting on Herbalife shares falling; he was banking on the company's demise—its death—something even those who agreed with his thesis thought was risky.

"I think he did a very good job, but when he made the comments about it going to zero, I think I said to myself, why is he saying that?" remembered the CNBC reporter Herb Greenberg, who'd also done work on Herbalife for a documentary project produced by the network. "He was drawing a line that showed so much hubris, but I thought it was a really good presentation."

Ackman accompanied the more than three hundred slides with a website that needled Herbalife even further. He called it "Facts About Herbalife," and it went into even greater detail about the fraud he was alleging. Ackman also pledged to give all personal profits he made to charity, lest he receive any "blood money" from the trade.

Back in LA, Herbalife's management was shell-shocked. Most in the office had expected Ackman to lay it on heavy, but not over several hours and with so many damaging accusations.

Then, there was the reaction of Herbalife's legion of distributors—its de facto sales force. Though few if any had any idea who Ackman even was, they sure saw the reaction of the stock and were left questioning whether their livelihoods were about to go up in flames.

John Tartol had been an Herbalife distributor for thirty-six years, rising through the ranks to become a top-selling Chairman's Club member. He earned millions of dollars a year from the business opportunity after having tried the product himself and becoming sold on its effects.

"I lost twelve pounds in a very short time," he said. "I had great energy, and I thought I'd start sharing it with others."

Tartol thought Ackman's allegations were false.

"We've been around for over thirty years, doing billions of dollars," he said. "You can't kid the public about a product for thirty years if it doesn't really work."

But no matter how much conviction Tartol and the other distributors had in Herbalife's products or the business itself, at that very moment, none of it mattered. It was Ackman the activist against Herbalife, and the market seemed to believe the billionaire investor. It was the reality of how the stock market had come to view activist investors in general and the power they had come to wield.

"It makes me angry because (Ackman) wanted to fill his own pockets," said Tartol. "There are certain people who have bad motives. There should be ramifications for people spreading misinformation and harming the business."

Tartol said the company reached out immediately to its rank and file to make sure they were well informed, even if slightly unsettled by Ackman's presentation and the dramatic stock drop that followed.

With his company's stock in free fall, Johnson, who'd never before been through such an exercise in his professional career, picked up the phone and called his mentor, Jerry Perenchio, the billionaire who once ran the television network Univision. Perenchio had watched part of Ackman's presentation and had heard the damning accusations. Right there on the phone, Perenchio made Johnson walk him through the business to prove it was legitimate.

Herbalife released a statement saying, "Today's presentation was a malicious attack on our business model based largely on outdated, distorted and inaccurate information."[20]

But Herbalife's executive team wasn't the only party stunned by the intensity of the takedown.

The research analyst Tim Ramey, who covered Herbalife for the firm D.A. Davidson, said, "I've never seen an investor spend three and a half hours of time at a major venue being webcast and then make TV appearances to make his point. It's the largest orchestrated bull or bear case that I've ever seen."[21]

"This is the highest conviction I have ever had about any investment I have ever made, full-stop,"[22] Ackman told a reporter before heading back to the office to watch the stock plummet even more.

"I thought the thing would be done in less than a year," Ackman said later. "I thought the stock would get crushed and the distributors would start to freak out, that the pyramid scheme would collapse and the distributors would move on to some other pyramid scheme."

Ackman soon learned it wouldn't be that simple.

On December 28 at 5:30 a.m., the Australian hedge-fund manager John Hempton published a blog post titled "Bill Ackman enters the city of Stalingrad," a reference to the epic battle in World War II that saw Nazi Germany face a catastrophic defeat.[23] Many historians consider the seven-month bloodbath to be the greatest battle of the war, and Hempton figured, at least metaphorically, that either Ackman or Herbalife would face a similar fate.

"Someone is going to lose big," he wrote. "And the victor will be so bloodied that the word victory will sound hollow. . . . For a short seller who is as risk-averse as me, watching this is pure hedge fund porn."[24]

Hempton then let it be known which army he was betting on. In a stunning postscript he wrote:

P.S. I am utterly convinced by everything in Bill Ackman's presentation except the final conclusion—that Herbalife's stock will collapse.
I took a long position on Christmas Eve. I suspect that Herbalife
is so profitable and so powerful they will see Mr. Ackman's attack
off—and the easiest way to do that is to buy back stock (and make
the stock go up). Mr. Ackman has given them the incentive to return
their huge (but tainted) profits to shareholders (and I plan to be a
recipient shareholder).[25]

The Hempton post caused Herbalife shares, which had sunk into
the $20s in the days following Ackman's presentation, to pop nearly
7 percent. Less than a week later, on January 4, 2013, Hempton
went on CNBC with Herb Greenberg to explain why he'd taken the
other side.

Of Herbalife, Hempton said, "It buys back stock regularly, it pays
a fairly hefty dividend. They're scumbags, but they're the stock market's scumbags."[26]

"I was surprised that he took the other side, because Herbalife
was typically the type of company where he'd have been the natural
skeptic," Greenberg remembers. "I knew that he had done his own
research, but I never thought he would make it so personal."

Hempton had underscored the debate some other investors were
having at that very moment—that Herbalife may in fact be a sprawling fraud, but that still didn't mean the stock would collapse to zero
under its own weight or that the government was going to shut the
business down.

Wall Street would soon learn Hempton wasn't the only notable
money manager skeptical of Ackman's thesis.

Out in Los Angeles, a man named Robert Chapman, who ran
money for his namesake firm, Chapman Capital, had followed
Herbalife since the late 1990s, when Mark Hughes had tried to take
the company private in the leveraged buyout. It had been a messy
process, and when it had become clear that the deal seemed unlikely,
Herbalife shares had sunk to near $8. Chapman had pounced and
gone long.

He said he traded in and out of the position every now and again but hadn't paid much attention to Herbalife in years—at least until Ackman's slideshow in New York, when his interest was piqued once again.

Chapman, who looks more henchman than hedge funder, had no great love for Ackman either. He thought the brash billionaire was more Barnum than Buffett, a sanctimonious schmuck who had Herbalife all wrong. Like Hempton, Chapman thought Herbalife could buy back stock or raise its dividend, with either event likely to drive the stock higher. He also went a step further, calling out Ackman's timing for the public presentation, which came just ten days before year's end, when hedge funds are marking their books to market or placing a fair value on their assets. Chapman's message was implicit. By sending Herbalife stock dramatically lower at the end of the year, Ackman could goose his annual performance numbers.

On December 29, 2012, Chapman put out a public letter that read, "Herbalife: Why I Made It a 35% Position after the Bill Ackman Bear Raid."[27]

Chapman called Ackman's public short a "circus show" and said he was likely to suffer a short squeeze—a quick jump in a stock price driven by others buying the stock, thus sucking shares out of the marketplace. Ackman had already taken away 20 percent, and if other investors took the other side en masse, he could be forced to "cover his short" (buy the stock), driving up the price at a potentially massive loss.

Chapman figured the government, which had given Herbalife the once-over before, had "been there, done that" and had already moved on. He'd also watched Ackman's interview with Sorkin on CNBC and was convinced the investor was relying too heavily on regulators to intervene.

Chapman concluded by writing, "Indeed, without the FTC (Federal Trade Commission) taking injunctive actions against Herbalife, Ackman's crusade toward 'zero' is doomed."

"He's an opportunistic trader and investor," Greenberg says of Chapman. "He went so far back in the story and because of that he did have a very interesting perspective on the company. . . . He saw the wave and the psychology of how things were moving in favor of Herbalife and he was going to be part of that."

Days later, Chapman said the stock could trade back to the $70s, and that $100 "was not far-fetched."

The bonfire had started. The only question now was whether Ackman could keep it from spreading.

7

THE POISON PEN

The Chapman and Hempton surprises had certainly created a buzz in the media and hedge-fund circles, but with the extended holiday break in full swing, and most on Wall Street still out of the city on vacation, many observers expected the brewing battle over Herbalife to take something of a hiatus.

It barely lasted a week.

At 12:37 p.m. on January 8, the always provocative business reporter Charles Gasparino tweeted, "Robert Chapman promises 'big news' regarding Herbalife sometime today or early tomorrow; possibly lawsuit against Ackman?"[1]

It was a tempting message for sure, even if no one had a clue what the news was going to be.

One thing was certain—Ackman wasn't sticking around in New York to find out.

The next morning, on Wednesday, January 9, Ackman made the nearly twenty-minute drive from the Upper West Side of Manhattan to Teterboro, New Jersey, where his private G550 jet was gassed and ready to go at Meridian terminal.

It was a much-needed break, considering Ackman's endless hours of work on the Herbalife short and the stress and scrutiny that had followed.

Scuba diving in Myanmar would be the perfect remedy, even if it meant a sixteen-and-a-half-hour journey, with a refueling stop, to get there.

Ackman and a group of eight, including an old friend, Leucadia's Joseph S. Steinberg, some Pershing Square partners, and the British financier Martin E. Franklin, would spend days on a luxury yacht enjoying some of the finest underwater action in the world.

But just before 10 a.m. Eastern time, as Ackman's jet was settling in for the long haul, his mobile phone blew up with an urgent message from the office.

The news was stunning.

Daniel S. Loeb, the chief executive officer of the hedge fund Third Point LLC, had filed a 13G disclosure form with the Securities and Exchange Commission revealing a massive 8.24 percent stake in Herbalife. Shares spiked 7.54 percent on the news to $41.24 before being halted under the new "circuit breaker" rules at the New York Stock Exchange, which prevent individual stocks from cataclysmic crashes.[2]

Ackman was blindsided.

Not only were he and Loeb friendly and even occasional investment partners, they were also two of the biggest stars on the hedge-fund scene—the Clooney and Pitt of the profession. Now they'd be trying to rip each other's heads off.

"This is one of those stories that now becomes perhaps as much about Herbalife and its future, as it does about the hedge fund world and both of these gentlemen," said CNBC's Sorkin, who broke into the network's morning programming to discuss the shocking revelation.[3]

Though Ackman had always suspected other "longs" could join Hempton and Chapman, he never figured Loeb would be among the opportunists. For one thing, he'd gotten an email from the financier following his Herbalife presentation, congratulating him on his work. Now Loeb was betting $350 million that the same research was a pile of garbage? Ackman was furious and thought it was "a shit move" from a guy he once considered a friend.

Loeb quickly made it clear he was out to win.

After the SEC filing became public, Loeb released a letter he'd sent to his investors. It included a scathing rebuke of Ackman's thesis, calling it "preposterous." He wrote:

"The pyramid scheme is a serious accusation that we have studied closely with our advisors. . . . We do not believe it has merit. The short thesis rests on the notion that the FTC has been asleep at the switch, missed a massive fraud for over three decades, and will shortly awaken (at the behest of hedge fund short seller) to shut down the Company."[4]

Loeb also went after Ackman's presentation at the AXA Center, which had lasted more than three hours, writing:

While the short seller's presentation was lengthy, it presented no evidence to show that Herbalife has crossed a line that would compel regulators to shut it down. Indeed, there was very little "new" news in the presentation and when pressed in later interviews, even the short seller conceded that the FTC was not looking at Herbalife's practices. In our experience, expert regulators like those at the FTC do not respond to sudden pressure from hedge fund whistleblowers by acceding blindly to their demands. Finally, even if there were some regulatory intervention that changed how the company does business, we are comforted by the fact that 80% of Herbalife's revenues come from overseas.[5]

Loeb made it clear that he had a much different price target for Herbalife's stock than Ackman, who said it was a zero.

Applying a modest 10–12x earnings multiple suggests Herbalife's shares are worth $55–$68, offering 40–70% upside from here and making the company a compelling long investment for Third Point.

The letter was about as thorough a "fuck you" as Wall Street had seen in years.

"This is shaping up to be potentially one of the bloodiest hedge fund battles of all time," Chapman told the *Wall Street Journal* when news of Loeb's new position hit.[6]

It was a battle Chapman had been all too happy to instigate.

Chapman had actually called Loeb, who was vacationing in Cabo San Lucas, Mexico, during Ackman's presentation, gave him the play-by-play, and told him how far Herbalife shares had fallen. Chapman knew that Loeb still had a long-simmering grudge with Ackman over the Target trade gone wrong. Loeb had intimated that he'd moved on from the disaster, but friends thought otherwise and believed he likely saw Herbalife as a win-win. He could buy the stock and fulfill his fiduciary responsibility to his investors by making money while at the same time sticking it up Ackman's ass for some long-awaited payback.

Loeb was intrigued enough by the Chapman call that he assigned one of his Third Point analysts to do some cursory work on Herbalife's business, knowing there was little time to waste. While Herbalife shares were in the high $20s and far down from the pre-Einhorn high of $70, Loeb knew they might not stay there for very long, certainly not the way the stock was being tossed around in the media.

Loeb called his office from Mexico and had his associates immediately hire former FTC lawyers with expertise in the field of multilevel marketing. The goal was clear—to decide whether Herbalife was a pyramid scheme or not and whether an investment and the risk that came with it even made sense.

It didn't take long for all involved to come to the same conclusion: Ackman was wrong. Convinced that Herbalife shares had been unfairly punished, Loeb started buying the stock at $28.[7] He then had to decide how much noise he really wanted to make.

That answer would lie in Los Angeles.

Just after Christmas, Loeb cut short his Mexican holiday and flew up to California to meet face-to-face with Herbalife's CEO. Loeb may have had it in for Ackman, but he also knew the guy was no idiot and wanted to cross off any lingering skepticism he had in his own mind about Herbalife's operations.

"Dan came to my office . . . and I think he wanted to put the finger on me to see who this guy was and who this company was," said Johnson.

Like Johnson, Loeb was also into cycling, and since he'd grown up in Los Angeles, the two even knew some of the same people. Johnson spent hours walking Loeb through as much of the business as he could on short notice.

"Everything," said Johnson of Loeb's queries. "[He asked about] the business, the legality, the structure, the compensation program, the product. He [Loeb] was highly inquisitive, and he spent a long time here."

Johnson even gave Loeb an Herbalife cycling kit to wear, jokingly telling him to wear it the next time he biked with Ackman. It was a reference to an unflattering story first documented in a *Vanity Fair* piece. It had recounted a bike-ride-gone-wrong years earlier between the two that had left Ackman sheepishly overexerted and embarrassed.

It was shortly after the meeting, which Johnson said lasted several hours, that Loeb began loading up on stock. On January 3, 2013, Third Point's position crossed the 5 percent threshold and triggered the regulatory filing with the SEC, which was done on the 9th.

Johnson was ebullient at the news of Loeb's filing. If Chapman and Hempton had given Herbalife some breathing room, Loeb had delivered a proverbial haymaker to the naysayers.

"We were looking for allies," Johnson said. "And to have people going long, when a short is out there—it certainly helps."

But Loeb wasn't just any white knight.

Like Einhorn, and even Ackman, for that matter, Loeb was a billionaire with a long and highly respected track record. In 2012, his Third Point Ultra fund was up 33.6 percent, with his main "Offshore Fund" up 21.2 percent, easily beating the market and most of his hedge-fund counterparts. Since its inception in 1995, Third Point's annualized returns were at least 21.1 percent, net of fees.[8]

Loeb was one of the best in the game, but it wasn't the numbers alone that made him one of the industry's leading men. He was handsome and witty, fit and feisty, and was known as much for his poisonous pen as for his annual performance.

In February 2002, Loeb wrote a scathing letter to the Penn Virginia Corporation, saying of its recent acquisition,

> The ill-conceived and poorly timed $112.0 million acquisition of Synergy Oil & Gas ("Synergy") appears to bode poorly for this management team's ability to complete accretive corporate transactions. . . . With all due respect, the sophisticated Texas oilmen that sold their interest in Synergy saw the Appalachian coal men coming with aspirations to wear crocodile skin cowboy boots, silver spurs and ten-gallon hats. No doubt the folks at NGP who sold Synergy so near the top tick of the natural gas bubble had quite a hootenanny at Penn Virginia shareholders' expense.[9]

In February 2005, he took aim at Star Gas Partners with this doozy;

"Sadly, your ineptitude is not limited to your failure to communicate with bond and unit holders. A review of your record reveals years of value destruction and strategic blunders which have led us to dub you one of the most dangerous and incompetent executives in America."[10]

Even some of America's most high-profile companies weren't immune to Loeb's reach. As an example, on September 8, 2011, it was Yahoo's turn to face his wrath. In a letter to the company's board of directors, Loeb announced his arrival. He'd acquired 65 million Yahoo shares, or a 5.1 percent stake in the company, which made him the third-largest outside shareholder.

Yahoo "has been severely damaged—but not irreparably—by poor management and governance," he wrote to the board.[11] It had been a painful few years for the one-time Silicon Valley anchor. In 2008, Yahoo had famously turned down a lucrative $31 per share takeover offer from Microsoft and since then had struggled to remain relevant against newer and more nimble rivals like Google and Facebook.

Just before Loeb came on the scene Yahoo had dumped its CEO, Carol Bartz. Loeb, who started buying the stock when it was near its fifty-two-week low of around $11 a share, made it clear from the outset he expected a say in who got the job next.

Loeb wrote:

> Third Point has held discussions with many highly respected entrepreneurial executives active in technology, internet, media and consumer-related businesses. From these discussions we have distilled an All-Star team of potential Director candidates, who would be indispensable in working with the reconstituted Board to pursue the three paths outlined in the recent company announcement: CEO search, business review and strategic options. We look forward to sharing our candidates with you shortly.[12]

It didn't take long for Loeb's patience to run thin.

On November 4, 2011, two months after his initial salvo, Loeb wrote another letter to the Yahoo board, this time taking aim at company founder Jerry Yang. Yang had personally turned down the Microsoft deal, and news reports claimed he was angling for private equity firms to swoop in and save his backside.

Loeb ripped the idea.

> We are deeply concerned by news reports that you are considering a leveraged recapitalization that will allow private equity firms to gain substantial equity positions that will, when combined with Jerry Yang's and David Filo's ownership, effectively establish a controlling position in Yahoo. More troubling are reports that Mr. Yang is engaging in one-off discussions with private equity firms, presumably because it is in his best personal interests to do so. The Board and the Strategic Committee should not have permitted Mr. Yang to engage in these discussions, particularly given his ineptitude in dealing with the Microsoft negotiations to purchase the Company in 2008; it is now clear that he is simply not aligned with shareholders. At a bare minimum, Mr. Yang must declare whether he is a buyer or a seller—he cannot be both. If we are correct and he is effectively a

buyer, corporate ethics require him to recuse himself from any further discussions on behalf of the Company. He should also be requested by the Company to promptly leave the Board and join Mr. Filo in solely an operating capacity.[13]

Loeb demanded Yang's resignation and two board seats of his own, and derided Yang's attempts to cut a "sweetheart deal" with the private equity firms.

Yahoo refused, calling Loeb a short timer, only out for his own interests.

Then, on January 5, 2012, without consulting Loeb, Yahoo announced they'd found Bartz's replacement. His name was Scott Thompson, a top eBay Inc. executive, known, according to an article that day in the *Wall Street Journal*, "for his cordial personality and thick Boston accent . . . a sharp contrast to his predecessor."[14]

If investors were excited, they certainly didn't show it. Yahoo shares closed the day down 3.10 percent, at $15.78 per share.

Loeb wasn't thrilled either, and on March 28, 2012, he fired off a letter to Thompson directly that hardly sounded like a detente. Loeb was now demanding four board seats, including one for himself, and slammed back against accusations he was a drive-by investor.

"At the risk of beating a dead horse," Loeb wrote, "we suppose that, by the Board's analysis, it would have been this dreaded 'short-term' thinking to have allowed Microsoft's $31 per share offer four years ago to be presented to shareholders. To the contrary, an unbiased observer might find Third Point's thinking quite 'additive.' Third Point has been a driving force standing up for shareholders since we disclosed our position in Company shares in September."[15]

Blood was in the water, and it was about to become a feeding frenzy.

On Thursday, May 3, in yet another letter to the board, Loeb dropped a bomb—alleging that Thompson had padded his resume with a degree in computer science he never earned. Loeb demanded Thompson's firing, by noon the following Monday.[16]

Yahoo confirmed the allegation, but said Thompson's error was "inadvertent."[17]

The facts were hardly on his side.

While Thompson had gone to Stonehill College, near Boston, he graduated in 1979 with a bachelor of science in accounting, not computer science. And according to a report from *allthingsd* reporter Kara Swisher, the bogus degree had been listed on Thompson's bios over the previous ten years.

Loeb had seen enough and pushed the board to send Thompson packing and welcome his own slate of directors. In another missive sent to Yahoo and publicly released, Loeb wrote:

> We urge the Board to stop wasting valuable company resources and drop its resistance to placing the Third Point nominees on the Board. . . . We are prepared to join immediately. Once on the Board, our first tasks will be to work with the remaining Board members to find Yahoo! a new leader with the qualifications and integrity to lead the Company and install best practices of corporate governance. The Company can ill afford to continue this misguided fight with its largest outside shareholder while it has so many other fires to put out. There has been enough damage already.

Eleven days later, Thompson, who'd been irreparably damaged by the embellishment, resigned.[18]

That same day, Loeb and Yahoo settled, with the financier getting three board seats: one for himself and one each for Harry Wilson, the CEO of the restructuring firm Maeva, and Michael Wolf, CEO of the media consulting firm Activate. Yahoo insider Ross Levinsohn was made interim CEO, while the board engaged in a formal search process for Thompson's successor.

On July 17, 2012, Yahoo named Google star, thirty-seven-year old Marissa Mayer, CEO. Mayer promptly exclaimed, "Yahoo is a terrific company with an amazing following, terrific brand and huge amount of potential."[19]

Yahoo shares rose 2 percent to $15.96 on the news, with investors betting the revolving door of CEOs had finally stopped spinning.[20]

Loeb had scored big again.

By the time the winter of 2012 rolled around, Third Point, with $10 billion under management and annual returns of more than 20 percent, had major positions in Yahoo, Delphi, American International Group, Ally Financial, and Murphy Oil.[21]

Now Herbalife had joined the list.

For CEO Michael Johnson, Loeb's landing, and his filing on January 9, couldn't have come at a better time. The following day, Johnson was scheduled to be in New York for an Herbalife investor day, the first public opportunity for the company to offer up its defense against Ackman and his takedown.

But Johnson and his executive team would soon learn they'd have more than just Ackman to contend with.

At 4:33 p.m. on the 9th, "S.E.C Opens Investigation into Herbalife," read the headline on the *New York Times*'s website.[22] *Times* reporters Ben Protess and Michael J. De La Merced said the agency's enforcement division had opened an investigation into the company, according to a source, and that the inquiry "was likely to examine the company's sales practices."

The *Wall Street Journal* had first reported the news, which initially caused Herbalife shares to fall before they recovered. At the end of the day, the stock finished higher by 3.7 percent, at $39.77 a share. Investors apparently believed the inquiry by the SEC's New York office was routine and was trumped by Loeb and his new position.

Ackman was elated. While the SEC had taken years to investigate his other big short, MBIA, here were regulators knocking on Herbalife's door after only two weeks.

"We were on a roll," Ackman said. "I was like, 'OK, this thing could be over fast.'"

The next morning, on January 10, with a cadre of television news live-trucks lining West 57th Street, Johnson and the other senior Herbalife executives—President Des Walsh, Chief Financial Officer John DeSimone, and Chief Operating Officer Richard Goudis—along with Moelis's Navid Mahmoodzadegan, lawyers from the firm Boies Schiller Flexner, and PR consultants from the crisis firm Joele Frank walked into the Four Seasons Hotel set to officially debunk Ackman's claims.[23]

Some considered the event a make-or-break moment for Herbalife.

At 8:46 a.m., Walsh gave investors a flavor of what to expect. He appeared via satellite on CNBC's *Squawk Box* program, telling host Andrew Ross Sorkin that Ackman's claims were a "gross distortion of reality," that "product results drive sales," and that Herbalife provided "a tremendous business opportunity." Walsh also claimed that Herbalife had "a huge customer base" outside of its distributor network, a reference to the accusations that had been made during Ackman's presentation.

In premarket trading that morning, Herbalife shares rose 3.1 percent, to $41.18, about $15 higher than they'd been after Ackman's initial speech.

At 9:02 a.m., Johnson, looking calm, walked onstage for what he called "a unique event." "There's a tremendous amount of misinformation about Herbalife," Johnson said. "This misinformation has found its way into the marketplace, and we're looking to correct that today."[24]

COO Goudas walked through some of Herbalife's products and how they were made, citing "misrepresentations" made by Ackman.

Then, it was Walsh's turn.

"If we're not a legitimate company," he asked, "why on Earth would we invest hundreds of millions of dollars in products and facilities?"[25] He continued, "Our business model is business-to-business. We sell to distributors. It's simply the nature of our business model."[26]

To counter Ackman's claims that the overwhelming majority of Herbalife's products were sold almost exclusively in-network, the company had commissioned a survey to prove otherwise. Kim Rory, a vice president with Lieberman Research, which had done the work, said 5 percent of the adults polled in the United States had bought Herbalife products. That equaled 5.5 million households and "clearly a large consumer base of Herbalife products,"[27] she claimed.

Walsh said it was a "myth" that Herbalife didn't have real outside retail customers.

"This is the picture Pershing Square would have you believe," he said. "The reality, of course, is very, very different."[28]

The pushback was working.

By just after 10 a.m., Herbalife shares had risen 7 percent to session highs.[29]

Then it was Johnson's turn again.

"This is a fabulous company with an incredible future," he said. "We've been here for thirty-two years, and we'll be here for another thirty-two years."

At 11:34 a.m., the presentation ended.[30]

Before leaving, each attendee got a goodie bag in the company's green corporate colors filled with Herbalife products, some of the same products Ackman had thrown under the bus a few weeks earlier.

Johnson hit the door, got into a waiting car, and headed to the airport for a flight back to Los Angeles for a distributor dinner that evening.

Ackman released a statement that day saying Herbalife "distorted, mischaracterized, and outright ignored large portions of our presentation."

At the end of a volatile trading session, Herbalife shares closed down 2.8 percent, at $39.24 per share.

Even so, Johnson thought he had nailed it and that the pushback would resonate on Wall Street. He climbed aboard the plane home and exhaled, assuming his fight with Ackman would soon be over.

8

THE BRAWL

Michael Johnson was in church.

It was Christmas Eve 2012, just days after Ackman made his presentation on Herbalife. Johnson had arrived early with one of his sons, hoping for something of a miracle—to save a dozen or so seats for family and friends who would join them for the pre-holiday Mass in fifteen or twenty minutes. Standing in one of the pews, Johnson and his offspring tried their best to wave off the inquiring eyes, when his mobile phone rang.

"No Caller ID" read the screen.

Thinking it was his wife calling, Johnson walked outside into the California night and hit the green "Accept" button on his iPhone.

"Hi Michael, it's Carl Icahn," said the voice on the other end in a friendly and engaging tone. "I don't get this Ackman thing."

Johnson had no idea how Icahn had gotten his number, but couldn't talk—his wife had just shown up and was waving for him to hang up.

It wasn't a request.

"But it's Carl Icahn . . . , it's Carl." Johnson said, unable to even finish the sentence.

Johnson sheepishly told Icahn he'd have to call him back the next day and hung up the phone, somewhat abruptly.

The next afternoon, on Christmas, Johnson went to a quiet spot inside his Malibu mansion and dialed Icahn's number. Not one to beat around the bush, Icahn got right to the point.

"'I don't think this guy Ackman is right,'" Johnson recalled Icahn saying. "He said he was going to take advantage of that and get in on the other side."

Johnson had never met Icahn but knew of his tough-as-nails reputation. He also figured that having the iconic investor in his corner was a potential game-changer in the fight with Ackman. It wasn't that Dan Loeb was chopped liver—he *wasn't*—but he also wasn't Icahn—a billionaire many times over who answered to no one. Plus, Icahn had something that Loeb didn't—staying power. Icahn's cash hoard, estimated to be nearly $20 billion at the time, was almost all his own, meaning he didn't have to worry about the interests of outside investors. Icahn's fiduciary responsibility was to Icahn himself. Icahn was also more than happy to mix it up anywhere, at any time, which Johnson knew could be a great asset against a guy like Ackman, who was loud in his own right.

"We had many people lined up against us that to have somebody lined up with us—it's a huge positive," said Johnson when we spoke about the development.

The substance of the Icahn/Johnson call remained a secret until January 16, 2013, when a *Wall Street Journal* headline splashed across the paper's website. It simply read: "Icahn Takes Herbalife Stake."[1]

The *Journal*'s Juliet Chung reported that Icahn had taken what amounted to a "small" position in Herbalife and that he, or one of his associates, had recently met with the company's management.

Despite the news, Herbalife shares fell 3.8 percent on the day to close at $45.06. Perhaps it was because most observers figured Icahn was simply along for the ride, content to ride shotgun on Herbalife with Chapman, Hempton, and especially Loeb, whom he had a great amount of respect for as an investor. It didn't take long for Icahn to make it clear that he had other plans.

One week later, on the afternoon of January 24, Icahn appeared on the Bloomberg business TV network but refused to even discuss whether he'd bought any Herbalife shares.

"I'm going to sort of duck that question," Icahn said coyly when asked by the show's host, Trish Regan, if he'd gone long on the stock.[2] But while Icahn may have been reticent to talk about Herbalife directly, he didn't hold back when it came to Ackman himself and his over-the-top tactics.

"Look, it's no secret to the world and to Wall Street—most guys on Wall Street I sort of like and get along with—it's no secret that I don't like Ackman. I don't respect him and I don't like him," said Icahn with stunning ease.[3] "But that doesn't mean that I'm going to go in and buy stock in a company necessarily just to get him—frankly I don't like the way he did this anyway. I think if you go short, you go short and hey if it goes down you make money—you don't go out and get a room full of people and badmouth the company. If you want to be in that business, why don't you just go join the SEC?"[4]

It was riveting television. Icahn lit into his nemesis in a barrage of insults.

"I will tell you—I dislike the guy, I don't respect him—I've done business with him and he wasn't forthright," said Icahn before the segment ended.

Icahn was alluding to the old Hallwood dispute, when he and Ackman had ended up in that ugly legal fight during the last days of Gotham. The beef ultimately cost Icahn $4.5 million dollars on what the financier felt was a technicality. The ruling had enraged him, partly because of the hefty check he'd had to write, but also because of Ackman's attitude afterward. Ackman had gloated about the victory in the *New York Times*, which Icahn felt had violated a decades-old code on Wall Street—never rub it in the other guy's face, no matter how gratifying the win.

Icahn had never forgiven Ackman for it, and the reported Herbalife position, no matter how small it was said to be, had many wondering if his long-awaited chance at payback had finally arrived.

While Icahn was going after Ackman on television, I was strolling through CNBC's newsroom, when I stopped by the desk of a show producer named John Melloy, who was watching the spectacle on one of the four TV monitors atop his desk. Melloy ran the *Halftime Report*, which I hosted. Neither of us could get enough of what we were seeing.

After the segment wrapped, I went back to my desk and impulsively emailed Ackman, whom I had never met before, asking if he wanted to respond to Icahn directly. I got my response later that evening, sitting at a table inside the lounge at the Surrey Hotel, on Manhattan's Upper East Side, waiting to have dinner with an acquaintance, thumbing through my emails to pass the time.

A message from Ackman suddenly popped up, saying he was putting the finishing touches on a statement and would send it to me first, momentarily. It was pay dirt, I thought.

A few seconds later, it appeared in my inbox:

On March 1, 2003, on behalf of my former fund, Gotham Partners, I entered into a contract with Carl Icahn, signed by him, to sell him a 15% stake in Hallwood Realty Partners. He paid my investors $80 per share and agreed to what he called "schmuck insurance." The agreement provided that he would pay my investors an earnout equal to 50% of his profit on Hallwood after he received a 10% annual return if he "sold or otherwise transferred" his shares for value within three years. Fewer than 13 months later on April 14, 2004, HRPT Property Trust acquired Hallwood. As a result, Carl and the other Hallwood shareholders received $136.16 per share in cash for their shares.

Under the terms of our agreement, Carl owed my investors about $4.5 million. He refused to pay. I was forced to sue him on behalf of my investors. On September 6, 2005, the court awarded us summary judgment and found the agreement to be "clear and unambiguous." He again refused to pay and appealed. We won on appeal and Carl was forced to post a bond for what he owed us and appealed again. In general, Carl waited to the last few days to appeal in order to delay the inevitable. After eight years and Carl's appeals of the judgment were denied, in 2011 the Court forced Carl to pay my investors the $4.5 million they were owed plus 9% interest per year from the date of the sale.

After Carl paid my investors, he called me up, congratulated me on winning, and said that he wanted to be my friend. I told him that I had no interest in being his friend.

Carl Icahn is a great investor, but, in my experience, he does not keep his word.

Within minutes, the release went public.

"Bill Ackman Fires Back at Carl Icahn" read the *Business Insider* headline that posted at 8:31 p.m. that night.

I asked Ackman if he'd come on my show the following day at noon to personally respond to Icahn's so personal takedown. To my surprise, Ackman readily agreed.

"Sure, I'd be happy to," he said.

I emailed the show's producers, telling them of my coup.

The stage was set—or so I thought.

Not even five minutes after Ackman had agreed to come on my show, my phone rang again. Again, it was Ackman.

"You know," he said, sounding exasperated by the evening's events, "I'm not going to come on. This whole Icahn thing is a sideshow. I promise that I'll come on your show when I have something substantive to talk about."

"OK," I responded, as I tried to hide the obvious dejection. I headed back to dinner, where my friend was waiting, when my phone rang again. Once again, I excused myself and headed into the small hotel lobby when the voice on the other end said, "Fuck it, I'll do it."

He didn't stop there. "Carl's an asshole . . . he fucked me . . . he's a fucking asshole!"

It was on.

The next morning, on January 25, 2013, as New York City was waking up to its first snow day of the season, I headed to the New York Stock Exchange to do *Halftime Report* from Post 9, CNBC's new set on the floor just under where companies ran the opening bell each day.

Shortly before noon, Ackman called in to the control room back in New Jersey, where the production staff checked his audio levels and made sure he was good for air.

At high noon, we went live.

"The war of words between two hedge fund heavyweights is heating up . . . " I began as I welcomed Ackman to the show. "Bill, it's good to talk to you," I said.[5]

"Sure, thanks for having me," he said, clearly ready to commence the rebuttal.

"Let's try to move the argument forward here," I said. "The fundamental one that Mr. Icahn seems to be making against you is that you were too aggressive—too public in the way that you attacked Herbalife in announcing your short position to the world. What would you say to that?"

"Do you know what's fascinating about it?" Ackman retorted. "In 2002 and 2003, Carl spoke at the Ira Sohn Conference . . . and talked about the same short idea both years. Trinity Industries, and he was short according to a *Fortune* story I just pulled up, 22 percent of the outstanding shares. I was there personally and remember him talking about the short and he gave a great story about why he was short. There was a room full of people, and it was the same conference, so I find it interesting our speaking at the Ira Sohn Conference in 2012 is somehow a bad thing."

Back in his office on the 47th floor of the General Motors Building, Icahn was watching the interview live and becoming angrier as Ackman spoke. If there was one thing that Icahn had no tolerance for, it was someone doing him wrong. "Don't fuck me," he liked to say when talking to me about a story or scoop.

Bill Ackman, it seemed, had fucked him.

Unbeknownst to me, Icahn had his assistant dial up CNBC's control room in Englewood Cliffs, New Jersey. Icahn said he wanted to speak to Ackman live right there on television.

It wasn't by accident.

I'd later learn that an enterprising CNBC producer named Maxwell Meyers had called Icahn's office that morning, told him of the planned Ackman interview, and floated the idea of a call-in. Meyers had known Icahn for years, even occasionally sending the investor delicacies from the smoked fish emporium Barney Greengrass on the Upper West Side as a "thank-you" for prior appearances on the network. Now, the pricey sturgeon was paying off.

At 12:25 p.m., Icahn called in.

Through my earpiece, John Melloy told me Icahn had been listening to the whole exchange and had called in to respond to Ackman.

"Carl Icahn wants to call in and respond to you directly," I said to Ackman. "I will give you two choices—you can hang on the phone and we can bring Mr. Icahn in and you guys can have that discussion with me on live television, if you're up for that."

In the heat of the moment, I forgot to give Ackman the other option of calling it a day and hanging up.

"You know, if Carl wants to come on, let's make it fun TV," Ackman said. "Let's put it to bed and move on. If you promise me we can move from here and focus on whether Herbalife is a pyramid scheme or not, for the future of CNBC Television, I'm happy to talk to Carl on TV."

We went to a commercial, while I gathered my thoughts and prepared for the moment the best I could. We came back live, and I welcomed Icahn and Ackman back in to the *Halftime Report*.

"Carl, we've been speaking with Bill for the last several minutes following the accusations you made yesterday, and he's essentially saying that you're a hypocrite, Carl, in your argument," I said.

"Listen," responded Icahn, with a fury in his voice I hadn't ever heard before. "I've really sort of had it with this Ackman guy. You know, why don't we go back over a little history with him. I'm not going to get into talking about short positions as much as maybe you'd like me to, but hey, let's start out with my history with this guy. Minding my own business and in 2003, I get a call from this Ackman guy, and I'm telling you he is like the crybaby in the school yard. I went to a tough school in Queens, and they used to beat up the little Jewish boys. He was like one of these little Jewish boys crying that the world was taking advantage of him. . . . He was almost sobbing, and he's in my office talking about how I could help him. And it was like in the old song, you will rue the day I ever met the guy."

Icahn breathlessly tore into Ackman as traders on the NYSE floor, watching from their posts, ooh'ed and aah'ed with each flying insult.

Trading virtually stopped.

I tried to ask Icahn whether he had taken a long position on Herbalife, but he refused to answer.

"I'm going to talk about what Ackman just said about me, not about Herbalife," he said. "And I'll just talk about Herbalife when I goddamn want to, not when you ask me."

"OK," I replied. But it hardly mattered that I had spoken. Icahn was on a roll. He went on, calling Ackman a liar and asserting that "he's got one of the worst reputations on Wall Street."

"I'm going to tell you this Herbalife is the classic example of what he does," Icahn said of Ackman. "He was down 2 percent, 3 percent. He probably woke up in the morning and said let's see what company we can destroy and put out a bear raid on it. It has happened from the late eighties till now and go do a bear raid, kill the stock. And now we can show our investors we made more money. Ackman has done that, if you read the articles about him, he's done it all his life. And he's basically lying. And I will tell you something. As far as I'm concerned, he wanted to have dinner once with me. I had dinner with him, and I got to tell you, I laughed. I couldn't figure out if he was the most sanctimonious guy I ever met in my life or the most arrogant. And that's Ackman, and that's the last time I met with the guy. I don't want to meet him—oh, yeah. And when it comes to friends, he called me and said, hey, we were friends, we could make a lot of money investing together. And I knew that even if I was a friend I would never invest with this guy. Because I tell you, the guy takes inordinate risks."

Icahn continued, "He goes short 20 percent of a company. Goes out there, and I will tell you this could be the mother of all short squeezes. I'm going to tell you this. That one day if somebody tenders for this company and wants all their stock back, what's Ackman going to do? History repeats itself. He'll be back where he was in 2003 with all the guys redeeming and where is he going to get the money in the stock for that? You know, as far as I'm concerned the guy is a major loser."

Ackman soon denied the various charges. "I think that Carl either has a very, very bad memory or he has trouble with the truth. We have a very—because we didn't make a verbal agreement on Hallwood, we made a written one. He's got very good lawyers as he says—just read the agreement. The agreement we put on the web. It's a ten-page agreement. Carl can say what he wants today about what he thought he said back then. But this was much more important to me than it was to Carl. Obviously, we read the agreement. Carl is a big boy. He signed the agreement, and then we had several courts conclude that we were right, and he held us up as long as he could. The big issue about Carl Icahn is he is not used to someone standing up to him. And particularly a little guy like me in 2003. Carl can try to orchestrate a short squeeze. He can do whatever he wants. He can try to scare my investors from investing with me, which it sounds like he is attempting to do on this call. We take prudent risks at Pershing Square. I'm going to end my—you know, I told Carl after the whole thing, he called me up and literally said, Bill, we can be friends now. I wish I had a recording of the conversation. I simply said to him, look, Carl, you are no friend of mine. And that was it. Every time he goes to TV, I will defend myself."

Icahn clearly had no interest in friendship. "I wouldn't do business with you if you were the last man on Earth," he replied.

"I will tell you about Herbalife. I will tell you what I will tell you and what I said before. You know, I think Ackman did Herbalife, because I—obviously I don't like Ackman. Ackman is lying about what happened. I didn't need the $4 million I made there. What incensed me was that he weaseled out of the deal. We'll leave that alone. You're right. Happened ten years ago, leave it alone. He weaseled out of it. I'll tell you that I'm known as a tough guy, but I think if you take my handshake you live by it. There's no one will ever say I went back on a handshake. Let's go back to Herbalife. This is the typical Ackman. I wouldn't care if it was anybody else but Ackman. But he goes into the room and gets three hundred people and tells them how bad this company is. It is a classic stuff. They did it in the nineties. You scare the hell out of people. Get the stock down. He marks the stock on December 31st and makes $600 million on paper. And tells the world how great he is. He is giving to charity and shows the world he has made 12 percent, which isn't so great anyway. I would like to say we made 28 percent last year without going and having to go pump and dump stocks and go and have rooms full of people. And in 2011, at the risk of being immodest, we made 33 percent without having to do what I consider to be manipulation, OK? And that's what he did in Herbalife. He got a bunch of innocent investors, retirees, they are going to lose their money so Ackman can show a good record at the end of the year and, by the way, took an inordinate risk because a company like Herbalife, you can ask almost any pro, you don't go 20 percent. And what the hell, he is not risking his money, he is risking his investors' money. You go in and you got 20 percent and if there is a squeeze, which well might be in Herbalife, what the hell does he do. I would like him to answer, where does he get the stock when they call back all the stock? Let's say there's [a] tender offer for Herbalife and they call back the stock. If you know, you know, Wall Street, on a tender offer, everybody calls back the stock you borrowed. If that happens, that stock could rush to a hundred. What the hell does Ackman do? Ask him. He is right here on the phone."

"I'm happy to answer it if I get a chance to speak," responded Ackman. "Number one, Carl is free to make a tender offer for the company. Carl, you want to bid for the company, go ahead and bid for the company."

"Number two, obviously we don't think there will be a tender offer for the company. We don't think the company is buyable. We don't think any person will write a check for five or six billion to buy a business we believe is fraudulent. That's number one. Number two, Carl Icahn says he doesn't like the behavior, it's bad. Meanwhile, 2003 at the conference in front of 500 people Carl Icahn pitched Trinity Industries, which he was short and short 22 percent of outstanding shares according to *Fortune* magazine. Carl, can you tell us whether that is true or false? But you did precisely that, so I find it interesting you have a problem with what we did in Herbalife. In Herbalife we simply provided to the public full transparency on this investment . . . 330 slides, in detail, not scaring people, but going through the facts on this company. We did exhaustive research over a year and a half. And we will either be proven right or we will be proven wrong. We shorted the stock. We have not covered our shares. And we have more to come, by the way. We have questions. The company has given us the opportunity to ask, and we will have responses for every issue they raise and their responsive presentation to us, and what I thank Carl for is he certainly helped highlight Herbalife and the issues at Herbalife, and my guess is that Carl bought Herbalife. If he did, because that's what someone in his shop leaked to the press and he flipped it out when the stock went up. He made a good trade. Congratulations on a good trade. I don't believe there is any good investor who can own this business long-term. We believe it's a pyramid scheme; we believe we can prove that to a high degree of certainty."

All in all, "The Brawl," as it soon became known, lasted for twenty-seven uninterrupted minutes.

Trading volume at the NYSE dropped more than 20 percent.

"Bill Ackman and Carl Icahn Just Brawled on CNBC in the Greatest Moment in Financial TV History" read the headline on *Business Insider* at 1 p.m.

I was shell-shocked.

Icahn was livid.

Michael Johnson, who went to church the night before Christmas, was about to get his divine intervention.

9

THE ICON

Carl Icahn strolled out of the back door of his sprawling seaside estate in East Hampton, the summer playground for New York's wealthy, sat down for breakfast, and grabbed a small white tube sitting next to his grapefruit.

It was August 2016, and he'd been nursing a cold.

Icahn grabbed the plastic cylinder, popped out a tablet, and dropped it into a tall glass of water, sucking down the effervescent potion once it had fully dissolved.

It was an Herbalife "Best Defense" pill, the company's supplement that boasted on its label that it could boost one's immune system.

"I really believe this stuff works," he said while looking out toward the Atlantic a couple hundred yards away.

Icahn had been an Herbalife believer since the last days of 2012, when the company first came across his radar and he had the famous brawl with Ackman.

On February 14, 2013, seventeen days after the televised tussle captivated Wall Street, the world learned exactly how serious Icahn was about Herbalife.

"Icahn Reveals His Stake in Herbalife" flashed a headline on the *New York Times*'s DealBook page shortly after word of his official filing hit the tape.[1]

Icahn had bought a 12.98 percent stake through common stock and options in a transaction valued at more than $200 million.[2] It was a massive position with a clear message: Icahn wasn't just backing up the truck for Herbalife—he was looking to run Ackman over in the process and wanted everyone on Wall Street to know it. Herbalife shares spiked 23 percent to more than $47 per share on the news,[3] nearly the exact spot where it had been when Ackman had started shorting it. But as stunning as Icahn's new position was for its sheer size, it was the timing of his trading activity that was most telling of his psyche.

Icahn had begun buying Herbalife stock on December 20, 2012, the same day Ackman had delivered his presentation on the company at the AXA Center. Icahn's top analyst, Jonathan Christodoro, had watched the event in real-time on the internet, saw the stock get pounded, and sensed the opportunity to make some easy money. Christodoro had been trained for moments like these. He had graduated with honors from Cornell, received an MBA with distinction from the University of Pennsylvania's Wharton School, and had worked for the legendary hedge-fund manager Steven A. Cohen at S.A.C. Capital Advisors. He had also served in the Marines, was built like a tank, and, most important, had followed Herbalife for years. Christodoro had even gone to the company's original "road show" when private equity firms J.H. Whitney and Golden Gate Capital were pitching the stock to investors ahead of its initial public offering. Christodoro knew the company inside and out and called Icahn, who trusted his young analyst's instincts. Icahn saw the stock dropping like a stone too and was compelled to take the other side.

"He said, you know this is crazy," said Keith Schaitkin, Icahn's then in-house attorney, who had spoken with his legendary boss about Ackman's presentation. "Ackman is explaining that he has this short position, and Carl said it's a very dangerous thing to do and let's start looking at this. We started buying it right away."

With the boss on board, Icahn's long-time trader, Edward E. Mattner, bought 748,308 shares at an average price of $33.41 in a real-time repudiation of Ackman and his wild assertions.

While Mattner bought, the others got to work on Herbalife itself.

Schaitkin hit the phones to call former FTC lawyers around the country while he quickly brushed up on years of murky pyramid-scheme law. Icahn's guys poured through Herbalife's financial statements, scoured the company's public filings, and studied other historical cases brought against multilevel marketers before ultimately deciding the government wouldn't shut Herbalife down.

On December 21, Icahn grabbed another seven hundred and fifty thousand shares, and three days later one hundred and seventy-two thousand more.[4] In the meantime, Christodoro flew to Los Angeles and spent almost two weeks meeting with Herbalife executives to turn over every stone he could find to refute Ackman's allegations.

In the days ahead, the more Herbalife shares fell, the more Icahn bought, until the position grew so large it passed the 5 percent threshold that required a filing with the Securities and Exchange Commission. On February 15, the day after Icahn revealed his filing, he called into CNBC for an interview with me on why he had taken the other side of Ackman.

"I buy things I think are undervalued," he said. "I think Herbalife is a very undervalued situation, and we've done a hell of a lot of research on this since Ackman has given me the opportunity by bashing it. It's a great company to take private. I think there's a great deal of money to be made here today."[5]

The comment was a shot at Ackman's suddenly precarious position, and the off-the-cuff remark Icahn had made during The Brawl, when he threatened the "The Mother of All Short Squeezes."

Such a move could happen if Icahn, or someone else, tried to buy Herbalife outright and take the company private. If he did this, it would bid up the stock and force Ackman to cover—that is, buy back the stock he'd sold in order to give it back to the investors he'd borrowed it from—at a much higher price than he had entered at. The financial pain could be endless, and Ackman knew it.

So did Icahn.

"I'm not going to lie to you and say if he gets squeezed, I'm going to cry and do penance," Icahn said during the live interview. "The fact that I don't like Ackman, you can say that is the strawberry on top of the ice cream."

Icahn was already getting his sundae.

Herbalife shares had risen more than 30 percent since he'd first started buying the stock, and Icahn seemed intent on keeping it that way. He pledged to meet with Herbalife management to discuss the business and consider any "strategic alternatives"—Wall Street speak for a deal.

Icahn also made it clear that while hurting Ackman would be a sweet treat after their decadelong feud, his real motivation for buying the stock in the first place was for the score.

"I don't like Ackman; everybody knows that," Icahn said. "I don't respect him, everybody knows that, and I actually thank him for calling me a great investor, so I think that comes to the point. I do not as a great investor buy things just to get even with anybody. I am not buying this company and putting money into it unless I've done a lot of research on it and believe in it, OK? I do not believe that the regulators are going to act because a guy comes out and says you're not doing your job properly and you better get moving on this. This company's been around for thirty years, and they're not waiting for Ackman to tell them what to do. And, by the way, I look at Ackman's arguments and to me, they are completely amateurish."

It was classic Icahn, who looked at investing much like a game of chess—you position yourself smartly through careful strategy until you can move in for the kill, which Icahn had a history of doing.

"He's the greatest fighter in the world," said hedge-fund manager and Icahn's former protégé Keith Meister of Corvex Management LP. "There's not a better situational investor. If you were a CEO of a Fortune 500 company and Carl was sitting there—there's no one who would be a scarier threat. There's no one who could be more intimidating or have better leverage in the world than Carl. Carl is just smarter than everyone."

Meister had first met Icahn in the late 1990s when, fresh out of Harvard, he'd gone to work for a real-estate private equity firm called Northstar Capital. Northstar had backed the takeover tycoon Asher Edelman in his hostile bid for Société du Louvre, the French holding company of the famed Taittinger family, but needed more money to fund the deal. Northstar had tried to sell the transaction to traditional private-equity firms known for that sort of business, but none wanted to get involved with a foreign-owned company, especially one with a convoluted voting structure. Enter Icahn, who not only had the money but was also willing to listen to just about any interesting pitch if there was a chance he could come out ahead.

"So, I was sitting in a bullpen with like five other associates, and the next thing you know," said Meister, "Carl is calling me because there was no one left at Northstar, and at Carl's shop he was dealing with it directly. Clearly the negotiation went Carl's way. Ultimately there was no deal we could do because his capital was too expensive, but I got to develop a relationship with him."

In May 2002, Icahn was so impressed with Meister that he hired him, but only after a slightly unusual interview process.

"So, the first day I come in and like two hours I sit in the waiting room," Meister said. "The next day he comes in and he's like half trying to hide from you because he doesn't want to talk to you but he feels bad. I think it was like the third day—I'll never forget it—it was the day WorldCom blew up, so I'm sitting there and you watch people come in and I'm sitting there and there's a bunch of bankers and Carl comes out and sees this kid who's been sitting there for like three days and he says, 'Hey you know what, come to the meeting with me and the WorldCom associates.' He was like, 'What do you think?' And that was part of the interview."

Meister sat wide-eyed, finding Icahn to be a highly engaged, out-of-the-box thinker who could read and assess an investment idea faster than most anyone. It was also apparent, says Meister now, that Icahn wasn't driven by emotion—even when it came to Herbalife.

"My view is, if this wasn't Bill on the other side of the trade, he never would have looked at it, but it's not about spite—it's about, 'I can win, and I'm going to beat a really fun foe.'" Meister said.

The point was clear—Icahn may have despised Ackman, but he wasn't about to risk losing a boatload of money just to prove it. It was a lesson Icahn had learned from more than fifty years on Wall Street in a career that, ironically, almost never happened.

Carl Celian Icahn was born on February 16, 1936, in Brooklyn, New York, the only child of Bella, a school teacher, and Michael, a cantor at the local synagogue. The family moved to the Bayswater section of Queens when Icahn was young, near Far Rockaway, a scruffy, mostly middle-class neighborhood not far from Kennedy Airport. Icahn was tall for his age, and lanky, liked baseball, and even early on was enterprising in how he made money.

At thirteen, he started a business making photographic matchbooks using a makeshift darkroom he'd set up in the family basement.

"I had a little camera to take pictures of people's homes. I would go knock on the door and go 'Mrs. Walker, Mrs. Walker I'll give you 150 matchbooks with a picture of your house.' . . . So then I'd take a picture of this guy's house to the darkroom and write the name on the picture. I'd get a buck fifty for the matchbooks I bought for a penny. I got to the point where I had three kids working for me."

Icahn would soon graduate to more lucrative endeavors.

During the summer after his senior year at Far Rockaway High School, Icahn worked as a cabana boy at Lido Beach on Long Island, often taking money off the leathered and more senior clientele during the Oceanside poker games. He was good with numbers, had a nearly photographic memory, and made thousands of dollars playing cards by the beach.

"I was a pretty good poker player," he said, with a hint of immodesty. He "made a lot of money."

Even then, Icahn loved a score and hated being crossed or taken advantage of.

"I had a temper," he told the *New Yorker*'s Ken Auletta in a 2006 profile. "I sometimes scare myself I'm so obsessive. If I go over a certain line, I'm like another person."[6]

He was also fiercely intelligent.

Icahn was the first graduate of local Far Rockaway High to attend Princeton, paying part of his tuition with the poker loot he'd won in Lido. He majored in philosophy, displaying the quick wit and deep thinking that would serve him well later.

"He was able to analyze a subject and come up with his own unique conclusion," said Peter S. Lieber, Icahn's roommate during his junior and senior years. "I think it presaged what he would do in the future."

Icahn spent hours in the library on his senior thesis, which was nothing short of a mouthful. Icahn called it "An Explication of the Empiricist Criterion of Meaning," winning top honors in Princeton's prestigious philosophy department.

"There was a special prize for the best senior thesis, and Carl certainly deserved it and won it," said Lieber.

Icahn graduated from Princeton in 1957 and, somewhat reluctantly, enrolled in New York University's Medical School to follow his mother's wishes. Icahn lasted a little more than two years before abruptly quitting.

"I really hated it," he said while recounting a story about his travails. "I quit twice and went back. And the third time I was reading a little about Tuberculosis, and I go to the Tuberculosis ward, and this doctor tells me go give me a diagnosis, so I go over and I tap this guy's chest and the guy coughs on me, and I said, I think I'm gonna get TB! The doctor was like, you psycho, you leave now and you are never coming back, which was fine with me. So I walked across the street—I think I'm going to die now anyway so it doesn't matter—and I go join the Army on 34th Street."

Icahn served six months in the Army reserves at Fort Sam Houston in Texas, where he was hardly your typical enlistee, considering it was poker games and not push-ups where he earned his stripes—and thousands of dollars.

In 1961, Icahn left the service and needed a job.

He chose the canyons of Wall Street and joined Dreyfus & Company as a broker trainee, getting the job with help from his well-connected uncle, Elliot Schnall, who was a wealthy businessman and had taken a liking to his neophyte nephew. Schnall had gone to Yale and seemed an ideal person for the younger and inexperienced Icahn to emulate. The two remain close to this day, often convening in the late afternoon for a cocktail when Icahn is out East.

"His uncle Elliot was not only a close family member, but Elliot's business success was clearly impressive to Carl," said Lieber, recalling their conversations while at Princeton.

The job at Dreyfus may have been a fresh start, but the timing was terrible. Icahn joined the firm shortly before the so-called Kennedy Slide began on Wall Street. Stocks were slammed for six straight months, and by the time the crash was over, the market had fallen 22 percent, including a 40 percent nosedive on a single day in the spring of 1962.[7]

Icahn lost everything, including his beloved Ford Galaxie convertible. Needless to say, Icahn's parents were less than pleased that their son, who'd already given up on being a doctor, was now financially in ruins.

"I lost everything. I was broke. I had nothing and I sold the car so I could live. And my mother said, 'You can't live at home—you can't go back to the house unless you go back to medical school again.' So I wasn't going to do that and so I rented an extremely small and cheap apartment with absolutely no view."

With his professional life in tatters after the '62 crash, Icahn joined Tessel, Patrick & Company, where he toiled in the options market.

Icahn mastered the arcane trading form, which was just like buying and selling stocks, only with a wrinkle. Options were often cheaper to own than stocks, but they were more speculative, since traders were essentially betting on the future price of a security rather than where it was at that moment. If the security in question hit the desired price by a specific date, the investor could win big, but if it didn't, losses could be steep. Icahn proved a deft risk manager and a year later joined Gruntal & Company, where he ran the entire options department.[8]

"He was quite bright, and very aggressive, which isn't a bad combination in this business," Icahn's former Gruntal colleague Howard Silverman told the *New York Times* in 1985.[9] Icahn was a perfect fit. His investing acumen and skill with numbers helped him excel in the volatile derivatives market.

Icahn was now making more money than he ever had, but longed to open his own shop. There was only one problem—he didn't have the money to do it. Luckily, he knew someone who did. Icahn turned to his wealthy Uncle Elliot for help. Schnall agreed to lend his nephew $400,000 for a coveted seat on the New York Stock Exchange, and in 1968, Icahn & Company opened for business on Broadway in Lower Manhattan.

In return, Schnall received 20 percent of the shares in the firm. Icahn was grateful.

"He was more like a best friend than an uncle," Icahn said of Schnall. "He was a great guy and he loaned me the $400,000 based on the fact that I would put up every penny of my net worth, which at that point was $150,000. His accountant advised me not to do it, but I didn't think twice. Somehow I knew I'd make it."

With the stock market still cooking during the decade's bull market, Icahn and a younger associate named Alfred D. Kingsley, whom he'd met at Gruntal and taken with him, hit the ground running. Kingsley had gone to Wharton at sixteen, had a master's degree in tax from New York University, and was a numbers whiz.[10] Icahn was a workhorse, keeping long hours and sometimes sleeping at the office to reach prospective clients early in the morning in time zones far from New York.

The two men also began dealing in the high-stakes game of arbitrage, a fancy Wall Street term that describes how investors buy securities like stocks or bonds in one market and sell them in another, pocketing the difference. At first, they dealt in closed-end mutual funds.

In a letter to prospective investors, the men laid out their hard-nosed strategy: "It is our contention that sizable profits can be earned by taking large positions in 'undervalued' stocks and then attempting to control the destinies of the companies in question by: a) trying to convince management to liquidate or sell the company to a 'white knight.' b) waging a proxy contest. c) making a tender offer. d) selling back our position to the company."[11]

Coined the "Icahn Manifesto" by the biographer Mark Stevens, the credo would prove to be an overwhelming success.

"I made a fortune," Icahn said. "I was up to making a million or two a year based on risk-less arbitrage which for some reason very few brokers at that time understood."

The kid from Queens had arrived. But the good times on Wall Street wouldn't last.

Between January 1973 and December of 1974, the Dow Jones Industrial Average lost 45 percent of its value. Billions of dollars in market cap were wiped out during the slide, which helped throw the United States's economy into a deep recession. The oil market was unsettled following OPEC's embargo, and then in the summer of 1974, the final blow—the resignation of President Richard M. Nixon following the Watergate scandal.

The period would go down as one of the worst bear markets in American history.

While others were picking up the pieces from the crash, Icahn and Kingsley found an opportunity. As documented in the book *Deep Value* by Tobias Carlisle, the two men began identifying undervalued stocks whose assets had a higher underlying value than they were trading for as a result of the sudden dislocation in the markets.

"We asked ourselves, 'If we can be activists in an undervalued closed-end mutual fund, why can't we be activists in a corporation with undervalued assets?'" Kingsley said at the time.[12]

So, Icahn turned arbitrage into an art, taking what he had learned dealing in stocks and bonds and turning to the companies themselves. Corporate takeovers were becoming the modus operandi for large and liquid investors, and Icahn was just beginning to broaden his shoulders. He wanted a piece of the action.

In 1977, in his first major foray into the takeover game, Icahn bought a 5 percent stake in the family-run appliance maker Tappan.[13] The Ohio-based company, founded in the 1880s, made ovens and stoves. Icahn bought the stock when it was near $8 per share, arguing that it was undervalued and that the company should sell itself. He launched a proxy fight for a seat on the company's board, which immediately put him at odds with Richard Tappan, the chairman of the company and grandson of its founder.[14]

"I wasn't going to let Icahn walk in and sell piecemeal an enterprise my family had spent their lives building," said Tappan in the book *The Titans of Takeover* by Robert Slater.[15]

Not by choice, anyway. Tappan would soon feel the force of the emerging antagonist. Icahn won the proxy contest and convinced Tappan's board to sell the company, which it ultimately did to the Swedish firm AB Electrolux for $18 per share, more than double what Icahn had paid for his stock.[16]

Icahn's initial investment of $1.4 million turned into a $2.7 million profit.[17]

He also gained an unlikely future ally in the process—Richard Tappan himself—who was so taken by Icahn's negotiating abilities that he'd join his one-time adversary in several future deals.[18]

But while Icahn was a burgeoning success in his new career and was well on his way to making billions on Wall Street, he found little appreciation for his newfound status back home. Icahn's mother had been heartbroken when he quit medical school, and he was never close to his father, who didn't quite understand what his son did for a living or how—only that he'd given away a chance to be a doctor.

To this day, the man who has made a living knocking heads with some of America's most iconic companies nearly tears up when recounting his relationship with his late father.

"Thinking about this makes me cry because we were never that close," Icahn said, his voice growing ever softer while speaking. "Then in the seventies—we had never discussed what I did—he comes up with a pencil, and he was terrible with numbers, but comes over with a pad, and he says, 'Come here, come here, son, write it down and tell me how you do it.' I said, 'You finally admit it.' He said, 'Yeah' and we hugged. I still cry every time I think about it."

Icahn's genius was in full force. He even figured out a way to make money when big deals didn't go his way.

In 1980, Icahn targeted the New York paper company Saxon Industries, buying more than seven hundred thousand shares for an average price of $7.21.[19] Icahn threatened a proxy fight, or a shareholder vote, for a seat on the company's board. While Saxon initially talked tough, the company settled after only six months and agreed to buy back Icahn's stock for $10.50 a share, more than three dollars above Icahn's average purchase price.[20]

Icahn made $2.2 million on the deal, and the scores kept coming.[21]

Icahn pocketed $10 million in a deal with Hammermill Paper the same year, $7 million from Simplicity Pattern in 1981, and $17 million on an investment in the storied department store chain Marshall Fields the following year.[22]

By the mid-1980s, Icahn had become a player on Wall Street's emerging takeover scene alongside the day's other dealmakers, such as Ivan F. Boesky, T. Boone Pickens, and Michael Milken, the Drexel Burnham Lambert banker whose infamous "junk bonds" helped finance the buying frenzy of the times. Milken's high-yielding securities had earned him the nickname "The Junk Bond King" since he had all but invented the market for the securities.

The men—coined corporate raiders by the media—were shrewd, often ruthless negotiators, stopping at nothing to shake up companies whose CEOs were deemed either too "imperial" or too "country-club," more interested in their golf scores than their shareholders. It was the era of the leveraged buyout (LBO), a time when deep-pocketed dealmakers like Icahn and others ran roughshod through the nation's boardrooms and there was little anyone could do to stop them. Milken's bonds were cheap, easy to access, and gave financiers a newfound power—power they were more than willing to exert.

On September 19, 1983, Icahn barreled into the railcar maker American Car and Foundry, or ACF, with an eighty-one-page filing with the Securities and Exchange Commission that immediately put the company on notice.[23] Icahn had amassed a 13.5 percent stake in the company and wanted control. He demanded a meeting with management, threatening to turn up the heat if they didn't come to the table willingly. Icahn continued to buy ACF stock in the meantime, and by December his stake had grown to 27.2 percent, only increasing his leverage.[24]

Early in 1984, Icahn pounced, buying the company outright for $469 million through an LBO. Icahn immediately sold off assets, including the company's expansive New York City offices when he couldn't figure out what the employees actually did there.

He later laughingly told of his adventures with the ACF investment and the real-estate enigma he had encountered in New York City.

"They've got 12 floors on 3rd Avenue . . . I spend the whole day, look at my yellow pad, can't figure out what the hell they do," Icahn recounted during an interview at a *New York Times* event years later. "I go back the next day, seventh floor, ninth floor, eighth floor, I say, I'm not an idiot, I can't figure out what they do. It's razzle dazzle. They say this is very arcane. I say, I want to go to St. Louis. I want to see the guy who is the Chief Operating Officer. Over martinis, I ask, how many of those guys in New York do you need to support your operation, because I honestly can't figure out what to do. [I] got rid of the whole 12 floors, sold the lease for $10 million. That was a lot then."[25]

Icahn became chairman, cutting even more costs. As a result, ACF's earnings soared, winning Icahn back his initial investment and then some.

Also in 1984, Icahn targeted Chesebrough-Ponds Inc., which had units in health care, food products, and apparel. Icahn mounted a fervent takeover attempt before the two sides settled on a deal a few months later. Chesebrough agreed to buy back more than a million and a half of Icahn's shares, scoring him a $68.6 million profit.[26]

Icahn then went hunting for even bigger game.

On February 5, 1985, Icahn attempted an $8.1 billion leveraged buyout of Phillips Petroleum. The company had just fended off another feisty financier, T. Boone Pickens, who'd gone hostile on the company the prior December. Phillips pushed back against the Oklahoma-born oilman, but when it looked like a deal seemed unlikely, it gave Pickens $90 million cash to buy back his shares, along with another $25 million for his expenses.[27]

When the stage cleared of Pickens, Icahn moved in.

He'd bought 5 percent of Phillips stock, declared that shares were undervalued, and proposed taking the company private through an $8.1 billion buyout. Icahn and Phillips battled for months and then, just like with Pickens, the two sides ultimately settled. Icahn agreed not to target the company for another eight years, and in return Phillips bought back his shares for a $52 million profit and gave another $25 million to cover his expenses.

Shareholders overwhelmingly approved the deal and hailed it as a monumental win.

"It's the single biggest victory ever won by stockholders on Wall Street because the big financial institutions finally decided they're not going to take a back seat," said large Phillips shareholder Irwin L. Jacobs.[28]

"He got a better deal for everybody; he's entitled to it," a trader said in the same *New York Times* article, discussing the deal Icahn had cut.

Others weren't as complimentary.

Critics began branding the exploits of Icahn, Pickens, and other big investors as "greenmail," likening the practice to a form of corporate extortion. Icahn angrily rejected the label, arguing that although he was motivated to make money, his efforts were akin to a night watchman keeping unscrupulous or lazy boards in check.

"They have tremendous bonuses, lavish offices, private dining rooms, jet planes and country-club memberships while the companies are falling apart," he said of directors during a 1985 news conference.[29]

No matter what critics thought, Icahn was proving himself a winner.

But in the summer of 1985, Icahn's takeover chops would be put to the test. In June, he targeted Trans World Airlines, the iconic but struggling carrier once owned by the legendary recluse Howard Hughes. TWA hadn't turned a profit since the 1960s, and by the time Icahn arrived on the scene, the St. Louis–based legacy liner was vulnerable. Icahn had bought 25 percent of the stock, then bid $18 a share for the company in a deal valued at $1.8 billion.[30]

TWA launched an all-out PR assault, running a full-page "Open Letter to Carl Icahn" in major newspapers around the country, making it clear it wasn't interested in a deal or the financier.

"If you thought we'd just stand by and do nothing while you try to take over our company, think again!" the hard-hitting ads read.[31]

TWA wanted a different deal—with a different person—and thought it had found its white knight in aviation industry pioneer Frank Lorenzo. Lorenzo's Texas Air Corporation bid $793.5 million for TWA, giving Icahn an immediate paper profit of $50 million through the stock he owned.[32]

The windfall was tasty, but Icahn had no intention of going away that quietly. He raised his bid. And when TWA's unions became skeptical of Lorenzo, the board backed Icahn instead, and the airline was his.

"We've got ourselves an airline! We've got ourselves an airline!" Icahn was reported to have said when the deal became official, wearing a pilot's jacket in his offices.[33]

TWA's rank and file were slightly less enthused.

Upset over Icahn's deep cost-cutting plans, four thousand flight attendants staged a ten-week walkout while wearing "Stop Carl Icahn" buttons. The work stoppage left the airline bare during a key travel season. Traffic suffered, and TWA had to borrow millions to keep operations going, which only increased its already heavy debt load.

Icahn didn't back down.

He pushed for TWA to grow its footprint and become more competitive with rivals. In 1986, he struck a deal with Ozark Airlines to acquire dozens of its planes and routes. Icahn's plan was to merge them through the Midwest with TWA's perfectly positioned hub in St. Louis.[34]

And he didn't stop there.

On July 22, 1987, Icahn went back to his playbook, announcing plans to take TWA private through a Drexel-led LBO valued at $1.2 billion.[35]

The deal was approved in 1988, and Icahn made $469 million, nearly $30 million more than he had paid for the airline in the first place. He also got control of 90 percent of TWA's outstanding shares. For its part, TWA got more than $500 million added to its debt load.[36]

Icahn continued to slash costs, canceling prior orders for dozens of new jets.

He sold TWA's lucrative London routes to American Airlines for $445 million, and early on, it looked like Icahn had the magic touch.[37]

After losing $193 million in 1985 and $106.3 million in 1986, TWA turned a profit in 1987 and 1988 as Icahn earned praise for orchestrating the airline's turnaround. It was a heavy lift, for sure, with some wondering why he'd even bothered getting his hands dirty in the first place.

Icahn said it was simple.

"I could have gotten out," he told the *New York Times* in 1986. "But I'm brought up in the Wall Street tradition. You make a deal and you stick with it."[38]

The good times were short-lived.

TWA's debt pile—heightened by the LBO—became insurmountable, and on February 1, 1992, the airline filed for Chapter 11 bankruptcy protection.

Icahn had a much more fruitful outcome.

As one of the top creditors, Icahn stood first in line to reap any profits from the sale of assets. He also cut what became known as the Karabu Ticket Agreement. It was an eight-year deal that let Icahn buy any ticket that connected through St. Louis for 55 cents on the dollar, with the ability to resell them at a discount.[39] It was a shrewd deal that helped solidify Icahn's reputation as the day's most formidable, if not feared, dealmaker.

"To the Raided, He's Icahn the Terror," screamed a headline in the *New York Times* during the period.

But by the mid-eighties, the dealmaking landscape was changing. Greenmail was under fire, and so too were some of the investors themselves. In 1986, Icahn admitted he was questioned as part of a broader investigation into insider trading that had also ensnared the arbitrageur Boesky and Drexel's Milken.[40]

Icahn was never named or charged in the case.

"No allegations have been made against me by the Securities and Exchange Commission and I have no reason to believe that any will be made in the future," Icahn said in November of that year.[41]

Boesky and Milken were less fortunate.

On November 14, 1986, Boesky plead guilty to insider trading and was sentenced to three and a half years in prison. He also agreed to testify against Milken, who was later indicted on six felony counts related to insider trading.[42] Milken also pled guilty, and on November 12, 1990, he was sentenced to ten years at the Federal Correctional Institution in Pleasanton, California, outside San Francisco.[43]

Drexel, the firm that had financed the decade's deluge of deals, soon met a similar demise. On February 13, 1990, the company filed for bankruptcy, a stunning end for what was then the nation's fifth-largest investment bank.[44]

In the wake of the crackdown and the change in public sentiment, Icahn began to change his own tactics. In 1988, he'd bought nearly 15 percent of Texaco and pushed for a takeover at $60 per share, or $12 billion.[45] Icahn also went back to his playbook, waging a proxy fight for five seats on Texaco's board of directors, and though he'd eventually lose, Icahn continued to buy shares and got the company to pay shareholders a special dividend rather than buy back his stock. It was a win-win, and in June of 1989, Icahn's stake in Texaco was worth a staggering $2.2 billion.[46]

As the 1990s began, Icahn showed no signs of slowing down. In 1995, Icahn and another investor, Bennett LeBow, bought big stakes in RJR Nabisco. It was Icahn's first of several attempts at the company that was infamous for being the center of the classic business story *The Barbarians at the Gate*. Icahn argued for a split of the company's food business, and though he'd ultimately lose a proxy contest, he made more than $130 million in profits when he sold his shares.

In 1999, Icahn was back with a new stake and the same calls for Nabisco to spin off its food unit. The company eventually agreed to a spin-off—just with its tobacco arm instead. Icahn sold again, with another $130 million in profits.

Icahn wasn't finished. He bought the stock again, making an additional $589 million when RJR finally sold the food division in 2000 to Philip Morris Cos. for $9.8 billion. Icahn emerged from the deal with a saying he still stands by and often repeats when recounting his many boardroom battles: "I fight with them. I'm friends with them. There's war and there's peace."[47]

And often, there's a lot of money.

By 2000, Icahn's net worth was estimated at more than $4.2 billion.[48] He owned a thirty-eight-acre estate in Bedford, New York, a silver Rolls-Royce, and other spoils worthy of his status as one of Wall Street's last standing titans.[49]

He began to reinvent himself, shedding the "raider" moniker that some had tagged him with in the eighties for the more civilized-sounding "shareholder activist." Icahn was also about to expand his exploits as a money manager.

In 2004, Icahn raised $3 billion from investors, a huge amount of money at the time, and started a hedge fund he called Icahn Partners.[50] It was hardly your typical hedge fund, but then again, Icahn was hardly your typical investor. According to the proposal sent to prospective investors, Icahn had generated annual returns of between 48 percent and 53 percent since 1990—astronomical by any standard. If investors wanted a piece of that action, they were told they'd have to pay up, and handsomely. $25 million was the minimum buy-in, and rather than the standard 1 percent or 2 percent in management fees that other funds were charging their investors, Icahn charged 2.5 percent. He also charged 25 percent of the net annual profits rather than the 20 percent that was the industry standard.[51]

Not surprisingly, Icahn had no problem raising the money for the fund.[52]

Icahn's war chest allowed him to think even bigger. On September 18, 2004, he began to show just how big. That day, Icahn revealed an 8.9 percent stake in the drug maker Mylan Pharmaceuticals, which was in the midst of a nasty takeover battle with rival King. Icahn had other plans for the company and offered $5.4 billion to take over Mylan outright. Icahn stood to score no matter what. He'd already pushed Mylan shares higher when he entered the scene and would profit even if the deal with King fell through. He'd also shorted King shares in the process, protecting himself even if the deal was canceled.[53] In July 2005, Mylan said it would buy back 94 percent of Icahn's stake at a hefty profit.

Later that year, Icahn went after Time Warner, the $85 billion media company that had had an ill-fated merger with AOL in 2000 during the last days of the dot-com bubble. Icahn owned thirteen million shares, good for a 2.6 percent stake, and had an audacious plan: he wanted Time Warner to split into four companies and buy back $20 billion worth of stock.[54]

It didn't take long for the relationship to grow contentious.

Icahn launched a proxy fight, asking shareholders to get rid of the company's current CEO, Richard D. Parsons, and the company's board of directors.

"I enjoy the war," Icahn told Ken Auletta in 2006 while in the midst of the battle.[55] "It's the greatest game in the world. It's like a poker game. Take Time Warner. I am on a battlefield against their best top lawyers, thirty P.R. guys are against me, and I'm here. I love being the underdog. Deep down—I know this sounds immodest, but I'm much better than them at this type of thing."

On September 12, 2005, Icahn made his case in an SEC filing, saying, "While [Time Warner] management has directed lip service toward these actions and taken an overly deliberate and slow path, we believe it is now time for action."

Time Warner resisted the Icahn-led split and on February 17, 2006, the day after Icahn's seventieth birthday, came to an agreement with the investor. Time Warner would buy back $20 billion in stock, instead of its planned $12.5 billion, and agree to appoint two independent directors to the company's board.

Though he'd won the bigger buyback, Icahn knew he'd suffered a setback in the bid to break up the company.

"Maybe I was a little off on knowing that the big investors did not want to see a complete change on the board," Icahn told the *New York Times*. "But I think you'd be hard-pressed to find a shareholder that does not think I created value here."

In fact, by 2007 Icahn had increased the market cap of his targeted companies by $50 billion, all within just a couple of years. He'd created wealth for shareholders far and wide—and, of course, for himself.

In 2008, Icahn was the forty-sixth-richest person in the world according to *Forbes*, and he aspired to climb even higher. In the year that followed, Icahn would go after Motorola, Yahoo, Biogen, and Clorox, among others, not always winning, but more often than not pushing share prices higher during his many campaigns.

And while he would never become a doctor as his mother had wished, he would contribute to the medical profession in another way. In November 2012, Icahn announced he was giving $200 million to Mt. Sinai Medical School in Manhattan. The donation would create the Icahn School of Medicine at Mt. Sinai.

By December 2012, when Herbalife hit Icahn's radar, he was considered Wall Street's most intimidating and savvy investor and was worth a reported $20 billion. Icahn's annualized returns had outpaced Warren Buffett's over a similar twenty-year period, solidifying his reputation as a true icon of investing.

Some wondered how Bill Ackman could survive in the ring with such a formidable opponent.

10

THE EXIT AND THE PILE-ON

By the middle of winter 2013, Icahn's emergence had helped push Herbalife shares back into the high $40s, hardly where Ackman thought they'd be just two months into his public campaign. Nevertheless, he remained steadfast that the story—and the trade—would eventually break his way.

On one frigid winter evening, it looked like it might.

On Saturday, February 16 at around 6:20 p.m. New York time, I stood on the darkened and quiet corner of East 65th Street and Park Avenue in Manhattan and broke the news, via an email, that, according to a source, Dan Loeb had started liquidating his Herbalife position. The selling had started a few weeks ago, I said in my report, which made no mention of exactly how many shares Loeb had dumped or the amount that remained in his fund.

It was surprising news to say the least.

Just six weeks prior, on January 9, Loeb had declared Herbalife a "compelling long-term investment" for his firm, Third Point, and said in a letter to his investors that "shares could be worth $55 to $68," representing a major jump from where he'd originally stepped in and bought the stock.[1] Now he was suddenly selling?

To Ackman the move looked like a classic pump and dump scheme, where an investor buys a stock, publicly pushes it up, then sells it soon after for a healthy profit. Loeb laughingly denied that claim months later during an interview with Andrew Ross Sorkin of the *New York Times*, saying that when Herbalife shares had reached nearly $44, the opportunity to sell was simply too good to pass up.

"That, for us, was a gift; we decided to take the money and run," Loeb told Sorkin. "There was no pump and dump."[2]

Three days after my report that Loeb had started selling down his stake, investors once again got a better look under Herbalife's hood. On Tuesday, February 19, shortly after 5 p.m. Eastern time, the company released its earnings report, which handily beat expectations. More important, the company raised its outlook in a sign of just how strong the business had been performing of late. On the earnings call the following morning, CEO Michael Johnson said as much to the analysts who'd dialed in.

"As we reported yesterday," Johnson said, "Herbalife enjoyed broad-based strength around the world. More specifically, in 2012 we achieved the following financial results: a record $4.1 billion in net sales, a record $4.7 billion in volume points, a record $736 million of EBITDA [a key metric of earnings], a record $477 million in net income, and a record $4.05 of Earnings per shares."[3]

Johnson also addressed Ackman, though not by name.

"Additionally, as noted in our press release," said Johnson, "our guidance excludes certain one-time costs, mostly legal and advisory services associated with our response to information put forth by a short-seller. The costs are currently expected to be between ten and twenty million dollars."[4]

Johnson also said he'd spoken to Icahn briefly, calling the discussions "short" with "nothing concrete to report."[5] Johnson sounded upbeat as he spoke, confident that, especially with Icahn's presence, he could outdo Ackman once and for all.

Two weeks later, investors would learn why Johnson had sounded so optimistic. On February 28, Herbalife announced it would add two new directors to its board, handpicked by Icahn himself. Herbalife also gave the investor the right to increase his stake to 25 percent from his current position of 14 percent.[6] The agreement also meant that Icahn would have access to critical information most typical investors wouldn't, a huge advantage if he ever wanted to buy the company outright.

"Over its long history, Herbalife has proven its ability to increase revenues and returns, and we will work with the Company to build on its results," said Icahn in a press release detailing the agreement he'd reached with management. "We conducted considerable research on Herbalife and its business before making our investment in the Company, and have great respect for its Board and management team, and believe in the Company's great potential. We expect our shareholder representatives to provide positive input into Board decisions affecting the future of the Company."[7]

Johnson heaped his own praise on the deal.

"We are pleased to have reached this agreement and look forward to working with the Icahn representatives as members of our Board of Directors," he said. "We appreciate the Icahn Parties' shared views on the inherent value of Herbalife's operations, products and future prospects."

Herbalife shares popped 7 percent on the news to close the day at $40.29.

To the experts who covered the stock on Wall Street, Icahn's board seats were more than simply symbolic.

"He has a board level opportunity to get some questions answered. That's worth something," said the D.A. Davidson analyst Tim Ramey, who covered the stock closely.[8]

The timing of Icahn getting his board seats was fortuitous to say the least, considering that only six weeks later Johnson would be dealing with another public crisis.

On Tuesday, April 9, one of the "big four" accounting firms, KPMG, abruptly quit as Herbalife's auditor amid reports that a former senior partner at the firm, Scott London, was being investigated by the FBI for insider trading. KPMG also withdrew three years' worth of Herbalife's audited financial reports.

Two days later, London was charged with conspiracy to commit criminal securities fraud for allegedly giving stock tips to one of his close friends in exchange for cash. The friend, a man named Bryan Shaw, had allegedly made $1.27 million on the illegal trades, with the two men pulling off an operation that sounded straight out of the movies. According to authorities, Shaw had routinely given London bags of cash in secret meetings on a street corner near his house. There were Rolex watches and other expensive pieces of jewelry in addition to concert tickets and cash.

In a statement, Herbalife defended its accounting practices and its management. Still, the timing of the announcement of KPMG's abrupt departure and the uncertainty it created was the last thing the company needed. Bad publicity was one thing, but throwing years of Herbalife's income statements into flux meant the company was essentially frozen financially. It couldn't borrow money to buy back stock as it hoped since no bank in its right mind would lend to the company without fully audited books.

To no one's surprise, Herbalife shares fell 3.8 percent to $36.95 on the day, with even the most bullish analysts suddenly rethinking their positions.

"This is and will be disruptive to the stock, but hopefully not the company," said Ramey in a research report detailing why he had downgraded the stock, for the first time ever, upon hearing the news.[9]

"I had been through this with other companies," Ramey said. "There was one I covered where they were in a three-year purgatory where they couldn't do anything. They couldn't provide earnings, they couldn't file, and that would be very, very bad for Herbalife."[10]

Though Ackman claimed it would be difficult for Herbalife to get another "big four" accounting firm on board, it actually didn't take long, relatively speaking, for the company to find another firm. On May 21, Herbalife announced it had hired PricewaterhouseCoopers to replace KPMG as its new auditor, which sent shares up 4 percent.

Two months later, shares would get an even bigger jolt.

On Wednesday, July 31, 2013, just after 11 a.m., I jumped on TV with news of yet another big-name investor getting involved. According to a source, George Soros's namesake firm had taken a large position in Herbalife—"one of its three biggest positions," I reported.

Shares exploded 10 percent higher, in heavy trading, to more than $65 per share.

Soros was the legendary investor who had famously broken the Bank of England on September 16, 1992. Soros had bet heavily against the British pound, forcing the government to withdraw the currency from the European Exchange Rate Mechanism, or ERM. It had thrown the Sterling market into chaos and transformed the Soros name into a thing of legend. He'd pocketed $1 billion on the trade on a day that became known in the United Kingdom as Black Wednesday.[11]

Now, some wondered whether Soros was looking to take Ackman down in a similar fashion. The elder statesman had all but retired from managing other people's money in 2011. However, he kept a mild interest in the firm's investments, leaving most of the critical decision making to a group of younger, hungrier portfolio managers.

One such investor was Paul Sohn, who'd graduated from Yale, studied economics, and had a top-notch pedigree in the hedge-fund business, working for Mark Kingdon and Soros disciple Stanley Druckenmiller, who was considered a god in his own right.

Sohn had started at Soros the first week of January in 2012, taking charge of two of the firm's portfolios—his own, which could comprise any investments he wanted, and the firm's biggest and most important Best Ideas fund, which he comanaged. The Best Ideas portfolio was mostly made up of concentrated positions, a few at a time, worth a few hundred million dollars each.

Sohn hoped to grow it and looked to hire an analyst to help him do it. Following a series of interviews, Sohn had whittled the talent pool down to three finalists and gave each a specific stock to analyze.

The stock was Herbalife.

Sohn had never invested in the company before but knew bits and pieces of its history and the controversies that had followed it over the years. It wasn't until Ackman showed up on the scene that Sohn decided to take a much closer look.

"When the Ackman thing happened, I thought it was worth dusting off again," said Sohn. "So I watched his presentation and like everyone else thought it was very convincing. He presents well and tells a good story."

While Sohn waited for the final analyst candidates to present their findings on Herbalife, it was ironically the company's own actions, during their rebuttal on the tenth of January at the Four Seasons Hotel, that proved seminal in his decision to buy the stock.

"A mental game-changer for me was the company's response," Sohn said. "I watched this thing and it was to me—it was as convincing as the Ackman presentation. But even if you thought both were convincing what stuck out to me immediately was there were many lies of omission and commission in the Ackman report. They had clearly annoyingly manipulated charts and manipulated data in a way that to me was a big red flag."

Buoyed by what he'd seen, Sohn immediately began an in-depth dive into Herbalife.

"The first big thing we did was commission a survey. And we basically asked 20 questions to a statistically significant number of Herbalife users and Herbalife distributors—thousands."

Sohn set out to debunk the core of Ackman's claims—that Herbalife preyed on thousands, if not *millions*, of unsuspecting people, mostly lower-income Hispanic immigrants who had joined with the idea of making big money but were left financially destroyed in what amounted to an elaborate scam.

"The initial short thesis was this is essentially a Ponzi scheme. No one is making any money off of it and everyone does it for the business opportunity," Sohn said. "There are no real customers. It's illegal."

Sohn spent $25,000 to commission a survey in both English and Spanish to make sure it was an accurate representation of Herbalife's customer base. The survey's first question, posed only to Herbalife distributors, read, "Would you recommend becoming an Herbalife distributor to family and friends?"

78.4 percent responded yes, with only 5.6 percent saying no, and the rest maybe.

Next, surveyors asked users of Herbalife products, "Would you recommend them to friends and family?" Again, the results were overwhelming.

62.1 percent said yes, with only 4.4 percent saying no.

The next item got to the heart of one of Ackman's chief accusations—that most who joined Herbalife for the business opportunity lost money.

"Would you say you have made money, lost money, or broken even as an Herbalife distributor?" they asked.

42 percent responded they had made money, and 21 percent reported breaking even, with 12.7 percent saying they had lost money. In addition, 71 percent said they had lost weight either temporarily or permanently because of Herbalife products.

"So, the answers that were coming from thousands of distributors just seemed to completely debunk the short thesis," said Sohn.

Even though he was convinced he'd done enough work to annihilate Ackman's assertions, Sohn wasn't quite ready to put hundreds of millions of dollars or more into the stock. He wasn't one to jump in without thinking carefully. He also knew of Ackman's reputation and track record as an investor, which constantly hung in his mind.

"I said we had done enough to know that the short thesis is wrong, but you know, he must know something we don't know. Ackman must be playing some cards that we don't know because otherwise this is crazy. I mean, that survey cost us $25,000. He committed a billion dollars without doing a similar survey?" Sohn asked rhetorically.

So Sohn did even more work on the company.

In early May, in the first of several trips out West, he flew to Los Angeles to meet face-to-face with Herbalife CEO Johnson and other company executives in one last "smell test" before going in.

On May 17, 2013, convinced that Ackman's claims were askew, Sohn slowly started buying Herbalife shares at an average price of $40.44.

Three weeks later, Sohn walked into a Midtown Manhattan steakhouse for a so-called ideas dinner. The oft-held events brought hedgefund managers or their top portfolio managers and analysts together, often in a restaurant's private room, to pitch investment ideas over expensive slabs of beef and pricy Cabernets.

Alongside the other men in the private room that night was a familiar face: Bill Ackman.

Sitting inside a clubby and dark-lit room, Sohn kept his Herbalife news to himself, pitching a tax-related stock called EM-Tech Co. instead while waiting for Ackman's run of the table. One after another, the analysts in the room pitched their ideas. When it came around to Ackman's turn, Sohn grabbed his pen, ready to take notes on anything he had to say about Herbalife.

Sohn was left disappointed. "He didn't even pitch Herbalife," said Sohn. "He pitched Howard Hughes Corporation."

Sohn stayed silent, but others in the room weren't letting Ackman off that easy.

"Then the rest of the dinner was all about Herbalife. All these other guys were very interested. It was very fanboyish—and I just clearly knew I was the only one at the table who knew anything about Herbalife other than Ackman, but I just kind of held back, and I asked him a couple of questions, and his responses were such that I remember thinking to myself 'The Emperor has no clothes,' like he truly knows less about this than I do."

But Ackman *did* know something that neither Sohn nor anyone else in the room that night knew. According to Sohn, "He pull[ed] out his Blackberry and sa[id], 'I'm going to read you a letter. It's coming from Linda Sánchez and it's going to take the company down,' or something like that."

Linda T. Sánchez was a congresswoman from California who Ackman said had sent a letter to the Federal Trade Commission the day before, urging the regulator's chairwoman, Edith Ramirez, to investigate Herbalife.

"Dear Chairwoman Ramirez," the letter, dated June 5, 2013, began.

"I am writing to express my concern about the marketing and business practices of Herbalife, Ltd. In particular, I am troubled by allegations that this company may be harming consumers especially those from our country's most vulnerable populations. Given the FTC's mission to investigate claims of fraud and potential pyramid schemes, I encourage you to investigate this matter. I have confidence that such an investigation will provide clarity to consumers and I expect you to aggressively pursue it in a timely manner."[12]

How Ackman had gotten the letter, which he quoted from word for word, was anyone's guess.

Sohn wasn't swayed.

"I didn't know who Linda Sánchez was," said Sohn, "but I went back and did a little more work. You know my conclusion after that dinner was there is no big smoking gun here. It was after that dinner where I really started to buy."

Over the next couple of weeks, Sohn quietly built his position, purposely keeping it under the 5 percent threshold that would have required an SEC filing, alerting everyone on Wall Street he was buying the stock.

On July 22, 2013, inside a Manhattan seafood restaurant for another hedge-fund event, Sohn went in search of more feedback. Once again, the conversation moved around the room until it was Sohn's turn to speak. "My idea is Herbalife," he said to the eighteen or so others who were around the table. Sohn made it clear he'd done weeks' worth of work on the company and could easily and thoroughly disprove Ackman's case.

"I was kind of hoping to get some pushback—you know, part of the reason you pitch something like that is that maybe there's something you hadn't seen or hadn't been a part of. But I didn't get much pushback."

What Sohn wasn't hoping for was for his position to get leaked.

Nine days after the dinner, through sources not related to Sohn or Soros, I broke the news of the position.

The headlines were juicy.

New York Post reporter Michelle Celarier, who'd been following Ackman's Herbalife investment since the beginning, reported that Sohn had been going around town telling other hedge-fund managers that "George Soros broke the Bank of England, he can break the back of Ackman."[13]

While the anecdote may have sounded good, Sohn swears it never happened. In either case, Ackman was incensed at the idea. The day after the news became public, Celarier wrote that Ackman intended to file a complaint with the Securities and Exchange Commission over suspect trading in Herbalife. It was a direct reference to the Soros stake.

Specifically, the *Post* report claimed Ackman said he was told by others that Sohn had tried to recruit other investors by pitching Herbalife to hedge-fund managers, promising to soon report a 5 percent stake in the company.

"There were people working together to try to squeeze me out," Ackman said. "How many times did Icahn go on TV and say this could be the mother of all short squeezes? That was a call to action for every trader to buy the stock."

On Monday, August 5, Ackman officially filed his complaint, but Soros and other long investors were becoming the least of his worries.[14] Days earlier, Herbalife had reported the best quarterly results in its history. Earnings and revenues surged past expectations, leaving CEO Michael Johnson gushing on the conference call.

"We've never been more confident about our business, and as a result, we raised our guidance for the third time this year. The new guidance range points to 2013 being another record year with double-digit top and bottom line growth," he said.[15]

Herbalife shares rose 5.8 percent to $64.05 in after-hours trading when the results were released, after having already jumped a few percentage points during the regular trading session.

Later that month, Ackman tried to turn up the heat on Herbalife again, writing a two-page letter to the company's new auditor, PwC, and its two chairmen, Dennis M. McNally and Robert E. Moritz. In the note, which was accompanied by fifty pages from Ackman's original Herbalife takedown, Ackman warned the firm of what could happen if his thesis about the company was true.

"If we are correct that Herbalife is a pyramid scheme and PwC fails to accurately inform investors of this risk, PwC may incur sub-stantial liabilities in the event of the company's failure," Ackman wrote. He also questioned the firm's independence, noting it had done "non-audit" services for the company.[16]

"We look forward to hearing from you and are available to respond to any questions that you may have," Ackman concluded.

Herbalife responded that it stood by its prior financial statements, but the company's best defense continued to be its surging stock. Herbalife shares, which Ackman had blasted into the $20s toward the end of 2012, was now up more than 80 percent for the year.

Ackman knew he needed to turn up the heat, so he grabbed his best suit and headed to Washington, DC.

11

THE LOBBYIST

On Wednesday, October 2, 2013, two impeccably dressed men walked into the Dirksen Senate Office Building on Second Street in northeast Washington, adjacent to the United States Capitol. They cleared through security and, briefcases in hand, headed down one of the long and hallowed hallways, counting off the numbers that marked each entranceway until they arrived at office number 225.

Bill Ackman and his longtime legal confidant, David Klafter, weren't classic K-Streeters—the consultants hired by large companies to influence policy decisions in Washington, known for having their offices on K Street—but their lobbying mission was no less important. Ackman and Klafter had come to see Senator Edward J. Markey's staff with one goal in mind—to press their case against Herbalife with hopes the Massachusetts senator would join their cause.

Markey was a liberal lawmaker who'd been elected to Congress in 1976 and had a history of consumer advocacy, even when it came to nutrition companies. Markey and other Democratic senators had previously targeted fourteen energy drink makers over their labeling in a report titled "What's All the Buzz About?" In the paper, Markey and the other senators had written, "It's time for energy drink makers to stop masking their ingredients, stop marketing to kids, and start being more transparent with their products."[1]

It was the reason Ackman and Klafter had sought out Senator Markey in the first place—they figured he'd listen. Ackman was also desperate for a catalyst to get the stock moving lower again after Icahn's untimely arrival had reset the narrative and sent shares surging in nearly a straight upward line.

The strategy to take the fight to DC had begun in earnest earlier that year. On Monday, March 4, 2013, Ackman and Shane Dineen had descended on Federal Trade Commission headquarters at 600 Pennsylvania Avenue to meet with the senior staff of Edith Ramirez, the FTC's chairwoman.

Carrying with them a distilled version of the original presentation from December 2012, Ackman and his team funneled into a conference room and began their pitch. As Dineen and the others walked staff members step-by-step through their research, Ackman grew more and more impatient.

Finally, he erupted.

Ackman began chiding the group on how they'd let Herbalife operate illegally—he alleged—for so long and how the government had a duty to stop it. Ackman's intensity and dogged determination were on full display.

But the aggressive tactic backfired.

FTC staffers were put off by Ackman's aggression, and he quickly sensed that the heavy-handed showmanship was a mistake. Ackman would leave the FTC building unconvinced that the regulator would ever take action, especially to appease what she perceived as a preachy hedge-fund billionaire.

Ackman wasn't getting the fast-track action he wanted, but it didn't mean he was about to end his campaign. If anything, he was ready to step it up. Since one of the central charges Ackman had made in his original presentation was that Herbalife defrauded low-income Hispanics, Pershing Square launched a secretive grassroots guerrilla campaign to create a groundswell in those communities.

Pershing blanketed consumer groups they figured would be favorable to their cause. They met with the National Consumers League (NCL), the League of United Latin American Citizens (LULAC), and the Hispanic Federation, which bills itself as the nation's "premier Latino nonprofit membership organization" in the United States.[2]

It didn't take long for their efforts to bear some serious fruit.

On March 12, 2013, the NCL's executive director, Sally Greenberg, wrote a four-page letter to Edith Ramirez, urging the FTC to investigate Herbalife.

"We believe that only the Federal Trade Commission has the resources and expertise to investigate these claims and determine whether Herbalife is, in fact, an illegal pyramid scheme rather than a legitimate multilevel marketing business," said the Greenberg letter.[3]

The NCL said it had met with representatives of both Pershing Square and Herbalife and had gotten conflicting points of view, which only muddied its viewpoint. It also seemed to suggest which way it was leaning in its vetting.

"As these conflicting statements from Pershing Square and Herbalife suggest, it is difficult for the typical consumer, and even for the National Consumers League—which has expertise in this area—to weigh these conflicting claims," said Greenberg. "We believe this necessitates an investigation of the kind that the FTC is well equipped to conduct. We therefore ask that the FTC launch an investigation to determine whether Herbalife is a legitimate MLM, as the company claims, or a pyramid scheme, as its detractors claim."[4]

The letters didn't stop there.

On May 17, 2013, it was the Hispanic Federation's turn when the organization's president, José Calderon, also urged Chairwoman Ramirez to investigate Herbalife.

"It is our understanding that the company's marketing materials promise riches for a few hours of work from home," the letter read. "You can imagine that for immigrants, particularly those who are underemployed or have no papers, this promise can seem like their ticket to achieving the American Dream. We understand, however, that when you add expenses to acquire the product, lists and marketing materials, most distributors appear to actually lose money."[5]

The letters from the Latino-leaning advocacy groups were an important start, but on June 5, Ackman's crusade got an even bigger gift. It was the news he had shared at that hedge-fund ideas dinner at the Manhattan restaurant where Paul Sohn and the other hedge-fund reps had gathered—the same night Ackman had revealed California Congresswoman Linda T. Sánchez had sent her letter to the FTC demanding action against Herbalife.

The news got even better for Ackman the next month when Linda's sister, Loretta, who was also a member of Congress, sent her own letter to Chairwoman Ramirez.

It read in part, "After careful consideration, we would like to request that the Federal Trade Commission look into Herbalife's business practices, specifically whether Herbalife's participants are deceived by exaggerated earnings claims, and whether profits are derived primarily from selling to outside consumers or from recruiting others," she wrote, along with Congresswoman Michelle Lujan Grisham.[6]

Ackman canvassed Congress, estimating he visited fifteen to twenty different lawmakers to plead his case. He even once ran into Arizona Senator John McCain in the hallway, then went back to his office and bent his ear.

"I spent fifteen, twenty minutes with him, and then we spent the rest of the time walking around his office, and he was showing me incredible mementos of his life. I thought he was great, but he ended up doing nothing," Ackman said. "But that's kind of what I did—told the story to anyone in Washington who would listen."

Ackman's campaign to drum up support in Washington eventually got to the point where he stood in danger of violating federal lobbying laws, which restrict the number of hours one can spend making one's case to elected officials. Ackman had an answer for that too—he hired professionals to do what he could not.

In 2013, Ackman had more than a dozen lobbyists from a handful of firms on the Pershing payroll.[7] One of those firms, according to a *New York Times* investigation, was the Global Strategy Group, which specialized in grassroots campaigns like the one Ackman hoped to start. Early in January, one of Global Strategy's "opposition researchers" sent a letter to the FTC asking for the number of complaints made against Herbalife since 2001. The regulator's assistant general counsel, Dione J. Stearns, wrote back, noting "721 pages of responsive complaints" against Herbalife.[8]

On February 22, the FTC received a similar letter from Sullivan and Cromwell. The letter cited "100 responsive complaints" that consumers had made to the commission during an undisclosed time period.

Pershing also hired the Ibarra Strategy Group, which was run by Mickey Ibarra, who'd served in the White House as director of intergovernmental affairs under President William J. Clinton. In 2008, *Hispanic Magazine* had named Ibarra one of the "25 Most Powerful Hispanics in Washington D.C.," and lobbying records from 2013 showed the group was paid $30,000 by Pershing for their efforts. Another $84,000 went to the Moffett Group, a firm describing itself as a "unique government relations and strategic consulting firm." Pershing also hired Wexler & Wexler, paying $150,000 for the firm's public policy services.

In some cases, Ackman went directly to the states, where he figured to make some quick headway. Pershing Square registered in Illinois for two lobbying firms to swamp the state's attorney general's office and members of the Illinois General Assembly.

Lastly, they hired the Dewey Square Group's Latinovations division, which claimed to have "deep and lasting relationships among the nation's Hispanic communities."[9]

Much like they had earlier, the lobbying efforts paid off in spades. Letters from mayors, council members from several cities, including Boston, New York, Hartford and Waterbury, Connecticut, and Carson City, Nevada, started pouring in to the FTC.[10] The majority leader of the Nevada State Senate, Mo Denis, even wrote to his state's attorney general, Catherine Cortez Masto, saying, "it appears that Herbalife has an important hallmark of a pyramid scheme."[11]

Small business owners took up the cause, writing to the regulator and urging similar investigations. One such letter was sent on July 13, 2013, from Xenia Perrica of Manchester, Connecticut, who wrote, "As someone who is a small business owner, I understand how difficult it is to be effective in retail sales. That is why what Herbalife is doing needs an investigation."[12]

Three days later, a woman named Mary Ann Turner wrote similarly, "I am urging the Federal Trade Commission to open an investigation into allegations that the multi-level marketing company Herbalife Ltd. is a complex and abusive pyramid scheme."[13]

There was only one problem—the letter from Ms. Perrica was identical to the one sent by Mary Ann Turner, which in turn was a word-for-word copy of those sent by others. The discovery raised questions over whether the authors were really victims or if they'd been given a form letter by a lobbyist, or Pershing Square itself, to sign and send to the FTC and others. By now, some were questioning whether Ackman himself was going too far in his crusade against Herbalife, as former Securities and Exchange Commission Chair Harvey Pitt openly wondered in the story describing the *Times* investigation.

"If you are trying to spread the truth, that is O.K.," he said. "If you are trying to move the price of a stock to vindicate your investment philosophy, that's not O.K."[14]

Ackman denied the assertion, arguing he was only doing what he set out to do in the first place—to show Herbalife as the fraud he claimed it was and get regulators to act against the company.

"So the risk we took in making this investment was could we get the world to focus on the company," he said at an event. "Could it get enough of a spotlight so that the SEC, the FTC, the 50 attorneys general around the country, the equivalent regulators in 87 countries, if any one of them, or at least any powerful member of that group, could we get them interested?"[15]

"Herbalife's a confidence game," Ackman told me. "When people lose confidence, it's done. It's a con game. So, if we could share information that would cause distributors to jump ship, that's one way [to attract regulators]. We basically ran a consumer protection campaign."

It may have been controversial, but Ackman's lobbying strategy was working. On July 17, 2013, the FTC's director of the Bureau of Consumer Protection, Jessica Rich, met with consumer activists for an hour, telling the group the bureau found Herbalife's business practices "disturbing," though it declined to reveal whether a full-scale investigation was in the offing.[16]

The meeting was well timed.

Later that day, Icahn was scheduled to appear at the Pierre Hotel in Midtown Manhattan for CNBC's "Delivering Alpha" conference for a live onstage interview. And since it had been weeks since the investor had talked publicly about Herbalife, the room was packed with journalists and bloggers waiting for an update on his investment. Icahn didn't disappoint, leaving little doubt about where he stood on the company. He even revealed he'd bought more shares and had already made a quarter of a billion dollars on the trade.

Icahn also didn't miss the opportunity to throw a few zingers Ackman's way.

"You're not going to get me to say bad things about Ackman. I like Ackman," he said as the room broke into laughter. "I've changed my thinking on Ackman. Anybody that makes me a quarter of a billion dollars I like."[17]

Icahn also revisited why he'd taken the other side of Ackman in the first place.

"To be honest with you," he told me onstage. "I never would have been looking at Herbalife if Ackman hadn't come out with that report, and because I'm not a great fan of his, I decided to look at it, and I'll tell you, when I read that report, what he wrote, I was looking at myself thinking, this makes no sense. . . . First of all, it's stupid to take that big of a short position anyway, but if you do, the dumbest thing in my mind is that you get a room full of people and tell them that you're short and then they tell you wow, wow, wow the stock is going to go down. I think the guy honestly believed that people were going to follow him, and you know he's not the best thought-of man on Wall Street. Hey, but I like him now, so I'm not going to say anything bad."

The hundreds sitting in the Pierre's Grand Ballroom ate it up, which only seemed to encourage Icahn to keep the one-liners coming—all, of course, at Ackman's expense.

"Carl Icahn Just Ended What May Be His Most Hilarious, Sarcastic, Awesome Interview Ever" wrote *Business Insider*'s Linette Lopez following the event.[18]

Icahn was also about to get some more backup.

On September 3, 2013, William P. Stiritz revealed in a regulatory filing that he'd taken a 5.2 percent stake in Herbalife.[19] Stiritz was a respected businessman who'd turned around the pet-food company Ralston Purina in the 1980s and was now the nonexecutive chairman of Post Holdings. He was also highly regarded both on Wall Street and in the business community, which is probably why Herbalife shares, which had been sharply lower on the day, pared their losses on news of his new position.

On October 28, Herbalife gave Stiritz reason to feel good about his investment when the company announced another strong quarter. (As it turns out, the company's actual employees and activities do have some impact on its stock price.) CEO Michael Johnson said the earnings results report "demonstrates our belief that the macro trend of global obesity will increase worldwide consumer demand for our products."[20]

While the Stiritz investment had given the company a vote of confidence, Herbalife was also making moves of its own to improve its image. Buried in the earnings report was news that the company had appointed the former surgeon general of the United States, Dr. Richard H. Carmona, to its board of directors. It was part of a broader strategy by Herbalife to surround itself with notable names with rich resumes who would help vouch for the company's legitimacy.

Only a month earlier, Herbalife had named the former mayor of Los Angeles, Antonio Villaraigosa, as a senior advisor. They'd also hired the new consulting firm run by former secretary of state Madeleine Albright. Albright had even attended Herbalife events while advocating for the company's products and its integrity.

Between the string of strong earnings results and the new Stiritz stake, Herbalife shares pushed up more than 100 percent for the year. While some investors may have run for the hills at that point, Ackman made it clear he was willing to go even deeper.

That fall, Ackman restructured his $1 billion short position to include over-the-counter put options, which could help protect him if Icahn followed through on the short-squeeze threat. In a letter to his investors dated October 2, 2013, Ackman explained the move:

In order to mitigate the risk of further mark to market losses on Herbalife, in recent weeks we have restructured the position by reducing our short equity position by more than 40% and replacing it with long-term derivatives, principally over-the-counter put options. The restructuring of the position preserves our opportunity for profit—if the Company fails within a reasonable time frame we will make a similar amount of profit as if we had maintained the entire initial short position—while mitigating the risk of further substantial mark-to-market losses—because our exposure on the put options is limited to the total premium paid. In restructuring the position, we have also reduced the amount of capital consumed by the investment from 16% to 12% of our funds.

"In my career, I have not seen a less attractive risk-reward ratio than a long investment in Herbalife common stock at current levels," Ackman said as he concluded.[21]

With Thanksgiving on the horizon and Ackman's Herbalife investment already down $500 million on paper, he appeared at the Robin Hood Investment Conference on November 22 to rip Herbalife yet again.

Ackman branded Herbalife "Robin Hood in Reverse" in a play off the title of the well-attended charity event. He detailed recent enforcement actions the SEC had taken against other alleged pyramid schemes and showed a slide of what the commission had designated as a "hallmark" of a pyramid scheme—an emphasis on recruiting. Ackman showed clips from some of the cheesy videos from Herbalife extravaganzas where distributors got up onstage in front of thousands of people and preached the virtues of the company.

"If you want to move the check, you need to find other people that want to make money and represent the Herbalife products and Herbalife opportunity," one of the company's Founder's Circle members said on the tape.

In roughly twenty minutes onstage, Ackman showed sixty-five slides before concluding with a piece of data purported to be from

Herbalife's own statements—that only "the top 1% of distributors received 87% of all commissions."[22]

Following his appearance, Ackman did a television interview and shot down any suggestions he'd soon be covering the short. If anything, he sounded more resolute than ever.

"We're going to take this to the end of the Earth," Ackman said.[23]

Herbalife responded that Ackman had presented nothing new at the event and pilloried the investor for what it said was "hundreds of millions of dollars of losses for his investors."[24]

Icahn had a similar reaction, telling another interviewer the same day, "I continue to believe Herbalife has a great future, and in my opinion, many of the things Ackman says about it are simply the rantings of a sore loser."[25] Icahn also alluded to what had become fodder for the media and the cadre of Ackman haters in the marketplace—that whenever Ackman spoke about Herbalife the stock seemed to move higher rather than the other way around. It was like schadenfreude on steroids.[26]

The investor Robert Chapman, who himself had gone long on Herbalife shortly after Ackman revealed his short position, described the climate at the conference in a memorable phrase: "Kill Bill." The list of Ackman's enemies seemed to continuously grow.[27]

By the end of 2013, Herbalife shares had risen an astonishing 139 percent, putting Ackman ever further on the defensive. As 2014 opened, Herbalife shares hit a high of $82.

Little did Ackman know at the time, but he was about to get the biggest break yet in his billion-dollar bet against Herbalife.

On Thursday, January 23, 2014, Senator Markey, whose staff Ackman and company had lobbied, sent off three letters—one to the Securities and Exchange Commission, one to the Federal Trade Commission, and one to Herbalife itself, calling for a probe into the company's practices. To the FTC, Markey wrote, "There have been suggestions that Herbalife may not, in fact, be organized as a multi-level marketing company, but instead may be a pyramid scheme, based on Herbalife's business operations."[28] Markey's letter to the SEC was similar in nature, but began with a more direct request. "I am writing to ask that you look into the business practices of Herbalife," he wrote to the agency's chairwoman, Mary Jo White.[29]

When news of the letters broke in the morning, Herbalife shares immediately plunged 14 percent.

Along with his letters to regulators, Markey put out a press release, saying, "There is nothing nutritional about possible pyramid schemes that promise financial benefit but result in economic ruin for vulnerable families."[30]

At the same time, some questioned Markey's motives and whether he was swayed to write them, in part, because he'd gotten a $500 political contribution from Ackman's sister years earlier. Ackman was incensed at the suggestion.

"The notion that a senator gets bought by a five-hundred-dollar mail-order solicitation from my sister is ridiculous," Ackman said. "And then they say, Mr. Ackman gave $30,000 to the Democratic National Committee on the same day of Markey's primary. First of all, the year before, I'd given to the Republican Senatorial Campaign Committee. So, by their calculation, if any senator got involved they would somehow have been influenced. I have never met or spoken to Markey. I certainly didn't know when his primary was. The whole thing was ridiculous. It drove me crazy."

The accusations aside, the Markey letters were a huge victory, and Ackman knew it.

So did Herbalife CEO Johnson, who got the news while in the most unlikely of places. He'd scheduled a weekend of exhilarating backcountry skiing with two friends in the mountains of Jackson Hole. Johnson had waited months for the trip—had secured the most sought-after guide—and was standing in the parking lot of Teton Sport, coffee in hand, waiting for the shop to open, when the emails began appearing.

After letting out an expletive as he watched the stock drop before his eyes, Johnson went back to his hotel to spend the rest of the day talking by phone with the team of lawyers and consultants Herbalife had hired. Johnson flew back to Los Angeles the next morning, a Friday, to face the hard reality of what the letter could mean.

A spokesperson for Herbalife, Barbara Henderson, said the company had received Markey's letter and looked forward to meeting with the senator to "introduce the company to him and address his concerns at his earliest convenience."[31]

While the Markey letter might have come as a surprise, ironically, Johnson had considered going to the FTC himself months earlier to ask for an investigation, to once and for all end the questions about his company. On one Sunday afternoon, Johnson had asked his executive team to come to his house in Malibu and, over cold beers, billiards, and football, they had hatched a plan to self-report—to take the whole thing out of Ackman's hands, believing they had nothing to hide.

With everyone in the room in agreement, Johnson had called Herbalife's lawyers to brief them on the idea. The suggestion was promptly met with silence, then a wholesale rejection by the attorneys, who thought letting regulators go down a rabbit hole could only bring more problems.

The plan was quickly dropped, and Herbalife went back to business. So did Ackman.

On February 13, 2014, Ackman appeared at the Harbor Investment Conference in Manhattan and addressed the run-up in the stock and his restructured position.

"If it [Herbalife] was to disappear tomorrow, we'd make a lot more than had it just blown up the day after I gave my last presentation—although life would be easier," Ackman said at the event.[32]

At least, more recently, Ackman had reason to be hopeful. The Markey letter had stopped the company's momentum in its tracks. By March 2014, Herbalife shares had fallen 17 percent from where they had started the year.

Then, on March 9, the *New York Times* ran a front-page story documenting Ackman's lobbying efforts and their own investigation, which revealed the great lengths to which he'd gone. Two days later, Ackman took the stage once again, this time to take on Herbalife's Chinese operations—a key area for the company's future growth. While Ackman was there to rail against China, he began his remarks by attempting to rebut what the *Times* reporters had concluded about the lobbying efforts in Washington, saying he had every right to ask the government to investigate Herbalife.

The dogged presentation gave the impression that Ackman was keeping up his relentless push against Herbalife, but behind the scenes, it was a far different story. Within the highest ranks of Pershing Square—reaching all the way to Ackman himself—doubt had emerged over whether the investment was worth pursuing. Pershing Square's advisory board had been discussing the position for weeks and whether it even made sense to keep going.

It all came to bear on March 12, 2014, when advisory board members Stephen Fraidin, Martin H. Peretz, Michael Porter, Edward Meyer, Allen J. Model, Matthew H. Paull, and Ackman himself gathered around a table in a Pershing Square conference room for something of a reality check. It was a sobering conversation, with several of the advisors openly suggesting it might be time to throw in the towel on Herbalife. Even Ackman, who'd always had the ability to remain resolute through the ups and downs of the investment, seemed to have reached a tipping point, believing that the firm had done great research and was content that they had given it their best shot.

Perhaps Ackman was thinking of the old pilot ejector seat that still sits in the corner of one of Pershing's conference rooms to remind him that sometimes it's safer to pull the ripcord than wait for a crash.

A decision to cover the short had been all but made when the phone in the room rang, indicating an internal call. One of Pershing's staffers was on the line and delivered what seemed like good news— Herbalife shares had been halted on Wall Street, with news pending from the company.

What could it be? The men in the room openly wondered.

"We had a debate in the board room," Ackman said. "Is this Carl Icahn announcing a going-private transaction? Then I said, no way, no way, Carl loves money more than he hates me, and that would be a terrible investment."

Just before 2 p.m., Ackman and the others found out the news, when Herbalife itself made a bombshell announcement. In a statement, the company said the FTC was opening a formal civil investigation into its operations.

Ackman, who had been only seconds away from moving to cover the short, was suddenly jubilant.

"There is a god!" he said, as he threw his hands into the air. "It was a great day."

CNBC's Herb Greenberg, an outspoken critic of Herbalife himself, jumped on television to react to the story in real time, while the rest of Wall Street tried to make sense of the shocker.

"This is a long overdue move by the FTC," Greenberg said, as the stock cratered nearly 10 percent to back under $60 a share.[33]

The probe had surprised Herbalife, which said in a statement, "Herbalife welcomes the inquiry given the tremendous amount of misinformation in the marketplace, and will cooperate fully with the FTC. We are confident that Herbalife is in compliance with all applicable laws and regulations. Herbalife is a financially strong and successful company, having created meaningful value for shareholders, significant opportunities for distributors and positively impacted the lives and health of its consumers for over 34 years."[34]

The statement did little to convince investors. Herbalife shares fell as much as 17 percent on the day before recovering to end the day down "only" 7 percent in heavy trading.

Herbalife was now under fire.

More important for Ackman, the investment he had almost terminated in his boardroom was suddenly looking good again.

12

THE DEATH BLOW

The news got even worse for Herbalife late in the afternoon on Friday, April 11, 2014, when the *Financial Times* reported that the FBI and Department of Justice had also opened probes into the company, this time criminal ones.[1]

Herbalife shares, which had been down a little more than 2 percent before the news, plummeted 14 percent to $51.48 when the story went public.

The agencies didn't comment on their investigations in the *FT*, but Herbalife put out a statement saying the company was completely in the dark about an investigation.

"We have no knowledge of any ongoing investigation by the DOJ or the FBI, and we have not received any formal nor informal request for information from either agency," the company said. "We take our public disclosure obligations very seriously. Herbalife does not intend to make any additional comments regarding this matter unless and until there are material developments."[2]

Later that evening, Reuters reported the investigation had been going on "for some time" and that so far no criminal charges had been filed against anyone. The outlet's sources also said the agencies were interviewing former distributors and seeking documents and information related to the company's business practices.[3]

Ackman was elated. After nearly hanging up on the trade altogether, he could now actually see a finish line.

Icahn, on the other hand, seemed unfazed by the news, giving no indication he was wavering on Herbalife even if the Feds had put the company under a brighter microscope. And even if Icahn *was* growing more skeptical, he was limited in what he could say publicly since the agreement that gave the investor seats on the Herbalife board came with strict regulatory rules.

That made the afternoon of Wednesday, July 16 all the more intriguing.

Shortly after 4:30 p.m., Icahn once again walked out from behind the golden curtain at the Pierre Hotel for a conversation at CNBC's Delivering Alpha event—only this time with a surprise guest lurking backstage. As he had been the previous year, Icahn was billed as the closer of the conference—the last speaker before the crowd would break for cocktails to mark the end of the event. Icahn had grown more nervous in recent weeks about the stock market's high valuation and worried that the Federal Reserve's easy-money policies of the previous years had artificially inflated the market. Icahn feared that once those policies ended it could get ugly.

"What happens when the low interest rate environment ends, no one knows. No one can know," Icahn said as he pondered worryingly of how stocks might react.[4]

The topic then turned to Herbalife, with Icahn admitting he now owned seventeen million shares of the company. Onstage with him, I pressed Icahn to elaborate on his position. He said he hadn't lightened up his stake at all and then made it clear he wasn't about to get too specific.

"I will say one thing, that we bought seventeen million shares at an average of $37 and we haven't sold one share. Now that's all I can say, and I think we have to drop it there," Icahn said abruptly as he gave me a menacing "move-on" look.

If only it were that simple.

Those in the audience had been promised a "mystery guest" in their programs, with the event's organizers remaining tight-lipped about who it might be. Few could have expected to see the man who walked onstage at my prompting.

It was Ackman himself.

Some in attendance gasped as Ackman, smiling along with the long-planned gag, eagerly made his way toward Icahn, who was in cahoots with the whole thing. The two embraced, somewhat awkwardly, before they each accepted a T-shirt that read, "Icahn and Ackman: Back Together Again." They shared a laugh, then sat for a twenty-minute chat that was perfectly cordial. The two exchanged pleasantries and spoke about Herbalife, agreeing to disagree on the company's outlook. Perhaps the ease with which the men handled the encounter was because they'd already broken the ice privately. In late April, Ackman had called Icahn to try to put their beef behind them. The two agreed to move on and even discussed the possibility of investing together in the future.

"I respect Bill," said Icahn on the Delivering Alpha stage. "It's almost crazy that we're at these loggerheads. . . . I mean, what the hell are we fighting ourselves for?" Icahn asked.

"It's not about winning," said Ackman lightheartedly before getting serious again. "Look, I would love to find a way to get Carl out of the stock. He bought seventeen million shares at $32 a share. He can get out at a very nice profit. That would be a great outcome for Carl, and that would be wonderful for us, so, Carl, maybe we should have a conversation."

For a moment, it actually appeared as though the war that had dominated Wall Street for the better part of a year and a half might be about to run its course—that Ackman and Icahn would make peace right then and there and head on to other things.

"Icahn and Ackman Publicly End Feud with an Embrace" read a headline on the *New York Times*'s DealBook site later that evening, reflecting the apparent detente.[5]

What no one knew that evening, as the two men sat and spoke on the Delivering Alpha stage, was that Icahn and Ackman had met in secret around two months prior in Icahn's offices atop the GM Building on 59th Street. Ackman had initiated the meeting and had come over to pitch Icahn on the idea of buying him out. After meeting as a group with their associates, Icahn and Ackman had retired to the titan's private office to talk some more, but the conversation had ended without a deal.

Even if Ackman wanted Icahn out, his actions less than a week later would make it crystal clear he was still going all-out to win. On July 22—six days after "The Hug" made headlines—Ackman appeared on CNBC's *Halftime Report* to set the stage for his next major presentation on Herbalife, which was set for the following morning in Manhattan, once again at the AXA Center.

This time, Ackman would go after Herbalife's nutrition clubs, which the researcher Christine Richard had painstakingly documented in her initial pitch of the Herbalife short. Asked on TV what investors would learn during the event, Ackman didn't hold back in the least.

"You're going to learn why Herbalife is going to collapse," he said before openly taunting the company's management. "And that's a pretty strong statement, but this is the largest fraud in terms of scale, of countries involved, doing harm to people. I want to make clear that Michael Johnson and his senior management team is welcome to come to the presentation. We'll be happy to sit them in the front row if they would like."[6]

Ackman had thrown barbs Herbalife's way for months, with the company mostly either staying silent or choosing to respond by a sharply worded press release. But less than twenty-four hours away from facing another Ackman onslaught, they'd clearly had enough.

The company took to Twitter to rip Ackman, saying, "Paying people to spread bad information isn't OK but Pershing Square thinks so," alluding to the intense lobbying he'd done. Herbalife concluded the social media shot with a hashtag that read "the worst of Wall Street" in reference to the man who'd relentlessly attacked them for eighteen months.

"We have not paid anyone to spread bad information about Herbalife," Ackman said, promising the information he had would be a "death blow" to the company.

"This will be the most important presentation that I have made in my career," Ackman said. "So how's that for raising expectations? But we won't disappoint."[7]

Ackman had thrown down the gauntlet.

The next morning, at 8:28 a.m., a metallic blue Mercedes sport utility vehicle pulled into the underground parking garage of the AXA Center on Seventh Avenue.[8] With a documentary film crew waiting for his arrival, Ackman climbed out of the front seat of the vehicle looking calm and confident. He threw on his suit jacket and walked alone through the bowels of the building until he wound up backstage, where an audio technician was waiting to put on Ackman's lavalier microphone.

"Count up," Ackman said to the engineer, referring to the digital time keeper that would track the presentation's length. Normally, such clocks would count down to keep a presenter honest, but Ackman was making it clear he planned to go as long as he could.[9]

Ackman wanted the made-for-TV event to be flawless.

He sat for makeup and had his hair combed perfectly into place while telling the artist doing the work not to go overboard. "I just need to be authentic," he said.[10]

Nearly ready to head out onstage, Ackman first wanted to watch the highly anticipated undercard happening at the same moment. Herbalife CFO John DeSimone had flown out from Los Angeles for a rare live interview with me on CNBC. Not wanting to miss the public appearance, Ackman had the interview fed live into the auditorium, where people, coffees in hand, were beginning to gather and get comfortable.

Surrounded by several of his Pershing Square associates, Ackman sat and watched as DeSimone spoke, staring at the TV as though he were transfixed.[11]

"He has made some outrageous statements," DeSimone said of Ackman. "He has made 435 accusations over the last 18 months— each one is the latest and greatest until it's proven not to be. I'm not worried about the substance of what he has. This is anecdotal. It's very propaganda based. What he's missing is that fundamentally we have millions of customers who use the product, who love the product. We have complete confidence in our compliance as it relates to regulations. I think the FTC inquiry will actually be something that kind of puts this behind us."[12]

Intent on using the appearance to debunk some of Ackman's expected ammunition, DeSimone cited a company-funded study released earlier that morning claiming to back Herbalife's long-stated view that it operated legitimately.

"It is a study we commissioned, but it's an independent person that had no ties to Herbalife. But we commissioned it so that a former FTC economist would look at our business."[13]

As the clocked ticked toward 10 a.m., the arranged start time of the event, Ackman made an ominous prediction about where Herbalife stock would go and what his response should be if it defied his expectations and actually went up instead of down.

"It's not going up, OK," Ackman said matter-of-factly. "The question is whether it opens again."[14]

Pressed again for a more thoughtful answer from his public relations consultant, Ackman wouldn't give in.

"The stock's not going up, OK. It's a certainty. The stock's irrelevant!" he said even more forcefully to make his point.

Then it was time.

"Ladies and gentlemen, please welcome the founder and CEO of Pershing Square Capital Management, Mr. Bill Ackman," said the announcer as Ackman walked out from behind the curtain to begin.

Ackman had spent months prepping and had stayed up until two or three in the morning putting the finishing touches on the presentation. With only four hours of sleep but looking fresher than the short night would suggest, Ackman began by zeroing in on Herbalife's nutrition clubs.

He questioned how they made money, saying Richard had visited ten shady sites in Queens alone to do her research.

"This doesn't seem to be a particularly good business model," he said.

Hour one went by, then hour two.

At 12:15 p.m., Ackman opened the forum for questions and was immediately put on the defensive.

"I don't understand something," said a man sitting toward the back of the room. "You got this nice presentation that you spent a lot of money on. Everybody's clueless except for you. I don't understand. Tell me. Why is Carl Icahn making a mistake? Show me every illegality Herbalife is doing to get this company shut down. I don't see it, and why is everybody else on the other side?"[15]

"It's a great question," Ackman answered. "We've had an army working on this project. Hundreds of people. Investigators, lawyers. Carl Icahn didn't do the kind of due diligence we did. The nutrition club thing is designed to be secretive. This is an ingenious fraud. You go after people who are the lowest income, the least sophisticated. Many of them are undocumented. You know you don't complain when you're an undocumented immigrant, because you're afraid you'll get thrown out of the country."[16]

But the skepticism wasn't limited to one gentleman sitting in the audience.

While Ackman spoke onstage, investors flooded into the stock—the exact opposite reaction Ackman had predicted earlier that morning. Herbalife shares surged 13 percent, then 20, and then even more, before closing the day up a stunning 25 percent.

It was as brutal a repudiation as anyone could remember, and Ackman knew it.

"Herbalife is going to use the fact that the stock price is up today to say that everyone is ignoring what we have to say," he said when confronted with the reality by a reporter in the room. "My advice to you is you probably shouldn't ignore it."[17]

"Next," said Ackman, who was now visibly agitated by the line of questions, which were more focused on the stock's rise than his marathon.

A friendlier inquirer then grabbed the microphone—perhaps in an attempt to break the ice. It was Ackman's own father.

"The definition of a pyramid scheme is what, Bill, and how close are you getting to be able to prove it's a pyramid scheme?" he asked.

"Dad, if you don't know it by now," he said, breaking into a laugh along with most others.

With the crowd now thinning out, some in the audience yawning, and Herbalife shares soaring, Ackman attempted to land one last blow. He referenced the Nazis and other totalitarian regimes while marveling at how Herbalife had stayed in business—how it had "gotten away" with its "big lie."[18]

He then turned the attack onto Herbalife CEO Michael Johnson himself, looking straight into the camera with one last message for his target.

"Michael Johnson is a predator, OK," said Ackman, his voice cracking as tears welled in his eyes. "This is a criminal enterprise, OK. I hope you're listening, Michael. It's time to shut the company down."[19]

However dramatic its ending, there was no hiding the fact that Ackman's promised "death blow" had fizzled.

Maybe tired from the long night or in denial at what the stock was doing, Ackman tried to put a positive face on the event, even if he was trying to convince himself more than anyone.

"What a day. What a day," Ackman said, now back in the Mercedes, which was driving off for the office. "It was a good day. It was a very good day."[20]

For once, Herbalife agreed.

The company issued a statement that read, "Once again, Bill Ackman has over-promised and under-delivered on his $1 billion bet against our company. After spending $50 million, two years and tens of thousands of man-hours, Bill Ackman further demonstrated today that the facts are on our side."[21]

Behind the scenes, Johnson and the other executives, emboldened by the reaction in the stock, joked that they wished Ackman could give another speech the following week.

Herbalife had reason to stick out its chest. One after the other, media headlines as far as London revealed the day's reality.

"Ackman Fails to Land Herbalife 'Death Blow,'" said *USA Today*.

"Herbalife Dodges Bill Ackman's Promised 'Death Blow,'" said the BBC.

Television commentators came to the same conclusion, as Ackman tried to figure out what to do next.

All he actually had to do was wait.

On July 28, a week after the death blow that wasn't, Herbalife released its latest earnings report after the close of trading. Though earnings per share rose double-digits from a year earlier, they had missed Wall Street estimates. Herbalife shares, which had closed up 2 percent to hit $67.48 before the numbers came out, got hammered, falling 11.6 percent to $59.64 in the aftermarket.

Even with the steep slide, Herbalife CEO Johnson remained as rosy as he could.

"Herbalife has once again delivered strong results in sales and profitability while demonstrating our continued ability to enhance our earnings per share," he said. "Our performance is a testament to the enthusiasm our millions of consumers and members have for our products."[22]

But the numbers continued to slide in the next quarter.

On November 3, Herbalife again reported quarterly numbers and again missed expectations—only this time the market's reaction was more severe. Shares fell more than 20 percent, or more than $11, to end the day at $44.44.

This time Johnson wasn't in spin mode.

"This performance is clearly out of character for us," he said on the conference call the next morning. "There is a confluence of factors, some external and some internal, that had an impact on our results."[23]

Johnson blamed the disappointment on the company's operations in Venezuela and a stronger US dollar, which had made its products more expensive overseas, and on so-called structural changes Herbalife was making to its business model.[24] Johnson had almost glossed over the changes during the November 4 call with analysts, but the market didn't, and with good reason.

Herbalife said it would start limiting the amount of product new members could buy on their first orders, a move that appeared to address one of Ackman's original criticisms—that new members were required to buy thousands of dollars' worth of Herbalife products to qualify for the title of "sales leader," at which point they could take advantage of big discounts.

"The rationale is that encouraging slower growth to sales leader increases the likelihood that the new sales leader will be successful and retained," said Herbalife's president, Des Walsh.[25]

It also meant the potential of lower sales, but if Johnson was worried about the new policy being a hit to future earnings, he certainly didn't show it.

"It's pretty simple here, folks. We've got a great business. We're in a great marketplace, and our distributors are confident, and we're moving forward."[26]

Wall Street wasn't convinced.

The next day, November 5, Herbalife continued its decline, closing at $39.78. In just two days, Herbalife shares had fallen nearly 30 percent.

Then, on November 25, Ackman let his investors know exactly what he thought of the rapid rollover in the stock.

"Recent developments at Herbalife reinforce our short thesis that Herbalife is an illegal pyramid that will collapse or otherwise be shut down by regulators," Ackman wrote.[27] "We believe that management's new 2015 guidance fundamentally changes the bull case prospects, both by reducing the projected earnings power of the company and the price-earnings multiple that investors will assign to a business in decline. Given the negative developments in the quarter, we believe that it will be increasingly difficult for institutional managers to hold (or initiate) positions in Herbalife."[28]

Ackman had reason to be bellicose.

Though many hedge funds posted only modest returns through October, Ackman's numbers had been so impressive they were near the top of the entire industry. Year to date, Pershing Square was up 35 percent, net of fees, thanks to Herbalife's sudden and sharp drop and sizeable gains in other key positions in Ackman's portfolio. The performance helped Ackman crack LCH Investments' list of the top twenty hedge-fund managers for the first time ever, joining an esteemed group that included legends George Soros, David Tepper, and Paul Singer. Since 2004, when Pershing Square was founded,

Ackman had made $11.6 billion for his investors, solidifying his place as one of the best and most trusted money managers on Wall Street.[29]

And it showed.

By the end of 2014, Ackman's total assets under management ballooned to nearly $20 billion, and as he entered the new year, he made it clear that he was on the hunt for his next big target. On Monday, March 9, 2015, the world found out what it was.

That afternoon, Reuters reported that Pershing Square had taken a more than $3 billion stake in the Canadian pharmaceutical company Valeant, becoming the company's fifth-largest shareholder.[30]

Valeant rose 2.5 percent to more than $200 per share on news of its newest investor. The position immediately became one of Pershing's biggest—yet another reminder that Bill Ackman never did anything small.

13

THE YEAR THAT WASN'T

Momentum on Wall Street is a powerful thing, but even the best investors know it can be fleeting—that the wave can break at any moment.

Bill Ackman knew that better than most.

After living through the Gotham death spiral more than a decade earlier, the JC Penney debacle, and the first eighteen turbulent months of his Herbalife crusade, Ackman finally appeared to catch a wave in early 2015. His fund, Pershing Square, had killed it the year before, scoring amazing returns that vaulted him to the very top of the hedge-fund industry.

"Bill Ackman Wins 2014," said *Forbes* of Ackman's incredible returns.[1] "Bill Ackman, Pershing Square Deliver Legendary Performance," said *USA Today*.[2]

"I told him at the beginning of 2015," remembered longtime friend and fellow money manager Whitney Tilson. "I said, 'Bill, you were worth a billion dollars, now you're worth two billion, your words move markets. Congratulations, you deserve it.' But I also said it's so important right now that you not be like Icarus and fly too close to the sun. That kind of thing can go to your head and lead to some terrible mistakes, and he assured me and said he appreciated me telling him that."

But before he even got a chance to soar too high, Ackman found his wings getting clipped. On March 12, the *Wall Street Journal* broke the news that several people tied to Ackman were being investigated by the US Attorney's Office and FBI over the possible manipulation of Herbalife's stock price.[3] The paper said the probe was looking into whether some of the many consultants and lobbyists hired by Pershing Square had made false and misleading statements about Herbalife and its business model. Ackman wasn't personally named in the probe and said during an interview with me the next morning that he didn't know anything more than what he'd read.

"We've hired a political consultant, a firm called Global Strategy Group. They in turn hire subcontractors around the country, and they assisted us in advocating on our behalf of our very firmly held view that Herbalife is a pyramid scheme," Ackman said. "And my understanding is that a handful of the people that they've hired or that work for them have been interviewed by the FBI."[4]

Ackman may have easily explained away the story, but its mere existence was evidence of how successful Herbalife had become in fighting back against his accusations.

In January, the company signed George Sard, whose PR firm, Sard Verbinnen, was known for repping businesses and people in crisis. Sard had worked for Martha Stewart during her insider trading scandal, and for the son of Bernard Madoff. He was a seasoned attack dog for his clients.[5] In Herbalife, he found a company willing to battle but unseasoned in its execution.

"It was like a club softball team playing against major league operations," said Sard. "We basically brought a discipline. This was a company that, even though it was out of its depth, was not afraid to be aggressive. Some companies may not have been willing to do it, but they had no problem being fighters."

Sard's plan was to take the fight to Ackman, something he had experience doing. It was Sard who had represented MBIA during its protracted war with the investor back in Ackman's Gotham days.

"We told Herbalife there was no way Bill was going to let go. He was well under water [on the investment] at the time, and we said you just have to expect that he's going to keep coming. It became clear that this is the kind of guy you have to play hardball with. There's no subtlety. You have to hit him with a two-by-four."

The point was clear. Ackman was too invested—emotionally and financially—to turn back now.

During the interview responding to the *Journal*'s bombshell story, Ackman revealed he'd already spent around $50 million on the Herbalife campaign—the vast majority, he claimed, going to legal fees and investigative costs.[6]

The dollar amount was staggering. But it was little compared to Ackman's next move.

On March 27, 2015, the investor and a group of friends closed on one of New York City's most expensive apartment purchases ever—a $91 million penthouse atop One57, a new ninety-story luxury highrise overlooking Central Park.[7]

The 13,554-square-foot duplex had six bedrooms, towering floor-to-ceiling windows, and monthly common charges of $24,000.[8] But even more stunning than the space was Ackman's plan for it.

He didn't intend to live in the property, but rather wanted to flip it to another buyer.

"The Mona Lisa of apartments," Ackman told the *New York Times* after confirming the deal. "I thought it would be fun so myself and a couple of very good friends bought into this idea that someday, someone will really want it and they'll let me know."[9]

Ackman had similarly grand plans for the high-flying new stock in his portfolio.

Earlier that month, Ackman had taken his $3.3 billion stake in Valeant, a Canadian firm known for its explosive growth.[10] The company had become a favorite of hedge funds for its aggressive cost-cutting and against-the-grain business model. Instead of investing heavily in the development of new treatments, Valeant spent next to nothing on R&D, relying instead on billion-dollar deals and piles of debt to grow. So many large investors had piled into the stock that some began calling Valeant a "hedge-fund hotel."

The architect of Valeant's ambitious strategy was its swashbuckling CEO, J. Michael Pearson, a crusty former McKinsey & Company consultant who loved making deals. Pearson had made more than a hundred deals during his tenure, including an $8.7 billion acquisition of Bausch and Lomb in May 2013.[11]

Investors couldn't buy shares fast enough.

From the time Pearson became CEO in 2008 until midway through 2015, Valeant shares had risen a stunning 1,000 percent, with Ackman fully believing the run was just getting started.[12] Perhaps it was because Ackman knew Valeant better than almost anyone, save for Pearson himself.

A year earlier, in April 2014, Ackman had partnered with Valeant in its $45.6 billion hostile bid for Allergan, the company behind Botox and other skin-care drugs. The deal had come with a twist.

In an unusual move, Ackman had secretly gone long on Allergan stock ahead of the overture, knowing the company was about to be approached by Valeant. Not surprisingly, the information led to quite a score. When the news of Valeant's advance became public, Allergan shares surged, reaping Ackman an immediate $1.2 billion on paper.[13]

Ackman pushed for the deal. He'd studied Valeant inside and out, laying out his grand plan for the merger with the usual Ackman flair—a 110-page presentation called "The Outsider" that portrayed Valeant as the perfect partner.[14] But while the case may have been convincing in its PowerPoint form, Allergan wasn't as optimistic. It rejected Valeant's offer, saying it undervalued the company, and did so again two months later when Pearson and Ackman came back with an improved bid.

Then the fireworks really started.

In early August, Allergan sued Ackman and Valeant in California civil court, accusing both of an "improper and illicit insider-trading scheme," an obvious reference to Ackman's taking a large position and knowing a bid was coming. But Allergan was hardly the only party scrutinizing Ackman's controversial tactics. "In Allergan Bid, a Question of Insider Trading," ran a *New York Times* headline.[15]

Faced with mounting criticism over the maneuver, Ackman went on TV to say he was not guilty of anything.

"The way the rules work is you're actually permitted to trade on inside information . . . as long as you didn't receive the information from someone who breached . . . fiduciary duty or duty of confidentiality, et cetera," Ackman said on CNBC's *Squawk Box*. "Valeant basically came to us and said, 'Look, if you can help us buy Allergan we can work with you.' We said, 'Great,' and we formed a partnership. The partnership has various terms. It gives us the right and permission from the company to go buy a stake in Allergan."[16]

Technically, Ackman was right. While the move might have smelled fishy, it wasn't illegal. Ackman had vetted the whole thing with a multitude of lawyers and even Robert Khuzami, the former head of enforcement at the SEC, who blessed the transaction.[17]

It all seemed moot when Allergan agreed to a deal with Actavis for $66 billion, thus nixing the transaction he was supposedly cashing in on. Ackman walked away with one hell of a consolation prize—$2.28 billion—which he promptly rolled into a new investment in Valeant, hoping for a similar outcome.

Others questioned whether more profits were in the offing. One such skeptic was the world's most famous, if not successful, short seller, James Chanos. Chanos was the guy who had helped uncover the massive Enron fraud and whose firm, Kynikos, took its name from the Greek word for cynic. Chanos had been betting against the stock since 2014, convinced that Valeant paid too much for its deals, was bloated with debt, and would eventually blow up altogether when the music stopped. Chanos called Valeant a "roll-up," meaning a company that buys another large business, then cuts costs dramatically to increase efficiency and keep growth and revenues climbing.

"Roll-ups present a unique set of problems," Chanos said during a CNBC interview on the topic. "Roll-ups are usually accounting-driven, and we certainly think that's the case in Valeant. We think Valeant is playing aggressive accounting games when they buy companies and write down the assets."[18]

Ackman knew Chanos was shorting Valeant when he bought the stock, and had even asked him for his research. When Ackman read it, he all but dismissed it, along with Chanos himself, during a CNBC appearance in June 2014.[19]

"He sent me a twenty-six-page analysis of the company. I went through every word in that document. I had access to inside information on Valeant. Unfortunately, Jim just does not have Valeant right," said Ackman.

Valeant's Pearson had heard from other haters through the years, but made it clear he wasn't about to alter his agenda. More proof of that came in January 2015, when Valeant bought Salix Pharmaceuticals for $14.5 billion in cash and debt. Shares quickly popped 15 percent on the news—a sign that, at least at face value, many on Wall Street liked the deal.[20]

After the transaction was announced, Pearson addressed the company's critics in an interview with CNBC's mergers and acquisitions expert David Faber, who asked Pearson point-blank whether the market was forcing him to keep the deal flow going, irrespective of whether it made good business sense.

"That's my job," Pearson scoffed. "It's our board's job to do whatever we can to create value for shareholders."[21]

Ackman was so smitten with Pearson's game plan that he even compared Valeant to Warren Buffett's hallowed Berkshire Hathaway and its own platform strategy of scooping up businesses and seamlessly adding them into the fold.

"You'd think after twenty-five years people would realize," Ackman said at the Ira Sohn Conference in May, alluding to Valeant's attractive value. "And Valeant is a very early-stage Berkshire."[22]

The comparison might have been hyperbolic, but the size of Ackman's stake backed up his conviction. Ackman had invested 20 percent of Pershing Square's capital in Valeant when the stock was near $161 a share, admitting he was "late to the party" since the share price had already surged dramatically in the previous year.[23]

By August 2015, Valeant sure looked like another home run. That month, shares hit an all-time high of $263, more than double the price at which Ackman had first bought the stock.

But while Valeant was making its investors and Pearson rich, it began to attract attention for a lesser-known but important part of its business model. When Valeant bought a new drug, it aggressively raised its price to consumers, even for life-saving treatments. In one case involving the heart drug Isuprel, it raised the cost for twenty-five ampules from $4,489 to more than $36,000 in just two years. It did the same thing after acquiring the diabetes drug Glumetza, hiking the cost of ninety 1,000-milligram tablets from nearly $900 to more than $10,000.[24]

Finally, in September 2015, a chorus of critics, including the Democratic presidential candidate Hillary Clinton, had seen enough. At 10:56 a.m. on the morning of September 21, Clinton tweeted about another company on the high-price hot seat, Turing Pharmaceuticals, which had similarly raised prices exponentially.

"Price gouging like this in the specialty pharma market is outrageous," read the tweet. "Tomorrow I'll lay out a plan to take it on."

At the very second the tweet hit the tape and media outlets mentioned it, the iShares NASDAQ Biotechnology ETF, the exchange-traded fund that tracked the sector, began falling, quickly losing more than 4 percent of its value.[25] By late September, investors were growing more and more nervous, with Valeant shares losing a quarter of their value since the spring.

At the same time, Pearson, who could be curt and abrupt with critics, appeared defiant on a company conference call when asked about the questionable price hikes.

"We will act appropriately in terms of doing what I assume our shareholders would like us to do," he said.[26]

In the weeks that followed, Pearson's communication skills would be put to the test again, only this time his company's future would arguably hang in the balance.

On October 15, the Australian money manager John Hempton, who'd bet against Ackman's short in the Herbalife trade, sent an email to Ackman that said, cryptically, "I just want to say one word to you. Just one word. Philidor."[27]

Ackman had never heard the name before, nor did he have any idea what Hempton was referring to. Neither did anyone else.

But on October 19, the Southern Investigative Reporting Foundation (SIRF), run by a dogged investigative journalist named Roddy Boyd, released an explosive report on its website titled "The King's Gambit: Valeant's Big Secret."

Inside the bombshell report, Boyd revealed Valeant's ties to a company called Philidor Rx Services, a "specialty pharmacy" firm outside Philadelphia that almost no one on Wall Street had ever heard of, even though billions of dollars' worth of Valeant products moved through its doors each year. Boyd claimed the businesses were virtually inseparable, all but intimating that Valeant owned the company.[28]

If that were the case, why hadn't Pearson mentioned it before? Boyd wondered as he noted Philidor's stark and simple website.

Philidor's business worked like this: Instead of getting a prescription for one of Valeant's expensive medicines the old-fashioned way—by going to a drugstore—patients were instead sent by doctors directly to Philidor's mail-order service. Philidor would then fill the prescription and deal directly with insurers, removing the physicians' need to haggle for reimbursements. The process also kept patients from getting prescribed lower-priced generic drugs, which in turn kept Valeant's healthy profits rolling in, especially on its expensive medications.[29]

Boyd's SIRF report was carefully timed.

Later that morning, Valeant was scheduled to hold its quarterly earnings call, which put Pearson on the defensive. Faced with questions about the business and its use of specialty pharmaceutical companies, Pearson admitted Valeant had purchased an option to acquire Philidor the previous year, and also revealed it had consolidated the firm's financial results into its own since then.

It may have been a shocking revelation, but Valeant's use of Philidor wasn't necessarily illegal, according to experts who opined on the topic. Still, the company's lack of transparency and the escalating outrage over the issue of its drug prices only raised more skepticism with investors.

Later that same morning, with chum already in the water, another attack came, this time from an antagonist in Los Angeles.

Andrew Left had founded Citron Research out of his Beverly Hills house in 2001 and was known for his scathing, if not hyperbolic, research reports touting short investment ideas. Left was a fast-talking idea machine with a credible track record among stock market watchers. He had drilled for-profit education stocks in the past as well as a company called Longtop Financial Technologies, which was ultimately delisted from trading over questionable business practices that Left had highlighted.[30]

Left liked to make a splash too, and when it came to Valeant he lived up to his billing.

"Valeant: Could This Be the Pharmaceutical Enron?" asked the title of Left's new report, alluding to one of the biggest corporate accounting scandals ever in the United States.[31]

"Citron Publishes the Smoking Gun!!" splashed another line just below in bold red ink, along with a shocking $50 price target, almost $100 lower than where Valeant was currently trading.

Left attacked Valeant for "covering up" its relationship with Philidor and another specialty pharma company like it, concluding that "Citron believes the whole thing is a fraud to create invoices to deceive the auditors and book revenue."

"Is this Enron part Deux??" Left asked.

It was an explosive accusation that sent Valeant shares plunging as much as 39 percent in heavy volume.[32] Valeant was suddenly reeling, and it put out a press release to refute Citron's allegations line by line.

"We categorically deny the allegations made in the Citron Report," said a company spokesperson. "Citron's false and misleading statements about Valeant appear to be an attempt to manipulate the market in an effort to drive down Valeant's stock price."[33]

Investors were running for the hills, at least most of them.

There was one in particular, though, who did the opposite.

In the midst of the storm, Ackman jumped in, buying two million more shares at $108 apiece, revealing the news to me by phone, along with a claim that he still believed in the company. As proof, Ackman touted that he had not sold a single share of the more than twenty-one million that he owned.

The news helped Valeant recover some of its losses, closing the day down 19 percent, at $118 a share.[34]

Days later, the Valeant story grew even more salacious when the *Wall Street Journal* reported that employees from Philidor not only kept in close contact with workers at Valeant but also used comic book–like aliases to communicate.[35]

Now Ackman was losing his patience, if not his mind. In the span of seven short months, his Valeant investment had lost more than $1.5 billion of its value, and he'd had it.

According to a detailed *Wall Street Journal* account, on Tuesday, October 27, while in Toronto for a board meeting of the railway Canadian Pacific, Ackman emailed Pearson and several members of Valeant's board, early that morning from his hotel room, to voice concerns about where the company was heading.[36]

"Your reputation is at grave risk," Ackman wrote to Pearson. "Valeant has become toxic. . . . Even we are concerned," he said.[37]

After reading the email, Pearson invited Ackman to join Valeant's board meeting by phone later that morning, which he did, urging that, according to the *Journal*, "management needs to come clean."[38]

Ackman encouraged the company to hold a conference call that day, which the company declined to do. Ackman then called Valeant's lead director, Robert Ingram, to raise an issue that once would have been unthinkable—whether Pearson should remain as the company's CEO.[39]

One week later, on Friday, October 30, Ackman held a four-hour conference call with more than nine thousand investors and reporters listening in. Ackman explained why he'd bought even more Valeant shares and continued to believe in the embattled company.[40]

Earlier that morning, Valeant announced it was severing ties with Philidor altogether, which was just as well with Ackman, who had criticized Valeant and Pearson for not being more transparent about the specialty pharmacy, admitting he didn't know of its existence when he originally bought shares back in March.[41]

Ackman pointed to other hedge funds that were still in the stock as validation for his support, calling shares "tremendously undervalued."[42] Indeed, ValueAct, a San Francisco–based investment firm run by Jeffrey Ubben, was still invested, and he said defiantly on CNBC that the scrutiny was nothing short of a witch hunt.

"The short-sellers and the media are dying for some new crisis like Enron," a frustrated Ubben told the CNBC host Kelly Evans.[43]

Ackman went even further, saying shares had an "89 percent upside" and could even be worth $448 in three years.

"Life will go on for Valeant," Ackman said on his call while answering more than two hundred questions from the media and analysts. "While this has been a very damaging moment for the company," he said, "we think the Valeant business is quite robust."

Others weren't so sure and began to worry about the hit Ackman was taking—both in the media and in his portfolio.

On November 4, Whitney Tilson wrote Ackman a personal letter, pleading with him over several pages to sell the entire position immediately, just as he'd done in the depths of the JC Penney crisis.

"I had tried talking to him and that didn't seem to work," said Tilson of the letter. "There were a lot of obvious red flags, and it still looked like the stock had plenty of downside, and I just wanted to warn him."

Tilson had done his own in-depth analysis of Valeant's balance sheet, identifying several worrisome signs he suspected Ackman was ignoring, including Valeant's high debt level.

As much as Tilson tried, the intervention failed. Ackman made it clear he wasn't selling.

"I tried to be the truth teller to Bill, but it didn't work," Tilson said.

To make matters worse, even Herbalife, which hadn't been one to engage Ackman directly in the press, couldn't resist taking a shot at the investor while watching the Valeant massacre unfold.

"I hope Bill Ackman has done more research on Valeant than he did on Herbalife, Target, Borders, and JC Penney," said Herbalife's executive vice president, Alan Hoffman, referring to some of Ackman's more infamous misfires.[44]

Hoffman had joined Herbalife in August after leaving a public relations role at PepsiCo. He had also previously served as Vice President Joe Biden's chief of staff and knew a thing or two about advocating against an opposition party. Though friends questioned his sanity for making the move from Purchase, New York, where Pepsi was headquartered, to Los Angeles and into the thick of the Herbalife war, Hoffman figured he was up for the challenge.

He also had a plan. Hoffman thought Herbalife had been too soft on Ackman and decided it was about time to change tactics.

The new hardline strategy had actually begun behind the scenes at the start of the year, when Ackman had traveled to Chicago to personally appear at an anti-Herbalife rally sponsored by the Waukegan chapter of LULAC. Ackman was slated to show up at a church in the city to hear from local Herbalife distributors who'd lost money. Herbalife wanted to mount a counteroffensive so that Ackman wouldn't get a free pass to control the narrative.

On the morning of January 10, 2015, Herbalife held a conference call, with Hoffman trying to convince other company bigwigs to support the public pushback.

It wasn't an easy sell.

Some of the executives were reticent to expose Herbalife's members to Ackman directly. Later that morning, Hoffman emailed Ibi Fleming, an Herbalife vice president who was one of the apprehensive executives.

"This is about supporting the company," Hoffman all but pleaded. "And during these times, folks have a tendency to band together. And to be honest the number matters. We need to show that we have significant support. They will have 100 and if we have 500, the press will report that. Finally, if [Ackman] is successful in this forum, we can expect others. We need to do everything possible to ensure that this does not happen."

"Why would we want our newest members exposed to this?" Fleming wrote back.

"They need to do this for the health of their businesses and the company," responded Hoffman. "This is going to be big news and not demonstrating that the company has support will have an impact on their sales. This is in their interest."

The pleas worked. Hundreds of Herbalife supporters braved freezing cold temperatures and snow, showing up outside the church with signs protesting Ackman and his assault on the company.

Buoyed by the turnout and the enthusiastic support the company had received at the rally, Herbalife executives felt they had reached a tipping point in their campaign to fight back against Ackman. President Des Walsh even suggested afterward that the company take out an open letter in *USA Today*, with Michael Johnson pushing all that Herbalife had meant to people while blasting Ackman for his JC Penney and Valeant support, saying the companies had lost jobs.

In June, Herbalife unveiled a website called *The Real Bill Ackman*. "Bill Ackman has made some jaw-dropping mistakes," the home page read, offering people a chance to "read and watch what people are saying about Ackman's blunders."

The company didn't stop there.

On July 20, attorneys for Gibson Dunn, Herbalife's outside counsel, wrote to the US Attorney for the Southern District of New York and the SEC alleging "suspicious trading" ahead of a story in the *New York Post* that was critical of the company.[45]

The confidential memo, first reported in the *Huffington Post*, highlighted the purchase of ten thousand put options contracts purchased on June 25 in the minutes before the story appeared on the publication's website.[46] The contracts would become profitable if Herbalife shares fell over the next two months.

"If true, we believe that this is market manipulation," Gibson attorney Barry Goldsmith wrote. "To the extent that you have not done so already, we would, therefore, respectfully ask that you investigate who is responsible for these (and other) large, suspicious put option trades and what their connection is to Mr. Ackman and/or Pershing Square."[47]

A Pershing Square spokesperson called Herbalife's accusations "false," but there was no denying that Ackman was squarely on the defensive.

By the fall, Valeant shares had lost nearly 50 percent of their value, with most on Wall Street expecting even more pain in the weeks ahead.

"There is a lot of headline risk there for investors," said Mark McCabe of KDP Advisors Inc. "And the tip of the iceberg? You just don't know. So there will be more pain in the short term."[48]

Ackman did whatever he could to stop the bleeding. On November 5, he sent an email to Pearson, pledging his continued support.[49] The note read:

From: William A. Ackman
Sent: Thursday, November 05, 2015 2:03 PM
To: J. Michael Pearson
Subject: You
    Dear Mike,
    In light of recent press reports, I thought it would be helpful for me to communicate my thoughts on your leadership of Valeant. We share the board's confidence in you and your leadership.
    While I have strong views on Valeant's communication strategy and would have taken a different approach, you and the board should not interpret this as a negative reflection on my view of you as the CEO of the company. I understand that the company's counsel and the board may have different views on what can be communicated in light of regulatory scrutiny. This is indeed a judgment call, and I respect the board's decision in this regard.
    You are one of the most shareholder-oriented CEOs I know. You have assured me that you and the rest of the board are considering any and all alternatives that would benefit shareholders and other stakeholders. That is very comforting to us.

                                          Sincerely,
                                          Bill[50]

The damage was mounting. In the third quarter, Valeant alone caused a nearly 5 percent drag on Pershing's overall performance, and to make matters worse, Herbalife continued to wreak its own havoc on the portfolio. By November, Herbalife shares had climbed more than 50 percent on the year.

Michael Johnson hoped to keep the pain coming.

On November 12, 2015, in a letter that has never before been made public, Johnson wrote directly to the SEC's chairwoman, Mary Jo White, asking her to join the FBI and US Attorney in investigating Ackman and his associates for manipulating Herbalife's stock price.[51]

"For the past three years," Johnson wrote in the two-page letter, "Ackman has engaged in a multimillion dollar campaign to manipulate and drive down the price of Herbalife stock, including by repeatedly 'putting out false information' relating to Herbalife, both directly and indirectly and through his paid operatives. . . . I respectfully urge the SEC (to the extent that it is not already doing so) to investigate Mr. Ackman's sustained and well-financed campaign to introduce false information into the market and manipulate the price of Herbalife stock."[52]

As much as Ackman tried to hide it, there was no denying that the year had taken a toll on the usually unflappable investor. On December 15, a contrite Ackman wrote to his investors with the sober reality setting in.

"If the year finishes with our portfolio holdings at or around current values, 2015 will be the worst performance year in Pershing Square's history, even worse than 2008 during the financial crisis when the funds declined by 12% to 13%," Ackman wrote.[53]

There was a bright side, Ackman said, as redemptions from angry investors in the fund had been modest. Ackman could thank himself for that.

Years earlier, Ackman had protected against large drawdowns by putting an eight-quarter "gate" on his investors' money, meaning if anyone wanted to redeem, they had to give two years' notice, in writing. The move was made to help protect for moments like these. Ackman had also taken his firm public back in 2014, doing an initial public offering (IPO) in Amsterdam. Pershing Square Holdings, as Ackman called the new vehicle, raised billions of dollars in so-called permanent capital that could never be withdrawn.

Still, the success of the IPO couldn't mask the obvious.

Thanks to the precipitous drop in the value of Ackman's investments, Pershing's assets under management had fallen from $20 billion at the start of the year to near $15 billion by year's end, evidence of just how tough that stretch of 2015 really was.[54]

"Despite the substantial decline in the funds' performance from August to the present, our net redemptions were nominal at $39 million or 0.2% of capital for the third quarter, and $13 million or 0.1% in the fourth quarter," he said. "As a result, we have not been forced to raise cash as the portfolio declined, but have been able to be opportunistic. The recent substantial increase in our economic exposure to Valeant at recent lows in the stock is a good such example."[55]

Ackman also addressed Herbalife saying that despite the sharp rise in the stock, his confidence hadn't wavered. He had reason to be at least a little optimistic. That August, the FTC sued the energy drink distributor Vemma, accusing it of being an illegal pyramid scheme.[56] At the very least, Ackman figured regulators were finally zeroing in on the industry, if not Herbalife itself.

"We believe that Herbalife will ultimately be subject to regulatory action or will collapse because of fundamental deterioration in its business, which relies on the continual recruitment of new victims. During the quarter, the potential for regulatory action increased while business fundamentals deteriorated," he said.

Year to date, Pershing Square Holdings was down 20.8 percent, net of fees.[57]

Even worse, Valeant continued to struggle publicly.

On Christmas Day, the company said Pearson had gone on medical leave to be treated for severe pneumonia. Howard Schiller, the company's former CFO, would take over in the interim while Pearson got the treatment he needed.

In another letter to his investors, this time summing up the awful year as a whole, Ackman was matter-of-fact.

"2015 is a year we will not forget," he wrote. "The substantial majority of our portfolio companies made continued business progress despite currency headwinds and a weakening global economic environment. Yet, the Pershing Square funds suffered their greatest peak-to-trough decline and worst annual performance ever."

Ackman admitted the "important mistakes" he had made during the year, such as "missing the opportunity to trim or sell outright certain positions," including Valeant.

"When the stock price rose this summer to the mid-$200s per share, we did not sell as we believed it was probable the company would likely complete additional transactions that would meaningfully increase intrinsic value. In retrospect, this was a very costly mistake."

Ackman also mentioned another, less glamorous position that caused its own considerable carnage.

"Our most glaring, albeit small, unforced error was buying additional stock in Platform Specialty Products at $25 per share to assist the company in financing an acquisition," he said. "We paid too much as we assumed the new transaction would create substantial value, and because we assigned too much platform value to the company. Our assessment was incorrect as execution difficulties, operating issues, currency effects, and financing issues have destroyed rather than created value."

Ackman concluded by looking ahead to what a new year might hold under the title "Humility":

I have often stated that in order to be a great investor one needs to first have the confidence to invest without perfect information at a time when others are highly skeptical about the opportunity you are pursuing. This confidence, however, has to be carefully balanced by the humility to recognize when you are wrong. While no one here is enthusiastic about delivering our worst performance year in history in 2015, it certainly does a good job reinforcing the humility side of the equation that is necessary for long-term investment performance. In 2016, we would like to generate results that reinforce the confidence side of the equation. Humility and skepticism will help get us there.

Whether Ackman's stocks would cooperate was the real question. At least he could commiserate with Icahn, who was having his own problems.

Global commodity prices had crashed, sending the price for a barrel of crude oil from nearly $53 at the end of 2014 to $34.95 late in 2015. The slide, and that of natural gas's own pullback, weighed heavily on several of Icahn's large energy-related positions, including Chesapeake Energy.

In mid-2012, Icahn had gone long on Chesapeake Energy, amassing a 7.5 percent stake to become one of the company's biggest shareholders. Icahn had demanded seats on the board and in a letter to the directors called out CEO Aubrey McClendon—a legend in the natural gas industry—for taking too many risks.

"Rather than act as a source of stability and provide assurance to shareholders, this board has led the company through a highly publicized spate of corporate governance breakdowns while amassing an astounding funding gap," he wrote in a letter to the company, effectively putting it on notice.

It didn't take long for the company to capitulate.

Less than ten days after revealing the massive position, Icahn won his seats. Whether he could use that muscle to help turn the company around was another question, especially given the historic collapse in commodities. Natural gas prices tumbled, leaving Chesapeake with a cash shortfall.

By late 2015, Chesapeake had lost more than 70 percent of its value.

Icahn's other energy plays weren't doing much better.

On August 6, Icahn revealed an 8.8 percent stake in Cheniere Energy, worth $1.3 billion, calling shares undervalued. Shares quickly rose 6.5 percent on the news.[58] The company had lost money for more than twenty consecutive years but stood to capitalize on the growing business of shale gas, which it hoped to export.

Even though Icahn got rid of the company's founder, the turmoil from the commodities crash crushed Chenier's stock. In a little more than six months, Cheniere shares lost 50 percent of their value from where Icahn had bought in. Investments in Freeport-McMoRan and Hertz had also fallen hard.

Even Icahn's top horse, Apple, which had been a home-run investment, hadn't been cooperating lately. Icahn had revealed the position back in August 2013 when he tweeted, "We currently have a large position in APPLE. We believe the company to be extremely undervalued. Spoke to Tim Cook today. More to come."

The news had sent Wall Street into a full-fledged frenzy. Apple wasn't just any stock; it was the market's crown jewel and the biggest company on Earth by market cap. Back in September 2012, shares had hit an all-time intraday high of $705, but had recently fallen on hard times as investors began to worry about Apple's margins and the pace of iPhone sales. By January 2013, shares had fallen more than 35 percent from those highs, including a 12 percent plunge in a single day.[59] Headlines even began talking about Apple's stock as a "bubble."[60] By February, shares had lost a third of their value from the top and didn't look ready to stop anytime soon.

By the time the summer rolled around, Icahn had clearly seen enough and stepped in.

Shares quickly rallied 5 percent on the news of his position to $489.57, the highest level they'd been in six months. Trading volume spiked more than 300 percent as investors rushed to grab hold of Icahn's coattails. Four minutes later, Icahn sent a second tweet that read, "Had a nice conversation with [CEO] Tim Cook today. Discussed my opinion that a larger buyback should be done now. We plan to speak again shortly."

Icahn had called Cook before going public out of respect for the CEO and to give him a head's up about what was about to hit the tape. Cook was in a meeting at the time and called Icahn back when he got out, finding the investor to be direct but cordial. Icahn said he wanted a large buyback and in short order. Cook explained that Apple had begun returning money to shareholders in 2012 after a long period of not doing so, had already expanded the program earlier in the year, and remained committed to the process, though at its own pace.

The call ended with the two agreeing to stay in touch and Icahn suggesting they should get together for a face-to-face meeting.

On Tuesday, October 1, 2013, Icahn called in to my show to discuss the new investment, making it clear he wanted Cook to take action.

"I feel very strongly about this," Icahn said of his proposal that Apple buy back $150 billion in stock. "I can't promise you the stock will go up and I can't promise you they will do the buyback. But I can promise you that I'm not going away until they hear a lot more from me concerning this," he said.

Icahn said the two had had dinner at the investor's penthouse the night before, and he'd told Cook directly of his hopes for the company's growing cash hoard. Icahn liked to meet over a meal, especially in the friendly confines of his own apartment, where he could avoid being seen doing business and at the same time disarm his counterparts. Icahn may have had a tough-as-nails reputation as a dealmaker, but as a dinner partner he was charming and at ease as he enjoyed a good chef-cooked meal and a cocktail—or two.

The dinner was the first time the two had ever met, with Cook only knowing what he had heard in the media about the billionaire and his supersized backstory. He knew from what he'd read that Icahn could be rough—how rough was the question. Cook figured he'd better find out and decided to do some recon. He called other CEOs who'd crossed with Icahn in the past, with nearly every one of them warning him not to take the meeting. While Cook listened to the warnings, he came to a far different conclusion, believing there was no harm in hearing Icahn out. Icahn had already praised the company and Cook's stewardship during their initial phone conversation. How bad could it possibly be to meet in person?

On the evening of the dinner, Cook, Apple's then CFO, Peter Oppenheimer, and the Goldman Sachs banker Glen Sykes made their way up to Icahn's apartment in Midtown. After sitting for drinks in the living room, which overlooked Midtown's vast skyline, the party moved into Icahn's regal dining room to get down to business.

Sitting three across on one side of the large rectangular dining table, the men were joined by Icahn, along with his son, Brett, and David Schechter, the two men who ran the Icahn fund and had invested in Apple in the first place; they knew the company like the back of their hands.

The men talked through Apple's business, with Icahn and the boys focusing mostly on the company's balance sheet, reiterating why Apple should do a huge buyback of its stock. Cook said that he agreed with their assessment that the stock was undervalued, but that Apple already had a cadence on the buyback issue and wasn't about to deviate, even for an investor as well-respected and seasoned as Icahn.

Though the conversation was heavy on Apple's financials, it wasn't all standoffish, with Icahn telling his trademark stories about his many investments of the past decades while the men at the table laughed in unison. After two and a half hours, the evening wrapped with Icahn and Cook agreeing to keep talking.

Cook came away with a polar opposite view of the man than what he'd heard from the other CEOs, and he left convinced the two wouldn't have a major problem in the months ahead.

"I saw no harm at all in meeting with him and listening," Cook said. "On the macro point we totally agreed that Apple was undervalued. On the sub point we thought that buying back stock was good too. The one debate we had was about the amount over what period of time."

It was a debate Icahn wasn't about to let go of anytime soon.

"It's a no-brainer and it makes no sense for this company with their multiple being so low not to do a major major buyback," he said during the interview on my show. "And there's another reason that I mention, that I think might go forgotten, the fact that you can borrow money so cheaply today. I don't think we are going to see this again."

Later that month, Icahn sent a letter directly to Cook mentioning their warm dinner meeting and an even bigger stake.

"When we met, my affiliates and I owned 3,875,063 shares of Apple," wrote Icahn. "As of this morning, we owned 4,730,739 shares of Apple, an increase of 22% in position size, reflecting our belief the market continues to dramatically undervalue the company . . . "

"We want to be very clear that we could not be more supportive of you, the existing management team, the culture at Apple and the innovative spirit it engenders. The criticism we have as shareholders has nothing to do with your management leadership or operational strategy. Our criticism relates to one thing only: the size and timeframe of Apple's buyback program. It is obvious to us that it should be much bigger and immediate," he wrote.

Icahn had spent decades sparring with large companies, often urging them to buy back their own shares or add new board members, but Apple represented something different. It was the richest company on Earth, and even though Icahn could only do so much given Apple's size, he proved unafraid to take on the giant.

Icahn even pledged to hold onto his shares, saying in the letter, "There is nothing short-term about my intentions here."

On October 28, 2013, Apple reported strong earnings, but margins fell to 37 percent, down from 40 percent the prior year. Shares fell 4 percent after hours when the numbers hit.

For the year, Apple shares still closed up 5.5 percent.

But on January 28, 2014, Apple suffered its worst one-day stock performance in months, with shares dropping 8 percent as a result of disappointing iPhone sales. Thankfully for Icahn, the declines were short-lived.

On April 23, the company blew away earnings estimates and announced a motherload of initiatives that sent shares surging 8 percent. Cook said Apple was increasing its buyback to $90 billion, raising its dividend by 8 percent, and initiating a 7-for-1 stock split in June to make shares more accessible to a larger group of potential investors.

Icahn quickly praised the moves.

"Agree completely with $AAPL's increased buyback and extremely pleased with results. Believe we'll also be happy when we see new products," Icahn said in a tweet.[61]

That summer, shares topped $600 as the company—which looked on its way toward becoming the first business to top $700 billion in market cap—continued to make Icahn happy by buying back shares in huge numbers. By December, Apple had spent the most of any company in the S&P 500 on the move, according to FactSet, which tracks such data.[62] Apple shares would close the year up more than 40 percent, scoring Icahn and other company shareholders a windfall.

Icahn had even grander ambitions. On May 18, 2015, with shares trading near $130 apiece because of the split, Icahn sent another letter to Cook, only this time the correspondence came with a stunning prediction of how high shares could trade.

"After reflecting upon Apple's tremendous success, we now believe Apple shares are worth $240 today," he wrote.

Apple shares ended the day up 1 percent at $130.19, adding more than $8 billion in market cap.

Though Icahn's Apple trade was shaping up to be one of the greatest investments ever—he'd made $3.4 billion since first buying it—2015 was a letdown. The stock barely outpaced the S&P 500, and by October was suffering through its worst year since the financial crisis, as investors seemed skeptical the company could keep up the pace of its iPhone sales. Shares fell 10 percent in December alone, with some analysts saying even more downside was likely.[63]

Both Icahn and Ackman headed into 2016 wondering what was next for their most prized positions. Little did Ackman know that he would first have to prepare for things to get even worse.

14

THE FLUSH AND THE FEDS

With his Valeant position imploding and his portfolio enduring its worst year ever, Bill Ackman was growing impatient. Would the FTC *ever* take action on Herbalife?

On one February evening, Ackman decided to turn hope into action. At 9:22 p.m. on February 10, 2015, Ackman typed out an email directly to FTC Chairwoman Edith Ramirez, urging her to shut Herbalife down.[1]

He wrote:

Dear Chairwoman Ramirez,

I have refrained from contacting you as I know you have many important responsibilities. I have chosen to do so now as the time has come for the FTC to shut down Herbalife. Every day the FTC fails to act, is another day for Herbalife to recruit 5,000 new victims who will shortly lose their life savings, and their hopes and dreams of success, along with their relationships with family and friends. In the United States, these victims are principally members of the Latino community, often undocumented and incredibly vulnerable.

It has been more than three years since we brought these issues to the attention of the FTC. During this period nearly 6 million more victims have been recruited, and about the same number have dropped out, often because they have run out of money.

Herbalife's business has begun to fail as it appears it is having greater difficulty attracting recruits to replace failing victims. If the FTC does nothing, and Herbalife fails first, its failure will destroy the FTC's reputation as a protector of consumers. The SEC ignored Harry Markopoulos' warnings about Madoff and its reputation has never recovered. I would hate for the same thing to happen to the FTC.

I am told that you and your staff have been reluctant to act here because Pershing Square is short Herbalife stock and will benefit from the company's failure. While it is true that our investors will profit, I have committed to give away any profits I make person- ally to the communities that have been harmed. While we only have incurred losses to date, I have already made $50 million in grants to the Latino community: $25 million to Dream US for scholarships for undocumented immigrants, and $25 million to Robin Hood toward their recent immigrant and other programs for poor Latinos.

Yesterday, we released a 13 minute video which includes inter- views of recent Herbalife victims. On our website, www.factsabout herbalife.com, you can hear each of their stories in greater detail. I only ask that you take 13 minutes of your time to watch the first video. It will remind you that this is not about Carl Icahn, the larg- est beneficiary of Herbalife's scheme as its biggest shareholder, or Pershing Square, the largest short seller of Herbalife. It is about pro- tecting those that are being harmed by this scam. And yes, tomorrow, another 5,000 victims will be recruited to this pyramid scheme.

You, perhaps more than anyone else in the world, can stop this madness. I respectfully ask you to fulfill the responsibility you as- sumed as the FTC Chairwoman and protect these victims.

Thank you for giving this serious consideration.

Sincerely,
Bill

Just fifteen days later, desperation was turned into deliverance.

On February 25, shortly after the market closed for the day, Herb- alife revealed in a regulatory filing that it was in discussions with the

FTC about resolving the twenty-two-month probe. The company said possible outcomes included "a contested civil complaint, further discussions leading to a settlement which could include a monetary payment and other relief or the closure of these matters without action."[2]

What few knew at the time was that the FTC had approached Herbalife the prior December, sending the company a formal complaint that did everything *but* call it a pyramid scheme.

When CEO Michael Johnson read it, he was shocked, believing the inflammatory and damning allegations made by the FTC's attorneys were not only a hit on the company itself but also a personal attack on his stewardship. The forty-two-page document, listed as Case Number 2:16-cv-05217 and filed in the United States District Court Central District of California, said Herbalife had operated while engaging in "deceptive and unlawful acts and practices," singling out the claims distributors had made about the wealth they'd earned through selling the company's products.[3]

Page by page, it attacked the company's compensation model, which went to the heart of the pyramid-scheme charge, saying Herbalife "does not offer participants a viable retail-based business opportunity" and that it "incentivizes not retail sales, but the recruiting of additional participants."[4]

It claimed that "the overwhelming majority of Herbalife Distributors who pursue the business opportunity make little or no money and a substantial percentage lose money."[5]

In one such instance, the complaint targeted a testimonial video that had been included in every new distributor's "starter pack" until January 2013. Called "Design Your Life," the video told of the expensive cars and "opulent" mansions some had attained.

"A year exactly after I started the business, my checks went up to $7,080, and that was the month I went on vacation, and came back, and got that $7,000 check! So, it's been amazing," said one testimonial.[6]

"The first nine months of really getting going, I had made a quarter of a million dollars," said another in one of the eleven pages documenting what the FTC called "misleading income representations."[7]

Not only did the document attack the claims of exorbitant wealth, it said "the overwhelming majority of Herbalife Distributors who pursue the business opportunity do not make anything approaching full-time or even part-time minimum wage because promised retail sales to customers simply aren't there."

Further, it said, "Half of Distributors whom the Defendants designate as Sales Leaders (those who were eligible for discounts on their purchases) average less than $5 per month in net profit from retail alone, and half of these Distributors lose money."

The nutrition clubs Herbalife had said were neighborhood meeting places to discuss health and wellness were, according to the FTC, "primarily a tool for recruiting new members rather than as a method for profitably retailing Herbalife products."[8]

The regulator summed up its case with four counts of violations of Section 5 of the FTC act, including; Unfair Practices, Income Misrepresentations, False or Unsubstantiated Claims of Income from Retail Sales, and something called Means and Instrumentalities, which covered the "false and misleading" promotional materials new members had been given.[9]

"Fuck them," Johnson said after reading it.

Alan Hoffman, the PR man who had been a federal prosecutor before the stints with Vice President Biden and PepsiCo, read the complaint too and thought it was just plain nuts—far from the company he had joined the previous fall.

Openly fuming, Johnson knew he had two choices—begin negotiating a settlement with the government or go to court and fight the case before a jury. Johnson preferred the latter, as did Des Walsh, the company's ever-optimistic president and the closest liaison to Herbalife's important distributor base—the ones who'd be most affected by the FTC's demands.

Icahn wanted to fight too, telling Johnson he thought Donald J. Trump was likely to become the next president of the United States and would usher in a more sympathetic regulatory environment that could benefit Herbalife.

Ackman barely had time to celebrate the news. Valeant was once again front and center for the wrong reasons. Shares had dropped into the low $80s after yet another attack by Mrs. Clinton on drug pricing—this time targeting Valeant directly, putting Ackman back on his heels.

On March 1, he once again turned to the media to try to put a positive spin on Valeant.

"We expect much of the uncertainty will be resolved in the relative short term, hopefully over the next few weeks," he told me in a live interview.[10]

The timing couldn't have been worse. Just two weeks later, on March 15, Pearson told Wall Street analysts during a conference call that it was cutting its outlook and wouldn't file its annual report with the SEC. If that weren't enough, Valeant incorrectly stated in a press release the amount of its adjusted profits, which only added to the uncertainty.[11]

This time, investors simply threw in the towel.

Valeant shares fell 51.5 percent to $33.51 in a flush few had ever witnessed. That day's slide alone cost Ackman $1 billion on paper.

Desperate to do something, Ackman sent a letter to his investors as the stock was cratering.

"We are going to take a much more proactive role at the company to protect and maximize the value of our investment," Ackman wrote. "We continue to believe that the value of the underlying business franchises that comprise Valeant was worth multiples of the current price. Getting to those values, however, will require a restoration of shareholder confidence in the management and governance of the company."[12]

Some were now wondering whether Valeant, whose stock had now lost 90 percent of its value, could even survive.

On March 18, Pearson tried to quell the concerns, telling his staff the company wasn't going bankrupt.

"I want to apologize directly to each of you for the distractions this intense scrutiny is causing you," he wrote.[13]

The apology was little consolation to Ackman, whose Pershing Square Holdings continued to suffer thanks to the nearly 60 percent plunge in Valeant alone. Through the end of April 2016, the vehicle was down 18 percent, with at least eight of his positions in the red for the first quarter.[14]

Whether Herbalife could provide a boost was far from certain. Even the company wasn't sure of what was going to happen. With the debate over whether to fight or settle raging behind the scenes, Herbalife and the FTC began secret negotiations, with company representatives making dozens of visits to Washington, convinced the commission was preparing to call Herbalife a pyramid scheme.

On May 2, Ackman let it be known during a live interview with me where he was placing his bets.

"If you find yourself as a Herbalife employee today, my advice is that you should leave the company because this is not going to be a good thing on your resume," he said snidely. "I'd go find another job."[15]

Rarely had Ackman directly addressed Herbalife's actual employees, whose actions and futures were ultimately at the center of the debate. But Herbalife's Hoffman was waiting and quickly shot back in a statement: "After spending hundreds of millions of dollars and having a negative return on his investment, maybe it is just time for Bill to move on."

Then, on May 5, Herbalife gave Ackman and everyone else a better idea of where things stood, both with the business and with the FTC's investigation. The company reported better than expected earnings, raised its guidance for the year, and revealed it was closer than ever to a resolution.

"While there are a number of open issues, those discussions have progressed to an advanced stage and the range of outcomes now includes litigation or settlement," the company said in a statement. "If a settlement is reached with the FTC, it would likely include injunctive and other relief as well as a monetary payment with our best estimate of a payment being $200 million."[16]

Shares surged on the news to more than $66 per share,[17] as investors figured a hefty fine, even in the hundreds of millions, was way better than a shutdown.

Ackman tried to do his part to make sure the punishment was more severe.

On May 24, at 12:14 p.m., Ackman again emailed the FTC's Ramirez to press his case.[18]

"Herbalife will never change its business model regardless of what it promises the FTC it will do in a settlement," he wrote in one passage. "The fact that the board keeps Johnson on as CEO speaks to how pervasive the corruption is at the board level."[19]

As summer fast approached, everyone, including Ackman, wondered when a final decision would actually come.

Herbalife tried its best to tip the scales in its favor.

The company met with former FTC economists and lawyers, producing charts and documents to support its case. It held face-to-face meetings with each of the three individual FTC commissioners in an attempt to make its case and, hopefully, sway their votes.

In the meantime, Herbalife's litigators prepared for a fight in court.

The company had even prepared a marketing campaign to surround the battle, should one occur, producing commercials and print ads ready to run in international newspapers and on television. Since only 20 percent of Herbalife sales were in the United States, the company knew it had to protect its turf across the globe.

The strategy of going to trial was risky. Going through a long and protracted spectacle could not only hurt business, it could also open up a can of worms during the discovery process. Did Herbalife really want hours of those disturbing testimonial videos, even if they were outdated, playing in a courtroom for the world to see?

There were intense battles within the executive ranks over what to do—a debate that continued outside among Herbalife's cadre of lawyers and paid consultants. Ultimately, the company decided that settling and trying to move forward was the best strategy.

With the decision made, Herbalife CFO John DeSimone, along with Hoffman the PR man, General Counsel Mark Friedman, and his deputy, Henry Wang, traveled to Washington on the weekend of July 9 for last-minute discussions with the FTC. CEO Johnson remained back in Los Angeles to prepare for what could be a turbulent week ahead.

With a settlement deal in hand, the Herbalife team returned to California to wait for word of an official announcement.

Whether word got to Ackman beforehand that a decision was getting closer, or it was just a coincidence, on July 13, Ackman let go one last barrage of emails to the FTC's Ramirez.

At 3:45 p.m., in a two-page note, Ackman said, "I have been told that the FTC is reluctant to litigate in light of Herbalife's high powered lawyers, but I am puzzled as to how our taxpayer financed government does not have the resources internally and/or externally to shutter a blatant fraud. This fraud cannot be allowed to continue. It is an embarrassment to our country."[20]

At exactly 12:30 a.m., Ackman sent another email, this time about Herbalife's distributors.

"Herbalife cannot survive without its distributors fraudulent conduct. As such, the company is highly incentivized to promote rather than police this kind of conduct," he wrote. "Until the incentives change, Herbalife and its distributors will never change."[21]

Ackman concluded:

"Herbalife should be shut down for being a pyramid scheme. The fraud is massive, blatant and ongoing. Litigating to stop Herbalife will also have a dramatically positive effect on the behavior of other MLM's whose distributors are operating fraudulently."[22]

Finally, forty minutes later, at 12:40:12 a.m., Ackman made one last push, urging Ramirez to watch the videos Pershing Square had made to prove its case that distributors were repeatedly making false claims.

"One last thought," he wrote. "If you watch the videos, you will note that the recruiting techniques of each distributor in each video are effectively the same. They use the same terminology and phrase-ology. They tell the same stories. We have yet to find one which em-phasizes retail sales over recruiting."

Later that day, Herbalife's board of directors convened and approved the agreement with the FTC, believing there was no way the regulators would go public on a Friday in the middle of the summer, especially with the Republican National Convention about to convene in Cleveland.

But at 7 p.m. that Thursday evening, Pacific time, Herbalife's counsel got a surprise call from one of the attorneys with the FTC. The news was stunning. The FTC said it was ready to go public and planned to announce the decision in the morning.

Just before 7 a.m. Eastern time on Friday morning, the *Wall Street Journal* reporter David Benoit emailed Hoffman, saying he had the scoop and was prepared to report the news. He also called Ackman, who was home getting ready for work.

"He says we're hearing and we're going to write that Herbalife settled with the FTC for 200 million bucks and found them not to be a pyramid scheme," said Ackman. "I said OK 200 million bucks . . . OK . . . there's no way the FTC found them not to be a pyramid scheme. Do not run with that story. And they ran with the story."

At 7:43 a.m., the first headline appeared on the newswires. It was from Dow Jones, which owns the *Wall Street Journal.*

"Herbalife, FTC Expected to Announce Settlement Friday—Sources" read the flash.

"Herbalife to Pay $200M over Claims of Misrepresentation—Sources" read another. Four minutes later, the final one hit—the one Ackman knew would be crushing to his crusade.

"FTC Determines Herbalife is not a pyramid scheme."

Herbalife shares surged past $70 a share in premarket trading to a two-year high.

I was in Manhattan that morning, cohosting *Squawk Box,* when the news broke. I did the first thing I could think of—I grabbed the phone and called Ackman.

"Did you see it?" I asked, frantically hoping for an on-the-record comment at that very moment.

"I'm reading it now," he said.

"I need something from you, NOW!" I exclaimed—the desperation in my voice evident.

"I'll call you back in five minutes," said Ackman as he abruptly hung up to finish reading the complaint.

Five minutes later, Ackman called back.

"The headline is bullshit," he said. "It's wrong. . . . It's totally wrong. Did you read the complaint?! Did you read it?! . . . They didn't say it's *not* a pyramid scheme."

Technically, Ackman was right. At 8:30 a.m., the FTC put out a press release detailing its settlement with the company, making no mention of the words "pyramid scheme."

The document was damning to say the least.

"Literally, the FTC confirmed every one of our allegations," Ackman said. "Every one."

Herbalife had agreed to a two-hundred-million-dollar judgment—the largest fine ever imposed by the Commission, money that would go to customers who'd bought product for the business opportunity and lost money as a result. It also mandated that Herbalife change its compensation structure to reward people based on whether participants actually sold products, not on whether they simply bought the products themselves.

"This settlement will require Herbalife to fundamentally restructure its business so that participants are rewarded for what they sell, not how many people they recruit," Chairwoman Edith Ramirez wrote in the three-page release outlining the agreement.[23]

"Herbalife is going to have to start operating legitimately, making only truthful claims about how much money its members are likely to make, and it will have to compensate consumers for the losses they have suffered as a result of what we charge are unfair and deceptive practices."[24]

Shortly after the FTC press release hit the wires, Herbalife released its own, with CEO Michael Johnson claiming victory and sounding defiant.

"The settlements are an acknowledgement that our business model is sound and underscores our confidence in our ability to move forward successfully, otherwise we would not have agreed to the terms," Johnson said, almost thumbing his nose in the FTC's face.[25]

For Ackman, the news was a stunning blow.

He'd held out hope since the beginning, spent tens of millions while pledging to go to "the ends of the Earth" to see to Herbalife's demise. Now the company he had called a "criminal enterprise" was allowed to keep operating.

Behind the scenes, the Pershing Square team broke into two factions—the media reach, led by Francis McGill, the in-house PR guy, and another group to read through the documents. Ackman told McGill to reach out to news organizations, hoping to get journalists to focus on what the FTC actually said in the complaint, rather than on what it didn't. They also drafted a statement.

"We expect that once Herbalife's business restructuring is fully implemented, these fundamental structural changes will cause the pyramid to collapse," Ackman said afterward.[26]

Ackman was so convinced he immediately shorted more shares, at $72 apiece.

"It was like the most profitable trade we had in Herbalife stock for some time," he laughed.

Icahn didn't exactly see it that way. Just after 10 a.m., the investor released his own statement and trolled Ackman directly.

"The FTC settlement announced today, coming after a two-year investigation also concluded that Herbalife is not a pyramid scheme—a conclusion that obviously vindicates our research and conviction," he said. "While Bill Ackman and I are on friendly terms, we have agreed to disagree (vehemently) on this subject. Simply stated the shorts have been completely wrong on Herbalife. I have the greatest confidence in Herbalife's CEO, Michael Johnson, and the entire management team, who have skillfully led the company through adversity, including holding firm against a high-profile PR campaign by Bill Ackman where it was alleged more than once that the company would be shut down."[27]

With investors on Wall Street clearly betting with Icahn and the company, another key voice weighed in on what the outcome meant for Herbalife and its shareholders.

Tim Ramey, the bullish analyst at Pivotal Research who had sparred with Ackman throughout his short campaign and had had a $90 price target on the stock for months, called it a profound victory.

"The deal is consistent with our long-held view that while the company had had certain historic weaknesses in its compliance and oversight, it is a legal and ethical business model with the best-in-industry compliance function today," Ramey said in his note. "This is a total victory for Herbalife shareholders and a total defeat for the short camp."[28]

Several months later, Ramey remained steadfast in his belief that the forced changes wouldn't hurt Herbalife's longevity.

"I think what the detractors will find is that the new paradigm will not detract from the profitability of the model or detract from the growth of the company. It will still be a growth company with very strong operating metrics."

But while Johnson and the others may have publicly declared victory, within the hallways of Herbalife's Los Angeles headquarters, there was no celebration or champagne corks flying through the air. The harshly worded FTC complaint had taken its toll on the company's psyche.

When specifics of the deal began to trickle out before 8 a.m., Herbalife knew it would spend the day attempting to control the message. Though Johnson and Icahn had made their defiant statements to the press, as if they'd read a different press release than the scathing and inflammatory one the FTC put out, big changes would have to be made.

Beyond the $200 million fine, Herbalife would finally be forced to bifurcate its membership into "Preferred Members," or those who signed up to get a discount on what they bought, and "Distributors," those who were pursuing the business opportunity.

Beginning in May 2017, Herbalife's two hundred and fifty thousand distributors in the United States would be required to get receipts for what they sold to prove that at least 80 percent of the products went to actual customers or were used for personal consumption.

The new standards didn't end there.

To make sure people who bought Herbalife products knew what they were truly getting into, every new member who signed up on the company's website would have to say on the spot whether they were buying the product for themselves or to be a distributor. To make sure the company complied with the new regulations, the FTC said Herbalife would have to pay for an independent compliance auditor (ICA) to monitor the changes for seven years.

The settlement also prohibited Herbalife from misrepresenting potential or likely earnings or claiming that members could "quit their job" to enjoy a lavish lifestyle.

The news was sobering.

Though Herbalife could finally move on after two years under the government's microscope, the company disagreed with each and every charge made in the complaint.

Johnson believed he'd cleaned up the company and that Herbalife had real customers and could easily prove it. In hindsight, if the company was guilty of anything, Johnson admitted, it was that it hadn't changed the way Herbalife referred to its members immediately after David Einhorn had asked his pointed and probing questions about sales back in May 2012.

As for Ackman, he remained convinced the new restrictions would ultimately cause the company to crumble, even feeling vindicated by how tough the FTC's language was. Even so, he was left to question whether his strategy had been a mistake from the start—whether going public in the first place had hurt his cause.

"Look, I can't know for sure if we would have gone directly to the FTC would they have done something and it would have become a big, high-profile thing, I don't know," Ackman said. "It was dangerous to be short this stock without the news out there. One of the things that mitigated our risk, I thought, was making the short thesis public. We didn't anticipate that Carl would come in and legitimize the bull case and make it into a short squeeze."

Ackman had made it clear by shorting even more stock that he wasn't ready to give up. The only issue was whether Icahn would follow through on his longtime threat to squeeze Bill Ackman until he crushed him.

15

FINALE OR FAKEOUT?

The thought of Icahn taking Herbalife private had hung in the air from nearly the beginning of the battle, ever since the investor had mentioned the "mother of all short squeezes" back in January 2013 in the infamous brawl with Ackman. Icahn had broached the subject several times with Michael Johnson, both on the phone and in person, with both men knowing nothing could happen until the FTC had finished its investigation. Now that it had, speculation was rampant about whether Icahn would actually follow through.

Few had even considered that Icahn might have another idea up his sleeve altogether—to take *himself* out rather than the company.

On Wednesday, August 3, 2016, Richard B. Handler, the chairman and CEO of the investment bank Jefferies, was walking on Manhattan's Upper East Side when his mobile phone rang. It was Icahn, asking him to drop by his office on the corner of East 59th Street and 5th Avenue for a chat.

Handler had done business with Icahn for years, often trading big blocks of stock for the investor, so it wasn't uncommon to be summoned for a meeting. The men often spoke several times a week to talk about the markets or the world at large. Icahn enjoyed the exercise, often sitting back in his large leather desk chair overlooking Central Park while spitting out names in his investment book for Handler to assess on the fly.

This time was no different, with Icahn shuttling through five or six stocks in his investment book, when he suddenly paused for a moment and mentioned Herbalife. The minute the name spilled off Icahn's lips, Handler sensed something was out of the ordinary. He'd been through enough of these sessions over the years to know the ins and outs of Icahn's inflection—the tone and pitch of his voice and how to read it. Handler instantly knew something sounded different. He also knew that Icahn could be cagey, even with those he liked and trusted.

Icahn then asked a question that only confirmed Handler's immediate suspicions. "Do I take the money and run?" Icahn asked, clearly fishing for some feedback from his friend. The two began brainstorming about a possible trade—how, and more important *if*, one would even work. "Let me see what I can put together," Handler said, knowing it wasn't going to be the easiest transaction he'd ever done. Icahn's stake was huge—seventeen million shares—and Handler knew it would take some creativity and the right trading partner. If Icahn was going to sell, which was still very much unclear, a prospective buyer would have to be willing to swallow the whole position at full price. If there was one thing Icahn didn't do, it was take a discount.

With his mind turning about a trade, Handler left, headed downtown to his apartment, and thought of the one person who could potentially help make it happen: Bill Ackman. Since Handler didn't have Ackman's number in his cell phone, he called a banker back at the office and got it. The two had crossed paths once at an event but barely knew each other, with Handler only knowing what he'd heard and read.

"Can we get together?" Handler texted Ackman the next evening in hopes of scheduling a quick face-to-face meeting. Ackman was out of pocket, traveling in Italy when the message appeared. He asked if the meeting could wait until the following week.

"It really can't," Handler said, and the two agreed to speak by phone instead.

"You and I don't know each other," Handler said to Ackman when they finally connected. "But I know Carl. I have no order, and this whole thing could be a pipe dream, but you have a problem with Herbalife, and I know the one guy who can get you out," said Handler, alluding to Icahn. Stressing that the entire trade could fall apart at any time, Handler told Ackman the ground rules for making a deal. Icahn would sell his entire 17 million share block, worth more than $1.1 billion, with Ackman agreeing to buy nothing less than half of the position.[1] Jefferies would then buy a quarter, with Handler taking the other piece to sell to institutions that might be interested in getting involved.

But with Herbalife shares trading in the low $60s at the time, Ackman balked and countered with an offer of near $50 a share. Now Handler was pissed.

"Don't even start with me!" Handler said, getting more and more irritated with Ackman's attempted negotiation.

"How little can I buy?" Ackman then asked.

"HALF!!" screamed Handler into the phone, making it clear the size wasn't up for debate.

Handler also didn't have time to screw around. Since Icahn held a large block of stock, he was limited in how much stock he could buy and sell without his having to tell the world he was doing so. There was also a loophole in the law. Since Herbalife's trading volume had spiked above a required threshold after the company's settlement with the FTC, Icahn could sell in one fell swoop without anyone knowing. There was another issue too. Since Icahn was an insider and served on Herbalife's board of directors, he was required to wait until after earnings to make a move, further compressing the time frame of what he could do and when. Since Herbalife had reported earnings on August 3, Icahn only had eight days to consummate a trade—and that's if he even wanted to, which remained uncertain.[2]

Ackman had his own timing issues. As much as he wanted to get Icahn out, he was also restricted lest he risk running afoul of the SEC, which could cause a delay in the trade if not kill it altogether. It wasn't long before the whole thing looked like the longshot Handler had predicted in the beginning. There was also the issue of buyers. Handler wasn't having much luck finding any, probably because anyone interested likely figured Herbalife shares would sink the moment Icahn's ejection became public. Nonetheless, Handler continued to pound the phones while making it clear to the Jefferies market-maker who was trying to arrange the trade to keep him informed up to the minute.

Sensing this could be his only real opportunity to get Icahn out, Ackman was growing impatient. "Where are we? Where are we?" he asked Handler several times over the course of the next couple of days.

Though Handler was more convinced than ever that Icahn wanted to do a trade—even if he hadn't put in an official order to do so—he was getting little traction in putting together a deal, especially since Icahn was unwilling to take a haircut on the price. The deadline to do a trade came and went without an agreement. Finally, on August 25, according to *Fortune*, Handler and his market-maker found enough buyers for 11 million of Icahn's shares at $51.50 a share, well below the stock's current price. Icahn said no, effectively killing the prospects for a trade.[3]

Ackman wasn't about to walk away quietly.

The next day, on August 26, the *Wall Street Journal* broke the story that Icahn had "mulled" selling his stake to a group of investors that included Ackman.[4] Shares dropped 7 percent on the report, to $57.60, with most assuming Ackman was the one who'd leaked the news to the *Journal* in hopes the stock would fall. He then decided to go public himself with the details of how the whole thing had come together in the first place.

Later that morning, Ackman dialed into CNBC's *Squawk Box* program to confirm he'd been contacted by Jefferies about buying a "few million" shares from Icahn's position.

"I think he knows this is toast," Ackman said of Icahn's alleged intent to sell his stake. "This is a confidence game. Carl is what creates the confidence in the company. If Carl sells, it can accelerate the demise of the company. I think the thing is over, and over quickly. The sooner he sells the better."[5]

When Icahn heard what Ackman had done on TV, he was livid. He hadn't given anyone at Herbalife a head's up that he was even considering getting out. Herbalife had heard rumors all week that something might be up but didn't know exactly what. Eventually, there was enough smoke that Herbalife's public relations executive, Alan Hoffman, pulled Michael Johnson into his office, and they nervously called Icahn's right-hand man, Keith Cozza, to ask him directly if Icahn was a seller. Cozza said he had no reason to believe Icahn was, but also stressed that his boss could decide to do anything at a moment's notice. Once Ackman went boasting on TV only days later that he had been contacted about Icahn's stake, Hoffman called Johnson at home to tell him what had just happened and what Ackman had claimed. Blindsided, Johnson then called Icahn, who told him to call back at the close of trading on Friday.

Herbalife executives spent the next several hours stewing over what Icahn might be up to—watching the clock and waiting for 4 p.m. Eastern to arrive—the time the market closed.

At 4 p.m. sharp, Michael Johnson, Alan Hoffman, CFO John DeSimone, President Des Walsh, COO Rich Goudis, Executive Vice President Robert C. Levy, and Herbalife General Counsel Mark J. Friedman dialed Icahn's office. Icahn's assistant answered and patched the group in. Icahn said hello, then said to hold. After several minutes Icahn came back on the phone and said, "Well guys, I hate to tell you this, but I sold everything."

Silence took over the room as the men looked at each other, stunned by what Icahn had said.

"Just kidding," he then said, as everyone, including Icahn himself, broke into laughter. "Not only didn't I sell, but I bought two million more shares," Icahn revealed. "Lemme tell you my thoughts," he continued, reading what appeared, to Hoffman, to be a statement. "What do you guys think of that?" Icahn asked.

"Thanks for the vote of confidence," a relieved Johnson exclaimed.

Icahn then released the statement publicly, which ripped Ackman once again.

"Ackman may be a smart guy," Icahn wrote, "but he has clearly succumbed to the same dangerous (and sometimes fatal) malady that afflicts many investors—he's developed a very bad case of 'Herbalife obsession.' It amazes me that a guy who hasn't any knowledge of my internal investment thinking believes he is in a position to go on television to tell the world what I AM thinking! Amazing! He has no right to do so, and even worse, I'm sure his unsubstantiated, obsessive comments, especially about Herbalife, have cost investors a great deal of money over the last few years."[6]

Icahn also claimed that he had never put in a direct sell order in the first place, which a person at Jefferies later confirmed. It was only after Ackman went on TV earlier that morning that Icahn became incensed and decided to stick it to his nemesis once more by buying more stock rather than selling.

"I went on to explain to make clear why we were buying. I thought it was bad for people to think we were trying to cover. That's why I went on TV. In retrospect, it was probably a mistake," Ackman said.

Later that evening, once Jefferies corroborated Icahn's story that he never took a bid, Ackman called Handler, who was up in Westchester, New York, screaming that he'd soiled his reputation publicly and threatening to release the original texts discussing a possible trade. Handler called Ackman a liar for downplaying the size of Icahn's stake he was interested in and told Ackman the whole thing was "an act of war."

The two men finally settled down, with Ackman eventually offering an olive branch. He invited Handler and his wife to the US Open tennis tournament to sit courtside, which they did, in full view of a global television audience for four hours.

On September 13, 2016, Icahn showed up at the Pierre Hotel for CNBC's Delivering Alpha conference, where I asked him onstage about the whole ordeal. Icahn was coy, refusing to answer a question on whether he'd entertained selling out of Herbalife. He did reveal that he'd gotten permission to load up even further on Herbalife shares if he wanted to.

"I am telling you that I'm not just playing games buying the stock," he said, "Here's a little secret for your show. I've asked permission—I've gone to the FTC to get accelerated treatment for the right to go to 50 percent, up to 50 percent, which is going way up. I only have the right to go to 35."

He then addressed Ackman.

"So, Ackman loves to think that I'm going away. But how do you go out on TV and say what a man thinks to someone else? I think it's absurdity."

I then asked Icahn about the endgame—how this Wall Street war would end, and whether he'd take the company private once and for all, leaving Ackman beaten and bloodied.

"I don't have any stated intention to do it," said Icahn, leaving the door open to changing his mind. "It's something I have thought about. Doesn't mean I will. And I think there are other people that might. I think Herbalife is certainly a candidate to go private."

Such a move was easier said than done, though, something Icahn knew as well as anyone. With Herbalife's market cap near $5 billion at the time, Icahn would have to put up the value of his 25 percent stake as well as deploy billions of dollars in additional capital from either his own coffers or from a lender like a bank or private equity fund. Given Herbalife's already high amount of debt and uncertain future following the FTC settlement, some, like Ackman, questioned whether the company could find a willing partner. Of course, Icahn could also find other large shareholders to join the effort. This was certainly a possibility, given the sizeable stakes both Stiritz and Michael Johnson owned, and the fact that the CEO would love nothing more than to participate in Ackman's ultimate undoing.

Ackman had other worries. On December 7, 2016, he released a new letter to his investors in which he revealed that Pershing Square Holdings was down 13.5 percent on the year, net of fees. He'd sold out of positions in Canadian Pacific and the animal health company Zoetis and had taken a new 9.9 percent stake in the fast-casual restaurant chain Chipotle at an average price of $405 per share. Ackman was betting that the company, which had been decimated by a customer revolt after an E. coli scare, could rebound.[7]

He also addressed what he termed "positive developments" at Valeant. Pershing's holdings of Valeant stock remained a significant weight on the firm's performance.

Ackman also announced a new "long-term incentive program" at Pershing to overhaul the way employees were being compensated. It was a way to maintain talent by rewarding long-standing employees with something other than a share of the firm's net profits.

"We recognize that the recent period had been a difficult one for our investors," Ackman wrote. "We are extremely appreciative of your support and patience."

In March 2017, Ackman had finally lost his own patience with Valeant, selling his entire stake of 27.2 million shares for a $3 billion loss. The investment would go down as one of the worst losses in hedge-fund history. Ackman said the investment—and the stunning loss—deeply affected him and those who relied on his decision making.

"Number one, I don't like losing money, but even worse is losing other people's money. You lose money yourself you feel like a jerk. You lose other people's money you feel way worse," he said. "I've never experienced anything like this. This was a significant moment, and it just makes me that much more motivated and vigilant. In this business you have to stay incredibly vigilant. The most successful people I know, every one of them had a moment. It's hard to think of a successful investor who hasn't had a major moment. You hope never to have it. This was mine."

Ackman, whose assets under management had sagged to $11 billion from a high of near $20 billion in 2015, says redemption requests among his firm's clients have been "basically normal," with the real fallout from his public losses coming via his ability to attract new investors and their hard-earned dollars.

In some ways, Bill Ackman has once again become a "show me" story; he appears to have accepted that. And while he now seems more introspective than I can remember, genuinely moved by the Valeant disaster and its impact on his employees, the firm, and his own reputation, Ackman's signature confidence hasn't waned or wavered. He says he believes he'll stage an epic comeback to prove everyone writing his obituary wrong.

"The life expectancy of a hedge fund is probably three years," Ackman said. "We've been in business now for thirteen years, and Buffett, the best, has been around for fifty years, so we're still early. We're in inning two and a half. The key is learning from your mistakes. I've had very difficult moments before. I had a very difficult moment in 2002 when we were short MBIA and the stock was going up every day, the company was all over us, and they convinced Spitzer to investigate us. That was a tough moment, and I said at the time this is a great experience. I will learn a lot from this. And I launched Pershing after that. We're going to come back. We'll be fine."

Michael Johnson is also looking ahead. He retired from Herbalife in June 2017 after twelve years. At one last gathering before his departure, twelve hundred of the company's distributors traveled to Charlotte, North Carolina, to raise money for the Herbalife Foundation. They brought in $1.6 million, with part of the evening serving as a tribute to Johnson's tenure and stewardship.

Johnson's team played a video during dinner set to the Andra Day anthem, "Rise Up." It depicted Johnson's journey and the challenges of the last many years. As tears welled in the eyes of the faithful, Johnson walked onto the stage, overcome with emotion and barely able to speak. He had taken Herbalife to a place that once seemed unthinkable, while managing to outlast one of the more formidable threats any corporate executive has ever had to encounter.

He'd come face-to-face with some of Wall Street's most ferocious wolves, and survived.

CODA: BIG THOUGHTS

Bill Ackman and Carl Icahn's war over Herbalife, which amazingly still rages, leaves many important questions, not the least of which is, who won?

While history's scorecard—and, for that matter, Wall Street's—will show that Carl Icahn got the better of Bill Ackman in this round, identifying a true victor proves much more complicated. There's no doubt that Icahn has profited handsomely from his investment in Herbalife. Perhaps you could say that Herbalife's legions of loyal shareholders are better off given the stock's rise, but what lives have truly been improved? Could all that money have been spent elsewhere, especially money from two men whose philanthropic endeavors are a key part of their personal fabrics?

Then there's the impact on Herbalife itself—its employees, customers, and contractors worldwide.

Though the government stopped short of shutting the company down, as Ackman would have liked, does it mean that he was entirely wrong in his assessment of the business? Herbalife is undoubtedly a different company than it was prior to the settlement with the FTC. Changing the business model was no doubt disruptive. Revenues fell by around 5 percent in 2017 and earnings declined in tandem, perhaps evidence that meeting the new guidelines won't be easy. Herbalife is no longer the hyper-growth business it once was, though some believe the company's challenges are beginning to stabilize and that even better days are ahead. It's been in business for thirty-plus years, has millions of loyalists around the global, and has truly changed some people's lives for the better. Still, some bears on Wall Street argue that Herbalife's comeuppance is coming sooner or later. Time will tell.

I'm often asked what I think—is Herbalife a legitimate business or not? My answer is undoubtedly more nuanced than some of you would like. I genuinely believe that the company has changed from its swashbuckling early years and that it has real customers around the world who use its products because they like them. Some do buy the shakes and teas and other things to make a little money on the side or to share with friends. I know because I met them and talked to them and heard their stories firsthand. At the same time, it's also possible that some people might still be using recruitment alone as their motivation to make money, preying on the naive. More broadly, I do often wonder what the lasting impact of this epic battle will be on the investment community as a whole. When pondering this question, I go back to what one famous hedge-fund manager told me in the hours that followed the now infamous brawl between Icahn and Ackman.

Late in the evening on January 25, 2013, when I finally had a chance to lie down and consider what had taken place only a handful of clock turns earlier, I emailed this particular person and asked who they thought had won.

The answer I got was striking and, frankly, unexpected.

"They both lost," he said, referring to the unflattering spotlight the episode was likely to shine on the business itself and ultimately on its deep-pocketed participants.

The bigger issue—perhaps far greater than what specifically happens to Herbalife from here forward—is the impact activist investors will have on our corporate culture in the decades ahead. Most of today's so-called Master Class of activists undoubtedly do good work, improving the businesses they've targeted and bringing a basket of fresh ideas into the boardroom. Still, it's unclear who actually benefits beyond the shareholders of these companies and the activists themselves. Do employees reap their own rewards throughout the hard-fought corporate struggle? A *BuzzFeed News* story that covered the fallout from another high-profile activist campaign cited a study from a few years ago that critics might say casts doubt on that question.

According to a 2013 paper titled "The Real Effects of Hedge Fund Activism: Productivity, Asset Allocation, and Industry Concentration," "employees of target firms experience a reduction in work hours and stagnation in wages despite an increase in labor productivity."[1] In other words, some experts say, while the activist investor may in fact cause positive changes that improve a company's performance, the actual rank-and-file employee may not feel those changes in their own experience.

Herbalife's shareholders have clearly done well, as the stock has remained resilient. Only the years ahead will decide whether there's a lasting taint on the business itself, one that employees will have to live with.

Good food for thought as we wonder who and where the so-called wolves will bite next.

ADDENDUM

On November 1, 2017, nearly five years after first going public with his $1 billion Herbalife short, Bill Ackman revealed during a live television interview on CNBC that he had modified the structure of his position once again in what some observers said was one step closer to closing out the embattled position once and for all. Ackman said he had converted the stake into put options, which would still pay off if the stock collapsed, but would eliminate the risk of being "squeezed" by Carl Icahn. "There's been a perception that Pershing Square will have to cover our position, and we've just taken that way," Ackman told me during a phone conversation following his TV appearance. But while Ackman may have inched toward the finish line, he made it clear that he wasn't ready to concede defeat. Ackman said his thesis on the company hadn't changed one bit, but that the circumstances around the investment had. "We still think it's a good investment," he said. "The fundamentals are deteriorating. They're actually getting worse, but the stock won't go down."

The truth is that Herbalife was no longer worth Ackman's time or money. He'd been busy on a new investment in his portfolio—one he'd hoped would make a splash and help spark a comeback. In August 2017, Ackman revealed an 8.3 percent stake in payroll processor Automatic Data Processing Inc., hoping to shake up the company and grab seats on the board of directors. Ackman waged a bitter proxy fight with the $50 billion company, but in a vote on November 7, 2017, at the annual meeting, shareholders sided with management.

That same week, Ackman also declared that he would never speak publicly about Herbalife again.

ACKNOWLEDGMENTS

Where to begin? I'm indebted to so many people who helped transform this dream into a reality. First and foremost, thank you to my amazing editor, Benjamin Adams, and the entire team at Public-Affairs for taking a chance on an unknown, unproven author. Risks aren't easy to take and I'm forever grateful that you were willing. Of course, none of this would have been possible without CNBC and the incredible platform CEO Mark Hoffman and Senior Vice President of Business News Nikhil Deogun have given me. Thank you for believing in me and all that the *Halftime Report* could be. Nik, your support, mentorship and unwavering commitment to strong journalism drives me. A special thanks to CNBC Executive Vice President, Public Relations, Brian Steel for supporting this project and for your friendship. *Halftime Report* Executive Producer Jason Gewirtz is this book's unsung hero for his willingness to read every word and critique them along the way. Thank you to CNBC Senior Producer Patricia Martell for the tireless hours she suffered through between the FOIA requests and critical research I needed done to make this happen. This book *literally* would not have happened without the quick thinking of Max Meyers, John Melloy, Lydia Thew, and my entire show team in the CNBC control room, on the day of the Icahn-Ackman brawl in 2013. I'd also like to thank my good friend and author, Mark Rotella, for sharing his own wisdom about the book writing process. Mark—it was invaluable advice! I owe so much to my team at United Talent Agency, most especially, my book agent, Marc Gerald, for "getting" this story before I even walked into his office. I couldn't have written this without his tutelage and guidance. How many pitch drafts did we go through? Thank you as well to UTA's Jay Sures for making that initial phone call over coffee that got this whole thing started in the first place. Thanks to UTA's Adam Leibner for his career guidance and excitement over this project. I'm especially grateful to my friend Michael Ovitz for his sage advice over the years including prodding me to step up and write a book. OK, Michael, now what? Finally, and most important, I am forever thankful to my wife, Nancy Han, a truly great and dedicated journalist and devoted mother of our two fabulous boys. Thank you for being my rock and always pushing me to do something big! Last but certainly not least—love to Dylan and Cameron, the two sweetest boys any daddy could ask for. Nancy, Dylan and Cameron: Your unconditional love and endless enthusiasm about the big project I was working on helped push me forward, especially in the toughest and most trying moments. And thank you boys for asking me more times than I can remember, "Daddy, what if you don't finish the book?" At least now we don't have to worry about that!

NOTES

Introduction: The Masters of the Universe

1. Leo E. Strine Jr., "Who Bleeds When the Wolves Bite? A Flesh-and-Blood Perspective on Hedge Fund Activism and Our Strange Corporate Governance System," *Yale Law Journal*, April 2017.
2. Jeffrey Sonnenfeld, "Activist Shareholders, Sluggist Performance," *Wall Street Journal*, April 1, 2015.

Chapter 2: The Pitch

1. William Cohan, "Is Bill Ackman Toast?," *Vanity Fair*, Oct. 17, 2016, www .vanityfair.com/news/2016/10/is-bill-ackman-toast; Gretchen Morgenson and Geraldine Fabrikant, "A Rescue Ploy Now Haunts a Hedge Fund That Had It All," *New York Times*, Jan. 19, 2003.
2. Gotham Partners, "Is MBIA Triple A?," December 9, 2002.
3. Joe Nocera, "Short Seller Sinks Teeth into Insurer," *New York Times*, Dec. 1, 2007.
4. Ian McDonald and Kara Scannell, "MBIA Accord Caught in SEC Delay," *Wall Street Journal*, May 22, 2006.
5. Katie Benner, "Bond Giant's $8.1 Billion Surprise," *Fortune*, Dec. 20, 2007, archive.fortune.com/2007/12/20/news/companies/benner_mbia.fortune/ index.htm.
6. Larry Doyle, "Are Student Loans an Impending Bubble? Is Higher Education a Scam?: Part II," *Business Insider*, June 22, 2011.
7. Roger Parloff, "The Siege of Herbalife," *Fortune*, Sept. 9, 2015, fortune .com/2015/09/09/the-siege-of-herbalife; FTC, "In the Matter of Koscot In-terplanetary," Docket 8888, November 18, 1975.
8. FTC, "In the Matter of Koscot Interplanetary," Docket 8888, November 18, 1975.
9. Grant Gross, "Burn Lounge Promoter Settles FTC Complaint," *PCWorld*, July 1, 2008, www.pcworld.com/article/147810/article.html.
10. Brian Louis, "Ackman's General Growth Sales Marks End of Investment Era," *Bloomberg*, Feb. 11, 2014, www.bloomberg.com/news/articles/2014-02-11/ ackman-s-general-growth-sale-marks-end-of-investment-era.

11. Christine Richard and Diane Schulman, "Herbalife Investigative Work," Feb. 22, 2012.
12. "A European Court Rules: 'Herbalife Is an Illegal Pyramid Scheme,'" *Pyramid Scheme Alert*, Jan. 5, 2012.
13. Richard and Schulman, "Herbalife Investigative Work."

Chapter 3: The Activist

1 William D. Cohan, "The Big Short War," *Vanity Fair*, April 2013, www .vanityfair.com/news/2013/04/bill-ackman-dan-loeb-herbalife.
2. Antoine Gara, "Baby Buffett: Will Bill Ackman Resurrect the Ghost of Howard Hughes and Build a Corporate Empire?" *Forbes*, May 6, 2015, www .forbes.com/sites/antoinegara/2015/05/06/bill-ackman-baby-buffett-howard -hughes.
3. Brett D. Fromson, "The Rookies' Big Score," *Washington Post*, July 10, 1994.
4. Cohan, "The Big Short War."
5. Fromson, "The Rookies Big Score."
6. Ibid.
7. Ibid.
8. Ibid.
9. Ibid.
10. Gara, "Baby Buffett."
11. Stephanie Strom, "Rockefeller Center Trust Gets New Plan," *New York Times*, September 29, 1995.
12. Ibid.
13. Gara, "Baby Buffett."
14. Linette Lopez, "Bill Ackman Is Acting a Lot Like He Did the Last Time He Blew Up a Hedge Fund," *Business Insider*, March 16, 2016.
15. Jonathan R. Laing, "Meet Mr. Pressure," *Barron's*, December 5, 2005.
16. Gretchen Morgenson and Geraldine Fabrikant, "A Rescue Ploy Now Haunts a Hedge Fund That Had It All," *New York Times*, January 19, 2003.
17. Ibid.
18. Deposition by Attorney General, State of New York, of William Ackman *In re Gotham Partners Investigation*, May 28, 2003.
19. Morgenson and Fabrikant, "A Rescue Ploy."
20. Ibid.
21. Gotham Partners Management, "A Recommendation for Pre-Paid Legal Services, Inc.," November 19, 2002.
22. Deposition by Attorney General, May 28, 2003.
23. Morgenson and Fabrikant, "A Rescue Ploy."
24. Deposition by Attorney General, May 28, 2003.
25. Ibid.
26. Ibid.
27. Ibid.
28. Ibid.

29. Unit Purchase Agreement by Gotham Partners and High River Limited Partnership, March 1, 2003.

30. Carl Icahn, "Icahn Unit Announces Proposal for Acquisition of Hallwood Realty Partners, L.P. at $222 Million," July 29, 2003.

31. Azam Ahmed, "Two Wall Street Titans, and a Seven-Year Tiff," *New York Times*, November 26, 2011.

32. David Benoit, "Icahn: Au, Contraire I Never Wanted to Be Ackman's Friend," *Wall Street Journal*, January 25, 2013.

33. Ahmed, "Two Wall Street Titans."

34. Ibid.

35. Ian Austen, "Wendy's Moving to Spin Off Its Canadian Doughnut Chain," *New York Times*, July 30, 2005.

36. Ibid.

37. Deborah Brewster, "Ackman Sells Off McDonald's Stake," *Financial Times*, December 6, 2007.

38. Parija B. Kavilanz, "Hedge Fund Takes Aim at Target," *CNN Money*, July 16, 2007.

39. Ibid.

40. Jennifer Reingold, "Taking Aim at Target," *Fortune*, May 28, 2009.

41. Ibid.

42. Jackie Crosby, "Shareholders: Target 4, Ackman 0," *Star Tribune*, May 29, 2009.

43. Heidi N. Moore, "Bill Ackman to Hedge-Fund Investors: 'I Neglected to Apologize,'" *Wall Street Journal*, February 9, 2009.

44. Joseph Guinto, "Who Wrecked JC Penney?," *D Magazine*, November 2013.

45. Drew Sandholm, "Howard Schultz Slams Ackman Over JC Penney Fight," *CNBC.com*, August 9, 2013.

46. William Ackman, "Harbor Investment Conference," February 13, 2015.

47. Pershing Square Capital Management Letter to Investors, June 12, 2012.

Chapter 4: Selling a Dream

1. Certificate of Death, Mark R. Hughes, State of California, May 21, 2000.

2. Ibid.

3. Ibid.

4. Mark Hughes Death Case Report, City of Los Angeles, Department of the Coroner, May 22, 2000.

5. Robert Welkos, "A Boy and His $400 Million," *Los Angeles Times*, September 13, 2005.

6. Matthew Heller, "Death and Denial at Herbalife," *Los Angeles Times*, February 18, 2001.

7. Ibid.

8. Ibid.

9. Ibid.

10. Ibid.

11. Heller, "Death and Denial at Herbalife."

12. Ibid.

13. Ibid.

14. Ibid.

15. Ibid.

16. Donnie Cannon, "The Biography of Mark Seyforth," *Ezine Articles*, September 30, 2010.

17. Ibid.

18. FTC Complaint, "In the Matter of Amway Corporation," March 25, 1975.

19. Heller, "Death and Denial at Herbalife."

20. Ibid.

21. Ibid.

22. Ibid.

23. Ibid.

24. Gieson Tandingan, "Mark Hughes Story," YouTube video, www.youtube.com/watch?v=YWdSenMF12s.

25. Mark Hughes Herbalife History Videos, YouTube, www.youtube.com/watch?v=rqr1i2FGYuU.

26. Eric V. Copage, "Mark R. Hughes, 44, Founded Nutrition Supplement Concern," *New York Times*, May 23, 2000.

27. "Mark Hughes Day 2010," *Today* magazine, Herbalife 30th Anniversary issue, US edition no. 146.

28. Heller, "Death and Denial at Herbalife."

29. Ibid.

30. Douglas P. Shutt, "Mark Hughes, Founder of Herbalife, Dies at 44," *Los Angeles Times*, May 22, 2000.

31. Robert L. Jackson, "Testifies at Stormy Senate Hearing: Herbalife President Calls Diet Powders, Pills Safe," *Los Angeles Times*, May 16, 1985.

32. Jube Shiver Jr., "Herbalife Settles Suit Filed by State on Medical Claims," *Los Angeles Times*, October 16, 1985.

33. Tina Fisher Forde, "Herbalife Owner Autopsy Inconclusive," *Malibu Times*, May 25, 2000.

34. Ibid.

35. Shutt, "Mark Hughes, Founder."

36. Heller, "Death and Denial at Herbalife."

37. Roger Parloff, "The Siege of Herbalife," *Fortune*, September 9, 2015.

38. Duane Stanford, "Herbalife: Pyramid Scheme or Juggernaut? CEO Michael Johnson Fights Back," *Bloomberg*, May 23, 2013.

39. Ibid.

40. Ibid.

41. Herbalife Press Release, PR Newswire, April 2, 2003.

42. Ibid.

43. Associated Press, "Founder of Herbalife Weight-Loss Empire Dead at 44?," May 23, 2000.

44. Parloff, "The Seige of Herbalife."

45. Ibid.

46. "Herbalife Ltd. Prices IPO at $14 Per Share," *Business Wire*, December 15, 2004, www.businesswire.com/news/home/20041215005958/en/Herbalife-Ltd .-Prices-IPO-14-Share.

47. Matthew Townsend, "Has Soccer Made Herbalife Unbeatable?" *Bloomberg Businessweek*, April 21, 2016.

48. Official Transcript from Herbalife 2008 Investor Day.

49. Ibid.

50. Dominic Rushe, "Michael Johnson of Herbalife: America's Highest Paid CEO in 2011," *The Guardian*, May 2, 2012.

51. Ibid.

Chapter 5: The Phone Call

1. *Leadville Race Series* website, www.leadvilleraceseries.com.

2. Herbalife International of America, Inc. Official Earnings Call Transcript, May 1, 2012.

3. Ibid.

4. Ibid.

5. Herbalife International of America, Earnings Conference Call, May 1, 2012.

6. Roger Parloff, "The Siege of Herbalife," *Fortune*, September 9, 2015.

7. Michael J. De La Merced, "Einhorn Questions Prompt Selloff at Herbalife," *New York Times DealBook*, May 1, 2012.

8. CNBC, May 1, 2012.

9. Ibid.

10. De La Merced, "Einhorn Questions."

11. John Vincent, "Tracking David Einhorn's Greenlight Capital," *Seeking Alpha*, November 9, 2011.

12. Ibid.

13. Ibid.

14. Helen Coster, "Einhorn Throws the Book at Allied," *Forbes*, May 16, 2008.

15. Nick Summers, "When David Einhorn Talks, Markets Listen—Usually," *Bloomberg*, March 21, 2013.

16. Gretchen Morgenson, "Following Clues the S.E.C. Didn't," *New York Times*, January 31, 2009.

17. Summers, "When David Einhorn Talks."

18. Morgenson, "Following Clues the S.E.C. Didn't."

19. YouTube Video of Herbalife President's Team Summit, March 24, 2012, www .youtube.com/watch?v=NuBbGSK-bGo.

20. Julia LaRoche, Linette Lopez, and Lisa Du, "The World's Top Hedge Funders Presented Their Top Picks Yesterday," *Business Insider*, May 16, 2012.

Chapter 6: The Big Short

1. Katherine Burton, "Defeat at JC Penney Hurts Ackman as Performance Trails," *Bloomberg*, August 14, 2013.

2. Letter to Investors, Pershing Square Capital Management, November 22, 2011.

3. Joseph Checker, "Bill Ackman Likely Takes $200 Million Bath on Borders," *Wall Street Journal*, May 19, 2011.

4. Ibid.

5. Ibid.

6. Letter to Investors, Pershing Square Capital Management, November 22, 2011.

7. Shira Ovide, "Bill Ackman Buys 12.2% Stake in Canadian Pacific Railway," *Wall Street Journal*, October 28, 2011.

8. Michael De La Merced, "Ackman Buys into Penney and Fortune," *New York Times DealBook*, October 8, 2010.

9. Investor Letter, Pershing Square Capital Management, November 22, 2011.

10. Brad Tuttle, "Why JC Penney's No More Coupons Experiment Is Failing," *Time*, May 17, 2012.

11. JC Penney Quarterly Earnings Report Conference Call Transcript, May 15, 2012.

12. Agustino Fontevecchia, "At Ira Sohn, Bill Ackman Defends JC Penney, Pins Hope on New CEO Ron Johnson," *Forbes*, May 16, 2012.

13. CNBC, *Street Signs*, December 19, 2012.

14. Ibid.

15. CNBC, *Street Signs*, December 20, 2012.

16. Ibid.

17. Ira Sohn Conference Special Event Video, December 20, 2012.

18. Pershing Square presentation on Herbalife, AXA Equitable Center, December 20, 2012.

19. Doran Andry "Testimonial," from Pershing Square presentation on Herbalife, December 20, 2012.

20. Svea Herbst-Bayliss and Sam Forgione, "Pershing Square's Ackman Escalates Fight with Herbalife," Reuters, December 20, 2012.

21. Stuart Pfeifer and Walter Hamilton, "Hedge Fund Manager Alleges Herbalife Is a Pyramid Scheme," *Los Angeles Times*, December 20, 2012.

22. Michelle Celarier, "Flare-Up in War of Words Between Ackman, Herbalife," *New York Post*, December 21, 2012.

23. John Hempton, "Bill Ackman Enters the City of Stalingrad," *Bronte Capital*, December 28, 2012.

24. Ibid.

25. Ibid.

26. CNBC, *Street Signs*, January 4, 2013.

27. Robert Chapman, "Why I Made It a 35% Position After the Bill Ackman Bear Raid," *Chapman Capital LLC, Takeovers & Turnarounds*, December 29, 2012, https://fm.cnbc.com/applications/cnbc.com/resources/editorialfiles/2013/01/02/HLF%20by%20Chapman%20Capital%2012-29-2012.pdf.

Chapter 7: The Poison Pen

1. Charles Gasparino, Twitter timeline, January 8, 2013.

2. Andrew Ross Sorkin and Michael De La Merced, "Loeb Explains His Herbalife Bet," *New York Times DealBook*, January 9, 2013.

3. CNBC, *Squawk on the Street*, January 9, 2013.

4. Ross Sorkin and De La Merced, "Loeb Explains His Herbalife Bet."

5. Ibid.

6. Juliet Chung, "Showdown Over Herbalife Spotlights New Wall Street," *Wall Street Journal*, January 10, 2013.

7. Agustino Fontevecchia, "Dan Loeb on Trumping Bill Ackman in Herbalife: It Wasn't Personal, There Was No Pump and Dump," *Forbes*, November 12, 2013.

8. Svea Herbst-Bayliss and Matthew Goldstein, "Hedge Fund Chief Einhorn Disappoints, Loeb Had Big 2012," Reuters, January 4, 2013.

9. Jaime Lalinde, "Dan Loeb's Top 10 Most Scathing Letters," *Vanity Fair*, October 31, 2013.

10. Ibid.

11. Ibid.

12. DealBook, "Hedge Fund Takes Big Yahoo Stake, Calls for Board Shake-Up," *New York Times*, September 8, 2011.

13. DealBook, "Loeb Calls for Yang to Quit Yahoo Board," *New York Times*, November 4, 2011.

14. Amir Efrati, Joann S. Lublin, and Stu Woo, "Yahoo Finds New CEO at PayPal," *Wall Street Journal*, January 5, 2012.

15. Michael De La Merced, "Loeb to Yahoo's Chief: I'm Not a Short-Term Shareholder," *New York Times*, March 28, 2012.

16. Michael De La Merced, "Third Point Demands Yahoo C.E.O. Be Fired by Monday," *New York Times*, May 4, 2012.

17. Ibid.

18. Amir Efrati and Joann S. Lublin, "Thompson Resigns as CEO of Yahoo," *Wall Street Journal*, May 13, 2012.

19. Amir Efrati and John Letzing, "Google's Mayer Takes Over as Yahoo Chief," *Wall Street Journal*, July 17, 2012.

20. Ibid.

21. Tabinda Hussain, "Third Point Up 21.2% 2012, AUM Reaches Another Record: $10.1B," *Valuewalk*, January 3, 2013.

22. Ben Protess and Michael J. De La Merced, "S.E.C. Opens Investigation into Herbalife," *New York Times*, January 9, 2013.

23. Steven Russolillo, "Live Blogging Herbalife's Investor Meeting," *Wall Street Journal*, January 10, 2013.

24. Ibid.

25. Ibid.

26. Ibid.

27. Ibid.

28. Ibid.

29. Ibid.

30. Ibid.

Chapter 8: The Brawl

1. Juliet Chung, "Icahn Takes Herbalife Stake," *Wall Street Journal*, January 16, 2013.
2. Allie Wickman, "Carl Icahn on Bloomberg TV: I Don't Like or Respect Bill Ackman," *Benzinga*, January 24, 2013.
3. Ibid.
4. Ibid.
5. CNBC, *Halftime Report*, January 25, 2013.

Chapter 9: The Icon

1. William Alden, "Icahn Reveals His Stake in Herbalife," *New York Times*, February 14, 2013.
2. Ibid.
3. Ibid.
4. Securities and Exchange Commission Schedule 13D CUSIP #G4412G101.
5. CNBC, *Halftime Report*, February 15, 2013.
6. Ken Auletta, "The Raid," *New Yorker*, March 20, 2006.
7. Colin Dodds, "Carl Icahn: Success Story," *Investopedia*.
8. Robert Slater, *The Titans of Takeover* (Philadelphia: Beard Books, 1999).
9. James Sterngold, "The Pawns Differ: Icahn Still Winning," *New York Times*, February 6, 1985.
10. Tobias Carlisle, "How Carl Icahn Became a Corporate Raider," *Investment News*, December 7, 2014.
11. Tobias Carlisle, "The Insight That Enabled Carl Icahn to Become a Corporate Raider," *Crain's Wealth*, December 8, 2014.
12. Carlisle, "How Carl Icahn Became a Corporate Raider."
13. Paul Richter, "Carl Icahn Relishes His Raider Role," *Los Angeles Times*, June 9, 1985.
14. Slater, *The Titans of Takeover*.
15. Ibid.
16. Ibid.
17. Ibid.
18. Ibid.
19. Carlisle, "How Carl Icahn Became a Corporate Raider."
20. Robert Cole, "Icahn Makes Dual Offer for Dan River," *New York Times*, October 26, 1982.
21. Slater, *The Titans of Takeover*.
22. Richter, "Carl Icahn Relishes His Raider Role."
23. Robert Cole, "ACF, Icahn Target, Prepares Next Step," *New York Times*, September 20, 1983.
24. Ibid.
25. Linette Lopez, "Carl Icahn Told an Amazing 8-Minute Story That Explains His Entire Philosphy About Activist Investing," *Business Insider*, November 4, 2015.

26. Times Wire Services, "Chesebrough Will Buy Stauffer for $1.2 Billion," *Los Angeles Times*, February 20, 1985.

27. Robert J. Cole, "Icahn Bids $8.1 Billion for Phillips," *New York Times*, February 6, 1985.

28. Ibid.

29. William Gruber, "Raider Carl Icahn—A Pirate or Patriot?" *Chicago Tribune*, May 12, 1985.

30. Fred R. Bleakley, "T.W.A.'s Brief, Futile Battle," *New York Times*, June 24, 1985.

31. Ibid.

32. John Crudele, "T.W.A. to Be Sold to Texas Air Corp for $793.5 Million," *New York Times*, June 14, 1985.

33. Agis Salpukas, "Icahn on T.W.A. Woe: 'We're at Crossroads,'" *New York Times*, February 10, 1990.

34. Winston Williams, "Carl Icahn's Wild Ride at TWA," *New York Times*, June 22, 1986.

35. Robert E. Dallos, "Icahn Proposes Buyout to Take TWA Private," *Los Angeles Times*, July 23, 1987.

36. Elaine X. Grant, "TWA—Death of a Legend," *St. Louis Magazine*, July 28, 2006.

37. Ibid.

38. Williams, "Carl Icahn's Wild Ride."

39. Grant, "TWA—Death of a Legend."

40. Robert J. Cole, "Icahn: No Charges Made or Expected," *New York Times*, November 20, 1986.

41. Ibid.

42. Scott McCabe, "Crime History: Wall Street Titan Boesky Pleads Guilty to Insider Trading," *Washington Examiner*, November 13, 2012.

43. The Associated Press, "Milken Assigned to Bay Area Prison," *New York Times*, February 22, 1991.

44. Kurt Eichenwald, "The Collapse of Drexel Burnham Lambert," *New York Times*, February 14, 1990.

45. Michael Quint, "Texaco and Icahn End Feud," *New York Times*, January 30, 1989.

46. Ibid.

47. Delivering Alpha, CNBC and Institutional Investor, Pierre Hotel, May 5, 2014.

48. James F. Peltz, "'80s Corporate Raider Hasn't Lost His Taste for Takeovers," *Los Angeles Times*, April 9, 2000.

49. Ken Auletta, "The Raid," *New Yorker*, March 20, 2006.

50. CNN Library, "Carl Icahn Fast Facts," April 2, 2017.

51. Andy Serwer, "Carl Icahn's New Life as a Hedge Fund Manager," *Fortune*, November 29, 2004.

52. Ibid.

53. Bloomberg News, "Icahn Bids $5.4 Billion for Mylan," *Los Angeles Times*, November 20, 2004.
54. Auletta, "The Raid."
55. Ibid.

Chapter 10: The Exit and the Pile-On

1. Linette Lopez, "Dan Loeb Explains Why Bill Ackman's Herbalife Short Thesis Will Go Wrong, and Why the Stock Is Going to Surge," *Business Insider*, January 9, 2013.
2. Julia LaRoche, "Dan Loeb Just Gave a Rare Interview and Revealed a New Position in FedEx," *Business Insider*, November 12, 2013.
3. Herbalife Earnings Call Transcript, February 20, 2013.
4. Ibid.
5. Ibid.
6. Stuart Pfeifer, "Herbalife to Let Icahn Add Two Directors to Board," *Los Angeles Times*, February 28, 2013.
7. Ibid.
8. Martinne Geller, "Herbalife Gives Icahn Board Seats, Right to Boost Stake," Reuters, February 28, 2013.
9. Martinne Geller and Emily Flitter, "FBI Probes Trading as KPMG Quits Herbalife, Skechers Accounts," Reuters, April 9, 2013.
10. Ibid.
11. Andrew Beattie, "How Did George Soros 'Break the Bank of England?'" *Investopedia*, March 16, 2017.
12. Letter from Congresswoman Linda Sánchez to the FTC, obtained through FOIA request with Commission.
13. Michelle Celarier, "Now, It Gets Ugly: Ackman to Sic SEC on Soros 'Trade,'" *New York Post*, August 1, 2013.
14. Julia LaRoche, "Report: Bill Ackman Filed a Complaint with the SEC Alleging George Soros' Fund Broke Insider Trading Laws," *Business Insider*, August 5, 2013.
15. Herbalife Earnings Call Transcript, July 30, 2013.
16. Lawrence Delevingne, "Ackman to PwC: Herbalife May Get You in Trouble," *CNBC.com*, September 11, 2013, www.cnbc.com/id/101026213.

Chapter 11: The Lobbyist

1. "What's All the Buzz About? A Survey of Popular Energy Drinks Finds Inconsistent Labeling, Questionable Ingredients and Targeted Marketing to Adolescents," April 10, 2013, Staffs of Senators Markey, Durbin, Blumenthal.
2. Michael S. Schmidt, Eric Lipton, and Alexandra Stevenson, "After Big Bet, Hedge Fund Pulls the Levers of Power," *New York Times*, March 9, 2014.
3. Sally Greenberg, "Petition for FTC Investigation of Recent Allegations Against Herbalife Ltd.," National Consumers League, March 12, 2013.

4. Ibid.

5. Letter from José Calderon, President of Hispanic Federation, May 17, 2013.

6. Letter to FTC Chairwoman Edith Ramirez from Congresswoman Loretta Sánchez and Congresswoman Michelle Lujan Grisham, July 26, 2013.

7. Schmidt, Lipton, and Stevenson, "After Big Bet."

8. Ibid.

9. Ibid.

10. Ibid.

11. Ibid.

12. Ibid.

13. Ibid.

14. Ibid.

15. Ibid.

16. Michelle Celarier, "FTC Herbalife Meeting Spicy," *New York Post*, July 17, 2013.

17. CNBC and Institutional Investor's Delivering Alpha Official Transcript, The Pierre Hotel, July 17, 2013.

18. Linette Lopez, "Carl Icahn Just Ended What May Be His Most Hilarious, Sarcastic, Awesome Interview Ever," *Business Insider*, July 17, 2013.

19. Duane D. Stanford, "Stiritz Sides with Icahn for 22% Surge in Herbalife Bet: Retail," *Bloomberg*, September 18, 2013.

20. Herbalife Official Transcript, "Herbalife Announces Record Third Quarter 2013 and Introduces 2014 Earnings Guidance," October 28, 2013.

21. Letter to Investors, Pershing Square Capital Management, October 2, 2013.

22. Robin Hood Investment Conference, Ackman Presentation, November 22, 2013.

23. Duane D. Stanford, "Ackman Says He'll Take Herbalife Bet to End of the Earth," *Bloomberg*, November 22, 2013.

24. Ibid.

25. Trish Regan, Bloomberg Television Interview with Carl Icahn.

26. Ibid.

27. William D. Cohan, "The Big Short War," *Vanity Fair*, April 2013.

28. Senator Edward J. Markey, Letter to FTC Chairwoman Edith Ramirez, January 23, 2014.

29. Senator Edward J. Markey, Letter to SEC Chairwoman Mary Jo White, January 23, 2014.

30. Office of Massachusetts Senator Edward J. Markey, Official Press Release.

31. Stuart Pfeifer, "US Senator Calls for Investigation of Herbalife; Shares Tumble," *Los Angeles Times*, January 23, 2014.

32. William Alden, "A Year Later, Ackman Sticks with His Bet Against Herbalife," *New York Times*, February 13, 2014.

33. CNBC, *Power Lunch*, March 12, 2014.

34. Nathan Vardi, "FTC Launches Herbalife Inquiry, Shares Fall," *Forbes*, March 12, 2014.

Chapter 12: The Death Blow

1. Dan McCrum and Kara Scannell, "Criminal Probe Launched into Herbalife," *Financial Times*, April 11, 2014.
2. Stuart Pfeifer and Richard A. Serrano, "Federal Investigation Target L.A. -based Herbalife," *Los Angeles Times*, April 11, 2014.
3. Emily Flitter and Svea Herbst-Bayliss, "FBI Conducting a Probe into Herbalife: Sources," Reuters, April 11, 2014.
4. CNBC and Institutional Investor, Delivering Alpha, The Pierre Hotel, July 16, 2016.
5. Matthew Goldstein and Alexandra Stevenson, "Icahn and Ackman Publicly End Feud with an Embrace," *New York Times*, July 16, 2016.
6. Julia LaRoche, "Bill Ackman Is About to Unveil the Most Important Presentation of His Career," *Business Insider*, July 21, 2014.
7. CNBC, *Fast Money: Halftime Report*, July 21, 2014.
8. *Betting on Zero*, Zipper Brother's Films, Gunpowder & Sky, Ted Braun, 2016.
9. Ibid.
10. Ibid.
11. Ibid.
12. CNBC, *Squawk on the Street*, July 21, 2014.
13. Ibid.
14. *Betting on Zero*.
15. Ibid.
16. Ibid.
17. Ibid.
18. Ibid.
19. Max Nisen, "Bill Ackman Just Enriched a Man He Loathes with His Failed Herbalife 'Death Blow,'" *Quartz*, July 23, 2014.
20. *Betting on Zero*.
21. Jonathan Berr, "Herbalife Wins a Round Against Bill Ackman," *CBS Money Watch*, July 22, 2014.
22. Herbalife Earnings Call Transcript, July 28, 2014.
23. Herbalife Earnings Call Transcript, November 4, 2014.
24. Ibid.
25. Ibid.
26. Ibid.
27. Letter to Investors, Pershing Square Capital Management, November 25, 2014.
28. Ibid.
29. Top 20 Hedge Funds, LCH Investments.
30. Svea Herbst-Bayliss, "Exclusive: Ackman's Pershing Square Makes $3.3 Billion Bet on Valeant," Reuters, March 9, 2015.

Chapter 13: The Year That Wasn't

1. Nathan Vardi, "Bill Ackman Wins 2014," *Forbes*, November 17, 2014.

2. Jordan Walthen, "Bill Ackman, Pershing Square Deliver Legendary Performance," *USA Today*, October 4, 2015.

3. Christopher M. Matthews, "Prosecutors Interview People Tied to Ackman in Probe on Potential Herbalife Manipulation," *Wall Street Journal*, March 12, 2015.

4. CNBC, *Fast Money: Halftime Report*, March 13, 2015.

5. Michelle Celarier, "Herbalife Hires New Crisis PR Firm to Fight Ackman," *New York Post*, January 8, 2015.

6. Matthew J. Belvedere, "Bill Ackman: I Haven't Traded Around Herbalife Short," *CNBC.com*, March 13, 2015, www.cnbc.com/2015/03/13/bill-ackman -no-fbi-doj-contact-over-herbalife.html.

7. David M. Levitt and Oshrat Carmiel, "Ackman Group Pays $91.5 Million for Condo at NYC's One57," *Bloomberg*, April 10, 2015.

8. Ibid.

9. Alexandra Stevenson, "Bill Ackman and His Hedge Fund, Betting Big," *New York Times*, October 25, 2014.

10. Svea Herbst-Bayliss, "Exclusive: Ackman's Pershing Square Makes $3.3 Billion Bet on Valeant," Reuters, March 9, 2015.

11. Nathan Vardi, "Bill Ackman Outs Valeant CEO Mike Pearson as a Billionaire," *Fortune*, April 22, 2014.

12. Devin Leonard and Caroline Chen, "Valeant's Boss Is Back: Can the CEO Save the Day, Again?" *Bloomberg*, March 3, 2016.

13. Allergan News Release, "Allergan Files Lawsuit in Federal Court Against Valeant and Pershing Square for Violations of Federal Securities Laws," August 1, 2014.

14. Investment Master Class, "Lessons from Valeant," April 8, 2017.

15. William D. Cohan, "In Allergan Bid, a Question of Insider Trading," *New York Times*, April 23, 2014.

16. CNBC, *Squawk Box*, April 23, 2014.

17. Cohan, "In Allergan Bid."

18. CNBC, *Halftime Report*, July 21, 2014.

19. CNBC, *Squawk Box*, June 9, 2014.

20. Ed Hammond, Scott Deveau, and Doni Bloomfield, "Drugmaker Valeant to Buy Salix in Deal Worth About $14.5 Billion," February 22, 2015.

21. CNBC, *Squawk on the Street*, February 24, 2015.

22. Jen Wieczner, "Bill Ackman: Valeant Could Be the Next Berkshire Hathaway," *Fortune*, May 4, 2015.

23. Gretchen Morgenson and Geraldine Fabrikant, "Hedge Fund Titan's Surefire Bet Turns into a $4 Billion Loss," *New York Times*, March 19, 2017.

24. Andrew Pollack and Sabrina Tavernise, "Valeant's Drug Price Strategy Enriches It, but Infuriates Patients and Lawmakers," *New York Times*, October 4, 2015.

25. Roberth Langreth and Drew Armstrong, "Clinton's Tweet on High Drug Prices Sends Biotech Stocks Down," *Bloomberg*, September 21, 2015.

26. Pollack and Tavernise, "Valeant's Drug Price Strategy Enriches It."

27. Jennifer Ablan, "Valeant's Crisis Fuels Feud Between Ackman and Australian Fund Manager Hempton," Reuters, November 3, 2015.

28. Roddy Boyd, "The King's Gambit: Valeant's Big Secret," *Southern Investigative Reporting Foundation*, October 19, 2015.

29. Andrew Pollack, "Drug Makers Sidestep Barriers on Pricing," *New York Times*, October 19, 2015.

30. Daniel Bases, Ryan Vlastelica, Claire Baldwin, and Mark Bendeich, "Special Report: The 'Shorts' Who Popped a China Bubble," Reuters, August 5, 2011.

31. Citron Research, "Valeant: Could This Be the Pharmaceutical Enron?," October 21, 2015.

32. Myles Udland, "Pharma-Giant Valeant Accused of Fraud, Denies It—Stock Still Craters," *Business Insider*, October 21, 2015.

33. Antoine Gara, "Valeant Plunges 30% After Short-Seller Citron Research Makes Fraud Allegation," *Forbes*, October 21, 2015.

34. Udland, "Pharma-Giant Valeant Accused of Fraud."

35. Jonathan D. Rockoff and Jeanne Whalen, "Valeant and Pharmacy More Intertwined Than Thought," *Wall Street Journal*, October 25, 2015.

36. Monica Langley, "Activist Investor Bill Ackman Plays Defense," *Wall Street Journal*, November 4, 2015.

37. Ibid.

38. Ibid.

39. Ibid.

40. Ibid.

41. Reuters Staff, "Valeant Severs Ties with Controversial Pharmacy Distributor," October 30, 2015.

42. Julia La Roche, "Bill Ackman Just Spent 4 Hours Defending His Giant Position in Valeant," *Business Insider*, October 30, 2015.

43. "CNBC Excerpts: CNBC Exclusive: ValueAct CEO Jeffrey Ubben Speaks with CNBC's Kelly Evans on 'Closing Bell,' Today," *CNBC.com*, March 14, 2016.

44. "Herbalife Issues Statement Regarding Bill Ackman's Presentation," *Business Wire*, October 30, 2015.

45. Gibson Dunn Letter, "Suspicious Trading in Herbalife (HLF) Puts in Advance of June 25, 2015 *New York Post* Article," July 20, 2015.

46. Ben Walsh, "Someone Made a Suspiciously Timed Bet That Herbalife Stock Would Plummet," *Huffington Post*, October 16, 2015.

47. Gibson Dunn Letter, "Suspicious Trading."

48. Ed Hammond, "Valeant Hits a Two-Year Low After Ackman's Presentation," *Bloomberg*, October 30, 2015.

49. Michelle Celarier, "Bill Ackman and Michael Pearson: The Inside Story," *Fortune*, March 27, 2016.

50. Ibid.

51. Michael Johnson, "Market Manipulation by Hedge Fund Short Seller William Ackman," personal letter in author's possession, November 12, 2015.

52. Ibid.
53. Svea Herbst-Bayliss, "Ackman Tells Investors That This Year Could Be His Firm's Worst Ever," Reuters, December 16, 2015.
54. Nathan Vardi, "Billionaire Bill Ackman's Pershing Square Hedge Fund Is Down 19% in 2015," *Forbes*, November 2, 2015.
55. Reuters Staff, "Bill Ackman Says His Fund Is Having Its Worst Year Ever," *Fortune*, December 16, 2015.
56. Federal Trade Commission Press Release, "FTC Acts to Halt Vemma as Alleged Pyramid Scheme," August 26, 2015.
57. Pershing Square Capital Management Letter to Investors, December 15, 2015.
58. Reuters, "Icahn Takes Stake in Cheniere Energy, Seeks Board Seat," August 6, 2015.
59. Maureen Farrell, "Apple Stock Plunges 12%," *CNN Money*, January 24, 2013.
60. Ibid.
61. Adrian Covert, "Apple Shares Soar on Increased Buyback," *CNN Tech*, April 24, 2014.
62. Jennifer Booton, "Apple Spent $56 Billion on Buybacks in 2014," *MarketWatch*, December 26, 2014.
63. Stephanie Yang, CNBC's *Trading Nation*, December 21, 2015.

Chapter 14: The Flush and the Feds

1. Ackman email to FTC Chairwoman Ramirez, obtained through FOIA Request to Federal Trade Commission. Information delivered on February 23, 2017.
2. Roger Parloff, "Herbalife in Talks with FTC to Resolve Probe," *Fortune*, February 25, 2016.
3. FTC Complaint, Case Number 2:16-cv-05217
4. Ibid.
5. Ibid.
6. Ibid.
7. Ibid.
8. Ibid.
9. Ibid.
10. CNBC, *Fast Money: Halftime Report*, March 1, 2016.
11. Linda A. Johnson, "Valeant's Stock Loses Half Its Value," *US News and World Report*, March 15, 2016.
12. Letter to Investors, Pershing Square Capital Management, March 15, 2016.
13. Jen Wieczner, "Valeant CEO Promises Company Won't Go Bankrupt in Staff Memo," *Fortune*, March 18, 2016.
14. Letter to Investors, Pershing Square Capital Management, May 11, 2016.
15. CNBC, *Fast Money: Halftime Report*, May 2, 2016.
16. Matthew Townsend, "Herbalife Soars After Saying It's Close to FTC Resolution," *Bloomberg*, May 5, 2016.
17. Ibid.

18. Ackman email to FTC Chairwoman Ramirez, obtained through FOIA Request to FTC, May 24, 2016.

19. Ibid.

20. Ibid.

21. Ibid.

22. Ibid.

23. FTC Official Press Release Announcing Herbalife Settlement, July 15, 2016.

24. Ibid.

25. Herbalife Statement, "Herbalife and the Federal Trade Commission Reach Settlement Agreement," July 15, 2016.

26. Kevin McCoy and Nathan Bomey, "Herbalife Agrees to $200M FTC Settlement," *USA Today*, July 15, 2016.

27. Carl Icahn, "Carl Icahn Issues Statement in Response to Herbalife's Settlement with the FTC," *carlicahn.com*, July 15, 2016.

28. Lindsay Rittenhouse, "Herbalife Settlement Is Profound Victory," *The Street*, July 15, 2016.

Chapter 15: Finale or Fakeout?

1. Michelle Celarier, "Inside Wall Street's Greatest Feud," *Fortune*, September 19, 2016.

2. Ibid.

3. Ibid.

4. David Benoit, "Carl Icahn Mulled Selling Herbalife Stake to Group That Included Bill Ackman," *Wall Street Journal*, August 26, 2016.

5. CNBC, *Squawk Box*, August 26, 2016.

6. Carl Icahn, "Carl Icahn Issues Statement Regarding Herbalife," *carlicahn.com*, August 26, 2016.

7. Letter to Investors, Pershing Square Capital Management, December 7, 2016.

Coda: Big Thoughts

1. Alon Brav, Wei Jiang, and Hyunseob Kim, "The Real Effects of Hedge Fund Activism: Productivity, Asset Allocation, and Industry Concentration," Abstract, p 1.

INDEX

VICTORIA TODIS

Scott Wapner is the host of the *Halftime Report*, which airs every weekday on CNBC. Known industry-wide as an expert in the area of activism and markets, Wapner is in regular contact with all the personalities in this book. Wapner has also reported several documentaries for the network, including, *Hotel: Behind Closed Doors at Marriott*, and *One Nation, Overweight*, for which he received an award from the Society of American Business Editors and Writers as well as a Sigma Delta Chi Award from the Society of Professional Journalists. He lives in New Jersey.

PublicAffairs is a publishing house founded in 1997. It is a tribute to the standards, values, and flair of three persons who have served as mentors to countless reporters, writers, editors, and book people of all kinds, including me.

I. F. STONE, proprietor of *I. F. Stone's Weekly*, combined a commitment to the First Amendment with entrepreneurial zeal and reporting skill and became one of the great independent journalists in American history. At the age of eighty, Izzy published *The Trial of Socrates*, which was a national bestseller. He wrote the book after he taught himself ancient Greek.

BENJAMIN C. BRADLEE was for nearly thirty years the charismatic editorial leader of *The Washington Post*. It was Ben who gave the *Post* the range and courage to pursue such historic issues as Watergate. He supported his reporters with a tenacity that made them fearless and it is no accident that so many became authors of influential, best-selling books.

ROBERT L. BERNSTEIN, the chief executive of Random House for more than a quarter century, guided one of the nation's premier publishing houses. Bob was personally responsible for many books of political dissent and argument that challenged tyranny around the globe. He is also the founder and longtime chair of Human Rights Watch, one of the most respected human rights organizations in the world.

·   ·   ·

For fifty years, the banner of Public Affairs Press was carried by its owner Morris B. Schnapper, who published Gandhi, Nasser, Toynbee, Truman, and about 1,500 other authors. In 1983, Schnapper was described by *The Washington Post* as "a redoubtable gadfly." His legacy will endure in the books to come.

Peter Osnos, Founder